Penned From the Heart
Volume xii

compiled by
Gloria Clover

Son-Rise Publications
New Wilmington, PA

Thanks again to a great crew for editing and proofing:
Evelyn Minshull, Audrey Stallsmith, Mom.
Thank you, Shirley Petrie, for helping me proof the index.
And a special thanks to my friend, Florence,
for the grand opportunity of
Penned From the Heart
for ten years.
I've been blessed by the experience.
God knows exactly what we need, always.
—Gloria Clover

"Scriptures quoted from The Holy Bible, New Century Version®, copyright© 1987, 1988, 1991 by Word Publishing, a division of Thomas Nelson, Inc. Used by permission."
"Scripture taken from the HOLY BIBLE, NEW INTERNATIONAL VERSION®. Copyright © 1973, 1978, 1984 by International Bible Society. Used by permission of Zondervan Publishing House. All rights reserved."

Son-Rise Publications and Distributing, Inc.
51 Greenfield Road
New Wilmington, PA 16142
©2006 Son-Rise Publications
1-800-358-0777
www.sonrisepublications.com
All rights reserved.
Printed in the United States of America

ISBN: 0-936369-53-1

Cover Art: Patricia Dunn
Cover Design by: Chris Fry

A PRAYER FOR THE NEW YEAR

Joseph Hopkins   **January 1**

We thank You, Father, for Your providential care over the past year—past years. You have sustained us in our times of sickness and sorrow, pain and disappointment, loneliness and loss. You have blessed us beyond our deserving with the love of family, friends, and pets; the joy of living in Your beautiful world and enjoying Your provision of ample food, clothing, and shelter.

We cherish many wonderful memories of 2005 even as we look forward with eager anticipation to future joys in 2006 and beyond. We thank You for making Yourself and Your love known to us by the written Word of Scripture and by the Living Word, Jesus Christ. By Him we have the sure hope of joy unlimited when time ends and eternity begins in Your glorious presence.

Father, as we enter this new year, help us to look beyond the horizon of our own comfort zone, to share Your concern for peace on earth and holiness for all people everywhere. Help us to do our part in fulfilling Jesus' Great Commission to evangelize the world. May we also be faithful in praying for peace and healing in Iraq, Afghanistan, Palestine, Sudan, Northern Ireland, Southeast Asia, and wherever Your children of all ages are victimized by war, famine, disease, death, and destruction. In Jesus' Name, we pray. Amen.

NEW BEGINNINGS

Donald L. Patterson   **January 2**

I could whistle the tune of the song "Mack the Knife" all day long and not get tired of it. It's the lyrics that drive me bonkers. On the other hand, the lyrics of the song "This Is A Day of New Beginnings" are great, but the music is not. If the words of "Beginnings" were put to the tune of "Mack," I would be happy.

This is the day of new beginnings, time to remember and move on

Time to believe what love is bringing, laying to rest the pain that's gone.

It's a brand new year. We stand in the light of the sunrise of 2006. Is our purpose to make new disciples?

Then let us with the Spirit's daring, step from the past and leave behind,

Our disappointment, guilt, and grieving, seeking new paths, and sure to find.

You have a new beginning in the year before you. What messes and failures need to be thrown into the trash? What are your goals for the year 2006? What new paths await you and where will you find the courage and the daring to travel them?

Christ is alive, and goes before us, to show and share what love can do.

This is our day of new beginnings; our God is making all things new.

(Lyrics quoted from the United Methodist Church hymnal, page 383)

MEDITATION ON RECYCLING

Charles A. Waugaman   January 3

Old Christmas cards! Such a strange phrase. Christmas cannot age; the story will not change; this birth is eternal. Yet every year we receive another set of greetings, and every year we ponder what to do with the accumulation of the past.

Clip them. Pack them. Send them to missions and hospitals; make them into scrapbooks to cheer the ill. Transform them into ornaments to bedeck the room or grace the tree. The suggestions are endless and consistently valid.

But I like the gift our nieces and nephew sent years ago. Place mats of red and green construction paper, irregularly divided with contrasting rickrack, glowing with pictures clipped from "old Christmas cards" under wipeable clear Contact paper—a treasure for our family of five children.

They were a fitting gift—blessed with the touch of personal effort—to celebrate the birthday of the Savior. The incarnate God come to renew—to seek and save that which was lost. Now we, too, can feed upon the past. Like a mulched garden. Like the renascent floor of the sea. Like a cracked acorn probing the moist leaf mold of spring.

Dear Father, let me join Your joy. Let me feast at Your celebration. I feel Your kiss upon my cheek, Your ring turns cleanly on my hand. So the used is not worthless. The lost has been found. I thank You for Emmanuel. Amen.

THE GLORY HOLE

Shirley S. Stevens   January 4

For I am fearfully and wonderfully made.
(Psalm 139:14 KJV)

We have often expressed our relationship with God in terms of the potter and the clay. We even sing hymns about this concept. On a recent visit to Wheaton Village in New Jersey where I watched a glassblower, I thought about how God breathes life into us and shapes us, as the craftsman blows into his pipe and shapes the glass with his steam pad. Out of the molten sand, He creates unique vessels. The analogy was confirmed for me when I learned that the glassblower's furnace is called the "glory hole"!

Thank You for creating and shaping me even as I go through the Refiner's fire. To thine be the glory!

CATCHING THE FOXES

Lorena Estep   January 5

Catch for us the foxes, the little foxes that ruin the vineyards, our vineyards that are in bloom.
(Song of Solomon 2:15 NIV)

I was looking out our sunroom window at the deep snow and ice that had built up heavily in the past week. Suddenly I heard a loud rumble and witnessed our aluminum picnic pavilion crumbling to the ground!

When I recovered from the shock, the wreckage became a visible reminder of the times in my life where I was suddenly flattened by circumstances. Just as our pavilion could have been saved by shoveling snow from its roof, so might I have kept my life from crumbling if I'd paid attention to the little signs.

Solomon warns in his book of songs of the little foxes that can ruin a vineyard. In the same way the little sins that we tend to ignore can grow to gigantic proportions until some relationship in our lives crumbles before our eyes. At that point, as with the pavilion, we may have to clear out the debris and start all over.

After having to rebuild in my own life, I'm now much more alert about the little things that can infiltrate to affect relationships or my walk with the Lord.

THE CUPBOARD
Dave Evans   **January 6**

Lord, please forgive my pride;
the cupboard in my heart
where I hide bottles
of stubbornness, arrogance,
and self-will

Be free
to restock these shelves
with jumbo-sized jars of
kindness, humbleness,
and obedience.

God has chosen you. You are holy and loved by Him. Because of this, your life should be full of loving-pity. You should be kind to others and have no pride. Be gentle and willing to wait for others.

(Colossians 3:12 NLT)

SHOWER
Barbara Ann Yonnotti   **January 7**

as I step into a sea of solace
water running as I cry
accept me
body as a web
veil of truth unfolds
I need to be whole again

Create in me a clean heart, O God; and renew a right spirit within me.

(Psalm 51:10 KJV)

GOD KNOWS OUR THOUGHTS
Janet R. Sady   **January 8**

If I regard iniquity in my heart, the Lord will not hear me.

(Psalm 66:18 KJV)

God knows the thoughts and intents of our hearts. We may fool ourselves and other people, but we can't fool God. If we have iniquity in our hearts, we may make excuses and give reasons. The truth is that we enjoy sin.

When Adam and Eve ate of the forbidden fruit, it wasn't because it looked horrible. It was beautiful and looked good to eat. They listened to Satan as he filled their heads with deceptive ideas. When they allowed themselves to lust after things forbidden by God, they sinned. The first thing they did when God asked them about their sin was to make excuses and try to blame someone else. This trait is still very much alive in our character today.

As we regard situations and things in this life that appear pleasant and desirous, may we not be deceived, but allow the Spirit of God to instruct and teach us.

Father, forgive me for blaming others for my sins and transgressions against You. I confess that I have allowed my desires to cause me to sin against You. Restore me to Your fellowship. Amen.

A SOFT ANSWER

Tiffany Schlichter January 9

A soft answer turneth away wrath: but grievous words stir up anger.

(Proverbs 15:1 KJV)

We had been traveling all day in the state of New Mexico, so we decided to break at a snow-covered rest stop. Because my siblings and I had never seen snow, we were eager to play in it.

Amidst the laughter and fun, however, a woman walked up who was responsible for cleaning the area. She looked irritated as she snapped at us to stop. She said, "Now I have to clean all this up!"

My first thought was selfish and judgmental. But I was convicted when I saw my father go to the lady, kindly take the broom, and begin to sweep the sidewalk for her. He told her he was sorry we had made a mess and would be happy to clean it up.

The woman was shocked, but suddenly became friendly and cheerful. She talked to us about the state she lived in, the children she had raised, and encouraged us to come back. I was amazed at the turn around I saw in her attitude.

It was all because someone gave a soft answer. My dad could have "stood his ground," or spoken harsh words, but either would have increased her anger. Instead he put self behind, and it wrought a wonderful change in this lady's day.

May we all remember to respond with soft answers as the Lord gives us opportunities. They bless others' lives and honor God!

A PRAYER OF REASSURANCE
Annettee Budzban — January 10

Heavenly Father,

Sometimes I feel as though I am alone and misunderstood in this vast world You have created. The defeats of life make me feel frustrated and afraid. I have a tendency to get bitter and resentful.

Then I sit and talk with You and I feel as though You understand my feelings. You don't criticize me as others do. As I listen for Your gentle voice to respond, You share Your thoughts with me and help me to put things into perspective. You strengthen me with Your words of encouragement. A loving companion, You tell me how to turn my fear into faith. You give me personal instruction on how to make myself better instead of bitter.

I enjoy the reassurance from Your Word that You hold me in the palm of Your hand, where my name is permanently engraved. I love the daily reminder of Your faithfulness as I watch the sun rise and set each day, according to Your holy timer. Thank You for being my daily companion. I don't know what I would do without You. You make my heart overflow with gratitude. In Jesus' name. Amen.

TRUST AND OBEY
Mary A. Koepke — January 11

"Trust and Obey"
We sing the old hymn—
and how do we respond?
With prayer and supplication
present preconceived plans
lifted on a silver platter,
expect granting of worldly wishes
we want but don't need
and answers as soon as possible—
to fit our time tables.

Do we accept His wise replies,
surrender self-centered desires,
wait patiently for His perfect word,

have faith in His providential care
and child-like walk His path?

Most times we don't, but—
"there's no other way."

STAY FOCUSED

Lanette Kissel January 12

And [Jesus] said unto another, Follow Me. But he said, Lord, suffer me first to go and bury my father. Jesus said unto him, "Let the dead bury their dead: but go thou and preach the kingdom of God.

(*Luke 9:59-60 KJV*)

The man gave a typical response to the call. "Jesus, I want to follow you, but first..." How many of us would have responded in that same way, "But first..."? Jesus did not desire to call hesitant, halfhearted people to the task of proclaiming the kingdom of God. If the potential follower Jesus called reacted with hesitation, he was not right for the task of discipleship.

Jesus required His disciples to be able to have a drop-everything-now-and-follow-me attitude, living in the here and now. He did not want disciples who would have one eye focused upon Him and the other eye looking backwards toward home. A follower of Jesus needs to have both eyes focused upon Him and upon the Father at all times.

How easy it would be for all of us to say, "But first, Lord..." Yet, it is preferable to try this response, "But, You come first, Lord, now and always."

Dear Lord, help us to follow You with our whole hearts, to have both eyes focused upon You at all times. Amen.

TIMID TRUST

Marion E. Gorman January 13

Trust in the LORD with all your heart and lean not on your own understanding.

(*Proverbs 3:5 NKJ*)

In her book, *Prayers & Promises for Every Day*, Corrie ten Boom cites a time when the Lord distinctly instructed her to go to Japan. In obedience, she went with no specific instructions. Upon her arrival, the Lord revealed the ministry He had prepared for her. *Would I respond to God's prompting with such trust,* I wondered.

My life was full and I loved it. I had a job, a large family, enjoyed a flower garden, and worked at a writing career. My contentment with my whirlwind life changed the moment my husband confronted me with, "I thought writers needed time to think." They do.

Writing is the purpose God gave me, so I knew immediately I needed to quit my job. But my job paid for health insurance and extra activities. What would happen if we got sick? Would we be satisfied with a simpler life? Could I say, "Yes, Lord"?

My mind was in turmoil. Was this the responsible thing to do? I procrastinated with a plan to retire in six months. God responded with a plan that began immediately with the threat of a layoff, testing my reluctance to trust Him. I retired.

Long days in my writing room exceed all expectations I had of fulfilling God's purpose for my life.

Lord, thank You for enabling me to trust Your faithfulness in supplying every need.

WASHING FEET

Kathleen Wolford   January 14

I liked the thought of servanthood, so noble and so neat,
Till Jesus bade me go at once and wash His people's feet.
I'd visions of important tasks that I might be assigned,
And now it seemed that wasn't what the Master had in mind.
I must confess I grumbled at this lowly, endless chore,
When feet I'd washed just yesterday were back again for more.
And then I paused, mid-grumble: these weren't just any feet,
But those that took the gospel to the family down the street.
Some other feet came calling on a single mom in need,
And stayed to help her teenage son bring schoolwork up to speed.
Still others found the lonely, the discouraged, and the lost,
And invested for eternity, not grudging what it cost.
There are more impressive titles, more high-profile work to do,
But truth be told, the limelight tends to fall on very few.
That's fine with me; what matters to the people whom I meet
Is that I be like Jesus, and that means washing feet.

WHAT'S YOUR EXCUSE?
Margaret Steinacker   **January 15**

So then, brothers, stand firm and hold to the teachings we passed on to you, whether by word of mouth or by letter.
(2 Thessalonians 2:15 NIV)

As we consider this scripture about standing firm and witnessing to our faith in Christ, what is our problem? Why are we so negligent in passing on the truths we know about Jesus Christ? How many of our excuses count for anything with God?

We use busyness, tiredness or our family's needs as an excuse. We say our demanding job gets in the way of witnessing. We would never want to push Christ's teachings on others. Although these may be somewhat legitimate, God's Word directs us to be prepared always to give an answer for the hope in us. [1 Peter 3:15]

We are so spoiled! With e-mails and telephones we have instant access to anyone in the world. If we do not know someone's number, the options are virtually endless in searching the web for information; a complete opposite to the available possibilities in the day Paul wrote this epistle. Let's forget the excuses and get on with God's work.

Lord, give us boldness to proclaim the glorious news of the gospel. Open our eyes to see the world through Your eyes. Help us to be prepared at all times to recognize Your voice prompting us to witness.

A TREASURED MEMORY
Ruth Baldwin   **January 16**

Well done, good and faithful servant!
(Matthew 25:23 NIV)

My first memory was of my mother carrying me to the Cradle Room, where I would stay while she attended church. When Mother set me down, I looked up at Mrs. Lienbach, our minister's wife, standing so-o-o tall above me. She smiled with such warmth and love that I felt no fear of going into her presence. She carried me into the room, where we rocked in a chair. I still feel her warmth as I recall the memory—at 80 years of age!

Mrs. Leinbach left our church to serve another church in town. I saw little of her through the years. When I finished high school, I started schooling in Chicago. For several days, thoughts of Mrs. Lienbach kept going through my mind, so I sent her a letter recalling the above memory, explaining that she had been a wonderful ambassador for Jesus Christ to this child in my beginning walk with the Lord.

I didn't receive an answer, and wondered how she had responded to it. Her son, now the town's doctor, stopped my sister on the street shortly afterwards and thanked her for my letter, saying it had surprised and comforted his mother. It arrived when she was on her deathbed. I didn't know she was ill!

How thankful I was that I had listened to the Holy Spirit's prompting to send it. Had I not listened, we would both have missed a blessing.

UNTO THE LORD

Marie DisBrow   **January 17**

> *Whatever you do, work at it with all your heart, as working for the Lord, not for men, since you know that you will receive an inheritance from the Lord as a reward. It is the Lord Christ you are serving.*
> (Colossians 3:23-24 NIV)

We all have chores or responsibilities that are unpleasant. Not everyone is fortunate to have enjoyable work. Certain people and circumstances may annoy us or try our patience.

Have you ever thought that these aggravations could be acts of worship? Worship is more than being present in church, praying, or singing praise songs. All our actions can become acts of worship, if they are offered to God with a humble and sincere heart. Even the smallest work can be dedicated to the Lord—and when offered to Him, it becomes meaningful and rewarding. Trying circumstances, even suffering, will be less difficult when given to Him, Who willingly suffered so much for us.

Day and night, the Lord sees all that we do. He even sees into our hearts and knows the motives for all our actions. Let us be motivated by His unseen eye to do everything for Him and for His glory. If we remember always that God sees everything, we would say only the words we'd say before His visible presence and we'd do only the things that would please Him.

Lord Jesus, You are always with me. Help me to speak, act, and think as I would if I could actually see You. Amen.

GIFTS AND GRACE
Bonnie J. Manion January 18

>Praise for the sunlight
>showering at noon
>
>Praise for dewfall
>flowering with the moon
>Praise for cloudbursts
>drenching the earth
>
>Praise for God's grace
>quenching human thirst

WHO'S AT THE DOOR?
Jana Carman January 19

>*The Judge is standing at the door!*
>*(James 5:9 NIV)*

My children's play had soured into arguments, loud voices, and tears. Heading upstairs to "reward the faithful and punish the wrongdoers," I found the bedroom door locked. Exasperated, I thumped it and ordered, "Open this door."

Suddenly all was quiet, except for one small voice. "Uh-oh, there's Mom."

Like my children, we tend to forget that "My Lord is listenin' all the time," and also that He is coming back. In the parable Jesus told in Matthew 24:42-51, Jesus Himself is the one standing outside, ready to reward the faithful and punish the evildoers. To paraphrase James, "Here comes the Judge!"

His return will be sudden and unexpected. A pastor asked his deacons if they thought Jesus was coming back that week. When one replied, "Oh, I think not," the pastor quoted Matthew 24:4.: "In such an hour as ye think not the Son of man cometh."

It could be this week, or even today. I wonder which will be our response. "Praise God, He's back!" or "Uh-oh, there's Jesus!"

A RACE TO RUN
Martha Rogers January 20

>*Therefore, since we are surrounded by such a great cloud of*

> *witnesses, let us throw off everything that hinders and the sin that so easily entangles, and let us run with perseverance the race marked out for us.*
> *(Hebrews 12:1 NIV)*

Each of us has a race to run. Paul tells us to run it with perseverance. To be persistent, we must also have patience. I don't think I'm alone when I say patience isn't one of my virtues.

I know God has a specific race for me to run, just as you have yours. He has it marked out for us. My problem is I don't want to wait for Him. I want to run ahead and see what's there, and I'm always checking to see how others are doing.

However, I am not to look around at others and their accomplishments. I must focus on my own lane and finish my race. As I look at it now, I realize that whenever I take my eyes off the finish line, and begin looking around at what others are doing, I stumble and fall.

Because of my impatience, I begin comparing myself with others in the race. Everyone is doing a better job than I am. They are forging ahead with victory. I become envious and discouraged. I've taken my eyes off the "author and finisher" of my faith.

God's timing is perfect. He will bring triumph and victory to our lives, but in His own plan and time frame for each of us.

Lord, I pray today for the patience to wait for Your perfect timing. Help me to focus on the race You set out for me and let me persevere to the end to bring honor and glory to Your name.

A RACE WORTH WINNING

Dan Nicksich   **January 21**

> *I have fought the good fight, I have finished the race, I have kept the faith.*
> *(2 Timothy 4:7 NIV)*

Former paratrooper, retired automotive engineer, beekeeper, local government official. Even in his early seventies, our friend Herb is active and always searching for new challenges. Recently he took up running and decided to enter a local 10K race, just for fun. Imagine his surprise when he was the winner in his age bracket! Herb's joy was just a bit tempered, however, when he learned he was the only contestant registered in the 65 and above age group. To win, all he had to do was finish the race.

If we are going to win only one race in this lifetime, let it be that race Paul speaks of when he says, "Run in such a way as to get the prize" (1 Corinthians 9:24 NIV). Like a single-entry race contestant, we need not fear competition in this walk with Christ; we need only to finish the race.

Lord, allow me to face each day with the awareness that it is simply another step in the course You lay before me. Help me to finish the race. In Jesus' name. Amen.

JUST ONE TAP
Charles E. Harrel   **January 22**

And He will place the sheep at his right hand, but the goats at the left.

(Matthew 25:33 RSV)

Bible-land shepherds often tended combined flocks, but they knew it was necessary to separate the sheep from the goats at particular times. The goats were headstrong, rambunctious, and preferred grazing the rocky foothills throughout the day. The sheep, however, needed specific times for rest and favored feeding in the grassy pastures.

Shepherds divided their flocks with a staff, tapping sheep on the right side and goats on the left. All the sheep would gather around the shepherd's right hand, while the goats moved to the left. The sheep found food and relaxation, while the goats continued to clamber around restlessly.

With this word picture, Jesus portrays a scene from the final judgment. The righteous inherit a kingdom filled with eternal rest, blessed by the right hand of promise. Since the left hand carries no such promise or blessing, the unrighteous depart to a kingdom of everlasting turmoil without rest. There will be just one tap—on the right or the left. Which kingdom we inherit is our choice, and we can make that decision now.

Precious Shepherd, I look forward to that final day when the flock is separated, and your sheep enter the kingdom of heaven. I can hardly wait to spend eternity with You. Amen.

TREASURES
Betty Redmon   **January 23**

For what will it profit a man if he gains the whole world, and

loses his own soul?
(Mark 8:36 NKJ)
What value be there in piles of gold
    If man gives up his heart and soul?
If cars and yachts and things like these
    Are all that man really sees.
What price, then, this world of fashion
    That drives man on without compassion?
Why must self be so imbedded
    To make man so empty headed?
He fails to see the things that are:
    The bird on wing, the evening star
    The kindness of his neighbors near,
    Who offer friendship, joy and cheer.
    The painting on the far off hill
    That only God is holding still.
How warped our mortal values be
    That we can't see what God gives free.

Do not lay up for yourselves treasures on earth...lay up for yourselves treasure in heaven.
(Matthew 6:19-20 NKJ)

AWFUL ATHALIAH

Audrey Stallsmith   **January 24**

Athaliah tore her clothes and shouted, "Treason! Treason!"
(2 Chronicles 23:12 NIV)

Athaliah was obviously not a grandmotherly type. After the death of her son, Ahaziah the king, she decided to murder *his* sons so she could ascend the throne herself. Only the infant Joash survived, smuggled from the palace to the temple by his intrepid aunt, Jehoshabeath, wife of the priest Jehoiada. After six years of hiding the boy, the priest conspired with some army officers to restore the young prince to his rightful throne.

The queen's screams of "Treason!" when she discovered the plot were disingenuous, to say the least. It was actually she who was guilty of treachery against her nation because she had killed the rightful heirs to the throne. And she suffered the execution that is the usual punishment for such perfidy.

The human race committed sedition, too, when it rebelled

against its Creator and, again, when it killed that King's Son. As a result, the world fell under the tyranny of a ruler even more evil than Athaliah. But we, like Jehoshabeath and her husband, can be the real patriots if we harbor the true King in our hearts—until such time as He also will take His rightful throne back from the usurper.

But every time we bow to the spirit of this world rather than to the Spirit of God, we're being disloyal to our true monarch. That isn't just sin; it's treason!

I'M YOURS, LORD

Debbie Rempel January 25

> I'm Yours, Lord;
> help me
> morning by morning
> to come to You
> with an open heart.
> I want to be the
> sanctuary you made
> me to be—
> faithful, true,
> and loving You.
>
> You designed me to
> follow You
> wherever You lead—
> even to the altar as
> a living sacrifice.
>
> That's me.
> I'll crawl on the altar, Lord,
> and leave my troubles there.
>
> So help me, Lord!

TAKING TIME

Shirley S. Stevens January 26

Having eyes, see ye not?
(Mark 8:18 KJV)

Georgia O'Keeffe once said it takes a long time to see a

flower.

On my morning walk, I stop to study the daisy. Some flowers are two inches across, each yellow disk depressed in the center. The leaves are dark, narrow, much lobed.

I think of the person who named the daisy for "the day's eye." He or she saw the sun from the heavens reflected in this earthly flower. I stop to pluck a dandelion, make a wish, and blow its white seed balls across the hillside. I examine the jagged leaves and remember that the name of this wildflower comes from the tooth of the lion, in French "le dent de lion."

Slow me down, Lord. Help me to put pen to paper today instead of dashing off an instant message or e-mail. Remind me to take time to truly see a flower and value a person.

LISTENING TO A LIE

Jennifer Kanode   January 27

Be self-controlled and alert. Your enemy the devil prowls around like a roaring lion looking for someone to devour.
(1 Peter 5:8 NIV)

I had arthroscopic surgery on my left knee in January of 2005, due to a skiing accident that had happened a year before. At the time of the accident, I did not have insurance. After I got married, I went under my husband's insurance. Numerous people believed that because it was a preexisting injury, it would not be covered by my insurance policy. So we began to pray.

In April, we got the papers from the insurance company. And what I had feared came true. I looked through the piles of bills that added up to about $12,000! I panicked. I thought God had not answered our prayers. My emotions took over. For a few days after that, I was depressed and wondered how we were going to pay.

My husband and I met with my parents later that week, and they looked at the papers. They soon discovered that I had been mistaken. Those bills were just a copy of what the insurance company had paid! The surgery had been covered.

This experience reminded me that believing a lie directs our thoughts and emotions off course. Satan can use what we believe to alter our emotions and reactions. When Satan gets us to believe in a lie, we don't recognize it until the Light shines on the situation and we hear, "This is how it really is."

Father, keep us from believing the lies of the devil. May our focus be on the words You have spoken and the Truth of Your Son. Amen.

MY PRAYER FOR YOU
Linda Mae Richardson　　　　　　　　　　　　　　　January 28

Today, my friend, I pray for you,
For God to grant you peace.
To stay your trembling heart and hand
That all your fears may cease.

And, though today you're feeling weak,
His strength for you I pray.
To face whatever lies ahead,
To help you day by day.

For every problem that you face
Remember there is hope,
That God is with you even now.
Together you can cope.

And, knowing that God loves you so,
I pray these words will be,
A messenger of love and hope
With love to you—from me!

HOW BIG IS GOD?
Joan Clayton　　　　　　　　　　　　　　　　　　January 29

Now to him who is able to do immeasurably more than all we ask or imagine, according to his power that is at work within us.

(Ephesians 3:20 NIV)

The vastness of God's creation is overwhelming. From outer space, planet earth is like a little blue marble, yet God provides every need for the earth's inhabitants.

At night my husband and I love to sit in our swing and look at the stars. One night Emmitt remarked, "People have been seeing these same stars for centuries. I wonder if they ever realize the scope of God's creation." We talked at length about God's greatness.

God knows each one of us. He knows every hair upon our heads. Realizing the sovereignty of God, we can see our difficulties as opportunities for God to show Himself strong. All things are possible for you and me, because He lives mightily in us. God is bigger than the illness of a loved one, a misunderstanding, a financial crisis, or any other problem that plagues the human soul.

God is able. He never grows weary and His supply never runs out. He is big enough to renew strength and to hear and answer prayers. He restores well being. Nothing can compare to our God. He is unequaled!

The next time you have a problem, step outside and look at the sky. Only God can make such magnificence, yet He has time for you and me.

How big is God? GOD IS BIG!

Thank You, God, for the wondrous beauty You have made.

PSALM 63
Tune of *Go Tell it on the Mountain*

Glenda Joy Race   January 30

Chorus:
Oh, God, you are my God,
Early will I seek after you.
I thirst after you,
As in a dry and thirsty land.

I want to see your power
And glory in this place,
Because your loving kindness
Is much better than life.

While I have breath to live
I will bless your name.
I will lift up my hands
And praise you with my mouth.

Because you are my help
I will rest in your shadow.
As my soul follows you,
Your hand will lift me up.

PEOPLE
Helen Kammerdiener   **January 31**

Thank You, Lord, for people.
Thank You for good conversations,
    for competition in games,
    for companionship
        in doing jigsaw puzzles.
Thank You for those who say, "Hello,"
    in the hallway,
And for those who stop long enough
    for a friendly comment.
Thank You for those whose door
    is always open to me
And for those who recognize
    when I need to be alone.
Thank You, Lord, even for those
    who seem to be no more than
        a small dot on the tapestry of my life.
Thank You, Lord, for people.

AS PARENTS LOVE A NEWBORN
Annette Budzban   **February 1**

See how very much our heavenly Father loves us, for He allows us to be called his children, and we really are!
(1 John 3:1 NLT)

As I performed my task as a nursery nurse, I gathered the newborn babies from their mother's bedsides and brought them back to the nursery for hospital visiting hours. I combed their soft, silken hair and bundled their tiny bodies in blankets of pink and blue, to prepare them for their initial presentation to family members.

Soon, groups of families began to gather outside the nursery viewing window. They proudly pronounced the last name of the baby they waited to see. Bending over the bassinet, I picked the baby up and held up their precious bundle of joy for everyone to see.

Tears of joy streamed down the cheeks of brothers, sisters, aunts, uncles, and grandparents. Their faces broke out with huge smiles and loving expressions that conveyed the pleasure that pierced their hearts.

God loves us the same way a family loves and welcomes their new arrival. Babies don't earn the love of their families; they simply receive it. It works the same way between us and God. However, many people think that they have lost the approval of God due to the mistakes of their past. We cannot make a mistake that will remove God's love from us. We need only to open up our hearts like a newborn baby and receive His love.

THE GIFT OF CHILDREN
Joan Clayton   **February 2**

Children are a gift from the LORD, they are a reward from him.

(Psalm 127:3 NLT)

I well remember when the nurse put each newborn baby in my arms. The love I felt I could not describe. Of course my husband and I were the proudest parents ever. Emmitt loved the nightly rituals, a story, a prayer, a hug and kiss. "Aren't they dolls?" he said to me every night. "Are we not blessed?"

Children forgive and forget, simply abandoning themselves to life. I shudder to think of a world without children. Their enthusiasm for life brings hope with promise for the future.

My students became my "teachers" by their childlike trust and faith. Somewhere between childhood and adulthood, we lose that faith. "The greatest person in the kingdom of heaven is the one who makes himself humble like this child" (Matthew 18:4 NCV).

I want to be that child.

Dear God, help me to be "childlike," not "childish."

OUR LITTLE ONES ARE LAMPS
Pat Collins   **February 3**

Oh, to have the heart and innocence of a child. We can learn so much from our little ones. Believe in God, without question, and be quick to forgive when hurt. Reach out in love to someone without needing a reason. Find something good in life when things go wrong. Never doubt that God will take care of us. Wonderful, simple trust and faith in God.

Dear Lord God, let me see and feel with the heart of a child. Blind me to the faults of others. Thank You for letting our little ones be a lamp unto You, so that we may see You through them.

> The spirit of a man is the lamp of the LORD, searching all the inner depths of his heart.
> (Proverbs 20:27 NKJ)

THE TIME OF FAMILY PRAYER
Mary Rose Pearson   **February 4**

When the evening shadows gather at the setting of the sun,
When the cares of day are ended, and the chores have all been done,
Then we all sit down together, and we look for blessings rare,
For we've come to talk to Jesus—it's the time of family prayer.
First the Word of God is opened, and a portion's clearly read.
Then we talk about its meaning; on God's manna we are fed.
Next we close the precious Bible, and we kneel together there—
Thus we seek the Father's blessing at this time of family prayer.
Each one takes a turn in praying—Father, Mother, children, too;
And the Heavenly Father's listening in His home above the blue.
How the family ties are strengthened! There are joys beyond compare!
Not another time is sweeter than the time of family prayer.
Would you have your family growing in their knowledge of the Word?
Do you want to see them walking in the footsteps of the Lord?
Do you seek their souls' salvation that for heaven they'll prepare?
Then join hearts and hands together at the time of family prayer.

THE BLESSING OF LIGHT
Betty Jane Hewitt   **February 5**

Once a month we provide a worship service for patients in our local facility. We select well-known hymns because we remember it is difficult for them to understand. This afternoon, I chose to read the familiar beatitudes...and found myself in tears.

These were precious children of God, the ill and the aged. They were positioned at tables in wheel chairs, with walkers, and wheeled beds with hanging IV bags. Some surveyed their surroundings with vacant eyes, trembling hands clutching their hymnals.

Henry, one of the regulars at the service, enjoys soloing, and this afternoon he lustily sang out "and He walks with me, and He talks with me and He tells me I am His own."

After the benediction, I felt my friend's arm on my shoulder, "I know, Betty, every time I'm here I think of my mother's final days." She glanced about the room. "We could be here too someday."

My emotional experience that afternoon wasn't a response to thinking "There for the grace of God go I." It was as if the Holy Spirit were in that dining hall and a light shone among us. That day when we ministered in the Lord's name to the disabled ones who could no longer take care of themselves, we allowed His grace to shine through us—if only for a brief moment in their lives.

> *You are the light of the world. A city on a hill cannot be hidden. In the same way, let your light shine before men, that they may see your good deeds and praise your Father in heaven.*
>
> (Matthew 5:14, 16 NIV)

LIGHT

Helen Kammerdiener February 6

Thank You, Lord, for light.
Thank You for the
    bright radiance of a summer day,
    the soft, clear moonlight on snow,
    watery sunshine peeping around the
        edges of storm clouds,
    the spectacular aurora borealis,
    and the serene beauty of the sunrise.
Thank You for electric lights
    and candles and flashlights.
Most of all, thank You, Lord,
    for the light of love that spills into
        my heart as I read Your word.
Thank You, Lord, for light.

THE HIDDEN LIGHT

Janet R. Sady February 7

> *You are the light of the world. A city on a hill cannot be hidden. Neither do people light a lamp and put it under a bowl. Instead they put it on its stand, and it gives light to*

everyone in the house. In the same way, let your light shine before men, that they may see your good deeds and praise your Father in heaven.

(Matthew 5:14-16 NIV)

My friend bought me a beautiful lamp. The black leather shade, however, hides most of the direct light. When I want to read, I take the shade off, allowing the full light of the bulb to shine.

God's Word instructs me to allow my light as a Christian to shine forth so that others might see Christ in me. If I fail to be an example and show Christ's love, I am like the lamp with the black shade.

Lord, help me to reflect Your light in my life, so that others may give You praise and come to know You as Savior and Lord. Amen.

VIRUS OF THE SOUL

Dolores Fruth   **February 8**

If there's a deep dark secret
That you cannot expose,
It's like a virus of the soul
Where steadily it grows.

It's ever hidden in the dark,
But you know it is there.
For it is eating at your soul;
It follows everywhere.

There is a cure that waits for you
And it is free for all.
Just ask forgiveness from the Lord
And He will heed the call.

Yes, you will get an added gift
For, as He will erase
The sins you lay before Him now,
He also offers Grace.

The virus that invaded you
Was such an ugly blight.
Our God can heal the hidden sore
And lead you to the light.

FEAR OF FALLING

Jana Carman February 9

Glory to him who is able to keep you from falling.
(Jude 24)

A baby barely minutes old will show a fear of falling. Some construction workers so completely conquer this fear that they can walk on open beams 100 stories above the street. Other phobics, like me, leave permanent finger indentations halfway up a six-foot ladder.

The Old Testament is full of semi-hopeful verses about falling. "Do not gloat over me, my enemy! Though I have fallen, I will rise" (Micah 7:8 NIV). "For though a righteous man falls seven times, he rises again" (Proverbs 24:16 NIV). "The steps of a man are established by the LORD ... When he falls, he shall not be hurled headlong; Because the LORD is the One who holds his hand" (Psalm 37:23-24 NAS).

But the doxology which ends Jude's short book is even more encouraging: God is able to keep us from falling. His strong arm helps us over, or out of, temptation's pitfalls.

To an elderly person, the specter of a broken hip makes falling a fearsome prospect, so he or she walks more cautiously. (Good advice spiritually, too.) A quad-cane offers more stability than an ordinary cane. In the same way, life built on faith, prayer, the Bible, and God's love is broad-based, and far less likely to come crashing down. Remember: an upright character seldom falls on his face.

SAVIOR, YOUR NAME IS HOPE

Charles A. Waugaman February 10

Jesus!
Jesus, Jesus, Jesus, your name means Savior.
To say Your name is to hope.
To pray is to look to God hopefully.
Oh, Lord, I need to be reminded. I need to remember that,
for there are many times that's all the prayer
I have strength for.
Jesus.
"Your faith has made you whole,"
you used to say to those who came to You.

And people suggest, even when it isn't spoken,
that faith is unwavering expectation.
Faith is belief unaffected by circumstance, appearances,
emotions.
> Pain robs me of such hope.

Anxiety drains away all expectation.
Failure of every kind saps my faith. That's when I need to remember that Your very name
is prayer, is hope, is healing. Jesus!
> Even when someone else speaks it,

I can feel the prayer.
Help my body accept hope, let my mind record
> Jesus!

A CLOSER WALK

Micki Roberts   **February 11**

> *O LORD my God, I cried unto thee and thou hast healed me. Weeping may endure for a night, but joy cometh in the morning.*
>
> *(Psalm 30:2, 5 KJV)*

Oh how gracious is the Lord, my God. For months I had allowed my hurt to grow and fester in my heart. My pillow had been soaked with bitter tears night after night.

But finally, moment by moment, my hurt was being healed. Yet, the healing could only begin when I immersed myself in His Word. For so long I had neglected the study of His Word. Still, "the balm of Gilead" was always there—waiting for me to partake of it. Now, at last, I had returned to it.

The healing waters washed away my hurt. God cleansed me anew with His life-giving water. I was able to release all of the bitterness and pain. Once more I was able to return to blessed fellowship with my Heavenly Father.

Is there something keeping you from a closer walk with God? Turn it over to Him, open His Word, and allow healing to take place in your life.

GIVER OF LIFE

Cheryl Wyatt February 12

>Giver of Life
>Sweet Living Water
>King of all Kings
>Merciful Father
>Lord of all Lords
>Faithful and Righteous
>Breathe on her Your
>Sweet breath of life.

WITHOUT FANFARE

Charles E. Harrel February 13

Many followed him, and he healed all their sick, warning them not to tell who he was.
(Matthew 12:15-16, NIV)

Normally I sleep well, but that night offered little rest. In the morning, I realized why. I was getting sick. By the time I finished dressing for work, my throat hurt, my muscles ached, and the chills of a low-grade fever had begun. Then a headache kicked in.

Knowing how my body reacts to illness, I realized there was just enough time to drive to the office, collect my files, and return home before the symptoms grew worse. I'm not sure why I didn't pray for myself or ask someone else to pray. I guess I was preoccupied with how bad I felt.

Once I arrived at work, several phone calls kept me busy until noon. That's when it dawned on me—I'm not working today—I'm sick. But the fever, sore throat, and headache were totally gone.

Isaiah prophesied God's chosen servant would heal the sick without fanfare. He would not ask for recognition, use loud speeches, or find the need to quarrel. These signs would confirm that God's Spirit was upon him. While humanity often needs acknowledgment for their deeds, Jesus never does.

Dear Lord, Your healing touch helps when we are sick or hurting, and at times, even surprises us. I wonder how many others You have healed without drawing attention. Amen.

WINTER RETREAT
Elizabeth M. Van Hook　　　　　　　　　　　　　　　February 14

> *But those who hope in the LORD will renew their strength.*
> *They will soar like eagles; they will run and not grow weary,*
> *they will walk and not be faint.*
> *(Isaiah 40:31 NIV)*

In winter's sunshine
I sit alone
on the damp sandy steps of the white gazebo
reading Isaiah's words,
praying for healing.

Waves pound the secluded Atlantic beach.
Driftwood is scattered around me,
tangled with the seaweed
from recent snowy north-easters.
A chilling wind brushes my face.
Eagles soar above me in the endless azure sky.
Here in my secluded retreat,
I reflect on the ancient prophet's promises,
which now assure me that God will answer
my pleas for healing
and grant me another spring.

Father, I am thankful that I have Your Word to go to when I need encouragement, reassurance, and healing. Amen.

FALLEN COMRADES
Lorena Estep　　　　　　　　　　　　　　　　　　　February 15

> *Go to the ant, you sluggard; consider its ways and be wise!*
> *It has no commander, no overseer or ruler, yet it stores its*
> *provisions in summer and gathers its food at harvest.*
> *(Proverbs 6:6-8 NIV)*

While taking a creative writing course that centered on contemporary poetry, I became very word conscious. During that period I found myself sometimes talking in poetic phrases.

We had an influx of ants in our house and set about trying to stop the invasion. What amazed me was seeing the live ones return to carry away the bodies of those who were down. I said to my husband, "Look! That ant's carrying a fallen comrade."

I recalled the words from Proverbs that advised us to consider the ways of the ant and be wise. Now I saw that not only could we take a lesson from the ant in hard work, but also in how they cared for their "comrades."

As Christians we are in a spiritual warfare, and need all the help we can get. Let's watch for any of our comrades in Christ who are down in any way, and help to lift them up with loving care and prayer.

Therefore encourage one another and build each other up, just as in fact you are doing.

(1 Thessalonians 5:11 NIV)

EULOGY FOR NORMA BROWN HALL
Gloria Hall Troup   **February 16**

Norma Brown Hall was a mother, grandmother, aunt, and friend to many. She was a giant of a Christian woman and a great prayer warrior. No request was too large or too small. When hearing of someone's problem, she would first quietly say, "Let us pray about it."

It was amazing to all that for at least forty years after her husband's death, she was able to keep living in her own home, regularly keeping it painted inside and out. She would always have an American flag in the front of her house. With joy she would lovingly water not only her inside flowers, but her front and back porch flowers.

Personally, she saw me through childhood, the adoption of her first grandchild, divorce, and the nursing home years with my ill health. I am especially grateful that God allowed my mother to live to see me healed by His grace.

At age 97, her mind was still sharp, and she read her Bible daily and still reached out to others. We all know she is in heaven with no pain and perfect peace, because she knew her Savior and lived in His grace. I imagine she heard Jesus' beautiful words, "Well done, good and faithful servant."

JUMPING JOASH
Audrey Stallsmith   **February 17**

But after his (Jehoiada's) death, the leaders of Judah came to King Joash and induced him to abandon the Temple of the

God of their ancestors, and to worship shame-idols instead!
(2 Chronicles 24:17-18 LB)

After so many had risked so much to put him on the throne, Joash should have followed their example by becoming a heroic king. But, although he made a promising beginning, his religiosity was apparently aimed only at pleasing the uncle who was like a father to him.

Once Jehoiada was dead, the leaders of Judah soon talked their monarch into "jumping ship" on all his previous convictions. Even a reproof from Jehoiada's son, Zechariah, didn't help. In a decision reminiscent of his wicked grandmother's, the king simply had his bothersome cousin executed.

But punishment wasn't long in coming. Joash suffered a humiliating defeat at the hands of the tiny Syrian army, after which his own officials assassinated him to avenge Zechariah's death. So the king's weakness won him only contempt from those he'd been trying to appease. They apparently had much more respect for the man who told them what they didn't want to hear.

If we're trying to please other people rather than God, we can lose our foundations as rapidly as Joash did. And, in our panicked rush to find new support, we too might sink to depths we would never have thought possible. Zechariah, who didn't lose his faith with his father, turned out to be Jehoiada's only true son.

SOCIAL SECURITY

Della Ray   **February 18**

On the way to work, I saw a church bulletin board advertising next week's sermon, "Social Security." As I pondered what the sermon might be, I was struck with the idea that many times we are more concerned with our Social security than we are with our Eternal security. Often we find ourselves making choices based on how others will react to us. We base our decisions on how it will affect our social standing. Will people like us, agree with us, and recognize us? We care very much what people think. It is important for us to be a part, an acceptable part, of the desired social circle.

"While you have the Light believe in the Light (have faith in it, hold to it, rely on it), that you may become sons of the Light and be filled with Light." Jesus said these things, and then He went away and hid Himself from them (was lost to their view)....

Isaiah has also said that God has blinded their eyes and hardened and benumbed their (callous, degenerated) hearts. He has made their minds dull, to keep them from seeing with their eyes and understanding with their hearts and minds and repenting and turning to God to heal them. Isaiah said this because he saw God's glory and spoke of Him.

And yet (in spite of all this) many even of the leading men (the authorities and the nobles) believed and trusted in Him. But because of the Pharisees they did not confess it, for fear that (if they should acknowledge Him) they would be expelled from the synagogue; for they loved the approval and the praise and the glory that come from men (instead of and) more than the glory that comes from God. They valued their credit with men more than their credit with God.

Where do you put your security? Do you put it in society or in Christ?

BE A CHEERFUL GIVER

Gloria Clover   **February 19**

At my home church we have a saying regarding our material possessions: It's all God's anyway. Like most pithy sayings, though I believe the truth in my mind, I find it difficult to live consistently. Recently our gracious God gave me an image to remember when I need convinced that He "loves a cheerful giver" (2 Corinthians 9:7 NIV).

Each summer for Vacation Bible School, I choose to shepherd the four- and five-year-old class. During this week I gather spare change from the top of the washing machine, my husband's dresser, the bottom of my purse, and I pass those coins on to any child within the group who doesn't have money for our mission's collection. Sometimes I barely have the coins passed out before the collection bucket arrives and they eagerly drop their change into it. Save one little darling. One tyke's fist remained closed around her newly received quarter.

Father, I am too often that child clutching a gift You had given to me to pass on, given simply because You wanted to see my joy in participating in building Your Kingdom. I'm sorry, Lord. I want to be an eager giver with my money, my possessions, my time, and Your Word. Bring that convicting image of a tight-fisted child to my mind when I am not the sieve in whom You find joy. Thank You in Jesus' name. Amen.

SHAPING FOR ETERNITY
Judy Barron   **February 20**

Blessed are those who are persecuted for righteousness' sake, for theirs is the kingdom of heaven.
(Matthew 5:10 NKJ)

Billy Graham tells the story of a workman shaping a small piece of stone for a church. He explained what he was doing. "See that little opening way up there near the spire? Well, I'm shaping this down here, so it will fit up there." And in just that way, God, the Master Craftsman, shapes us down here to fit in "up there" in heaven. Whatever we have to endure down here only helps to prepare us for the time when God will call us home to that place which He is making ready for us. When we, our family or our friends, go through tough times and face extreme difficulties, let us remind each other that we are being shaped for that perfect place in the only home that really matters.

Father, I ask You to chisel away my faults and fill in my rough spots, so that I will be more fitted for my place in heaven. While You prepare a place for me as You have promised, please remind me that You are also fitting me for that place. Amen.

BRAIN MATTERS
CJ Hitz   **February 21**

Above all else, guard your heart, for it is the wellspring of life.
(Proverbs 4:23 NIV)

Ready to brush up on human anatomy? What part of our brain stores memory? If you said, "Hippocampus," you're correct. Studies have shown that once information is loaded into our hippocampus, it's almost impossible to erase. In a sense, our brains are the most sophisticated computer systems on the planet. The last I heard, no company has created a computer with unlimited hard drive memory. My laptop has 60 gigs of storage space, which is nothing compared with the latest technology. But even the most sophisticated computer we have at our fingertips pales in comparison to the human brain. As long as we're alive, we're able to load as much information as possible into our brains. But unlike a computer, our brains do not have a delete button. How many times have you loaded images or words into your brain and wished you could delete them?

I was nine years old when a kid next door brought over his dad's *Hustler* magazine. At that age, I barely comprehended what I was looking at, but those images were burned into my brain. Television, movies, video games, and the Internet have a profound impact on our lives. I know people who say they have trouble sleeping at night. The first question I ask them is what were they doing right before going to bed.

Because, remember this: Whatever you load into your brain will either be your friend or your enemy...*for a lifetime.*

STORY WITH NO END

Tom HarshbargerFebruary 22

I am sure you have heard the old, old story
How our Lord came from Glory
To seek, to save, and show us the way
It is one story that has no end.

God created the Heaven and Earth
And all that is therein,
Giving us light which He did send.
It is the story with no end.

Giving us blessing each and every day
When to Him we go and pray,
Warning us, stay straight, don't bend.
From the story that never ends.

Walk tall and with a smile,
As you travel each and every mile,
Showing all, a hand to lend,
As in the story with no end.

Live good, love all,
Preparing each, for a call.
Some day His angels He will send.
As told in the Story with no end.

Be prepared to answer His call.
Under your burdens do not fall.
Your love, your forgiveness, what a blend,
From the Old, old Story with no end.

PROCLAIM THE PRIZE

Audrey Kletscher Helbling   **February 23**

Now there is in store for me the crown of righteousness, which the Lord, the righteous Judge, will award to me on that day—and not only to me, but also to all who have longed for his appearing.

(2 Timothy 4:8 NIV)

His joy shone in the wide smile that stretched across his face, revealing the braces on his top front teeth. He couldn't hide his enthusiasm as he unzipped his coat. Pinned to the front of his fleece shirt was a bright yellow tag announcing in red letters, "3rd Place Disgusting Sneakers."

Caleb had ranked high in a fourth grade contest that pitted classmate against classmate to see who had the smelliest, dirtiest, yuckiest shoes.

Caleb's teenaged sisters could barely contain their laughter. They secretly wondered why their little brother, notorious for his sweaty feet and stinky shoes, had not placed first. Unaware of their snickers, Caleb raced upstairs and tacked the award onto his bedroom bulletin board.

We too should feel such unbounded enthusiasm for a prize that awaits us—the prize of Heaven. We should be bursting with joy, smiling from ear to ear, spreading the news of God's salvation. But more often than not, we feel undeserving of God's grace. After all, why should we receive an award for being smelly, dirty, and yucky?

God, however, views us as pure, clean, and sweet-smelling. And He sees us that way for one reason. His beloved Son, Jesus, washed our sin-soiled clothes with His blood and dressed us in the clean clothes of righteousness. Only because of Jesus can we claim the promised prize of eternal life.

Lord, thank You for sacrificing Your Son so that we might receive the ultimate prize, everlasting life. Let us joyfully proclaim the good news of salvation on the bulletin boards of our lives.

LIVING THE WONDER

Shirley S. Stevens   **February 24**

Make me to understand the way of thy precepts: so shall I talk of thy wondrous works.

(*Psalm 119:27 KJV*)

Albert Einstein observed, "There are only two ways to live your life. One is as if nothing is a miracle, and the other is as if everything is a miracle."

When was the last time that you noticed a miracle? Have you walked the beach and found a whole shell which survived the pounding surf? Have you looked closely at a sand dollar to see the finely etched flowers there? Have you broken open the shell to find the miniature doves inside? If you have, you understand why some call the sand dollar the Holy Ghost shell.

Have you picked up a feather and wondered at the way in which each section interlocks with the other? Have you seen a premature baby who weighed less than three pounds grow into a healthy child? Have you looked into a bathroom mirror and asked yourself, "How could he love this face?" And then you go out into living room, and your spouse comes over and kisses you and says, "I love you"?

Help me, O Lord, to find the miracles in each day. Help me to renew my sense of wonder.

PRAISING GOD

Christi McMath   **February 25**

Praising with
Reverence to the Lord Jesus
Always works.
It makes me
Smile,
Even when I don't feel like it.
Today's troubles go away, and I soon find myself
Relaxing, with my heart filled with peace and
Understanding that the Lord's
Everlasting love for me replaces my despair with a new
Hope, and I realize the
Awesome fact that the

Power of
Praise will help build my faith
In the fact that
Nothing can
Ever
Separate me from the
Security I receive when I trust in Christ. I will
Praise Him
Even when I can't find
A reason, knowing in my heart my
Cares will
Eventually depart.
When I PRAISE Jesus, even in difficult circumstances, He fills my heart with TRUE HAPPINESS and PEACE.

DUSTY CORNER

Peter Paulson   **February 26**

I am a wood mangler. No wood scrap is safe from my radial miter saw, table saw, band saw, seven hand saws, two drills, five sets of bits, one inch sander, orbital sander, or three-inch sander. I have four types of glue, four trays of nails, screws, bolts, and nuts. There are four tool boxes as well as a large peg board of tools over my workbench. When my wife asks for "the pointy thing you need when you fix..." I can bring her three dozen different pointy tools. If I want to hammer something, I have two for each hand. When I purchase brads, I buy them in 5k boxes and I have lots of boxes.

Last night, I fussed over a birdhouse with a frying pan lid, "Bed, Breakfast, and Bath." The battery pack on my drill went dry. I reached for the pack in the charger. It sat out of sight in the back corner of the workbench, dust laden and unpresuming. A pencil point red light glowed at the base to confirm its functioning.

All of the tools, a lumber yard of wood, and there it sat, almost buried, unseen, quietly doing its job. It is a mirror of the Holy Spirit. We live under avalanches of doings and things. Somewhere underneath it all, our personal, spiritual battery charger works away to keep our lives going. Oh ...you do need to plug into it, though. Have you?

Power me up, Spirit.

CONSTRUCTION WORKER JOY

Thomas Dallio   February 27

Today God has given us tools and provisions to build His house on earth as it is in heaven. No matter where we are, every person who has been saved by Jesus Christ is a hired construction worker on God's team.

When we wake in the morning, we must prepare to go to work. God's Word offers specific instructions, which we can reason together with God in prayer to develop a wise strategy for building up a solid foundation.

The Lord is our foreman. He can teach us how to build a highway home to the glorious dwelling. Architecture is God's specialty. Jesus said, "In my Father's house are many rooms; if it were not so, I would have told you. I am going there to prepare a place for you" (John 14:2, NIV).

Let's together be construction workers with joy!

HE IS THE MASTER CRAFTSMAN

Evelyn Minshull   February 28

When a potter takes lifeless clay—kneading and shaping it into a work of beauty and service...
Can God not easily coax our sometimes-reluctant spirits into shapes that please and glorify Him?

When a quilter creates an heirloom from fragments of fabric and lengths of thread...
Can God not take the remnants of our hours and fashion them for His eternal use?

When a sculptor takes a block of wood...or marble...or ice—freeing from its solidity a fluid shape, suggesting movement ...
Can God not find within our paralyzing fear and doubt an energy, joy, a flexibility, bursting to soar in praise?

He is the Master Craftsman. Whatever art we practice, our product is a muted imitation of His Works—around us and within.

May the Master Craftsman, Creator of all that is, guide the creative works He has placed in our minds and on our hearts. Amen.

A NET FOR CATCHING DAYS
Shirley S. Stevens   **February 29**

To everything there is a season, and a time to every purpose under the heaven.
(Ecclesiastes 3:1 KJV)

Native Americans make dream catchers, sinew strands in a web around a tear-shaped frame. They believe that the web will catch bad dreams to protect sleeping children. I have been thinking about a web for my waking hours. Annie Dillard suggests that we should create a net for catching days.

I have found that I accomplish more when I make a list or schedule each morning. There is something satisfying about being able to check off completed tasks. I find that by ordering my day, I use my time more productively. In capturing minutes, I catch hours and days before they slip by.

Dear Lord, help me to schedule my days so that I make time for You. Amen.

GOD'S TIMING
Connie A. Ansong   **March 1**

Our God is never late or too early.

Often, when we pray, we are not sure of what we want and whether we are being realistic or not. There are times when we even wonder if we deserve to receive answers to our prayers. God has been so good to us by revealing to us that, whatever we pray for, He responds to our prayers as soon as He hears our voice. We need to take courage when we set our hearts to understand the "word" and to humble ourselves before God. Our words are heard and our prayers are answered. Our God is faithful to His words.

We need to learn to rest totally in His will when we are waiting for answers to our prayers. Our God is never late or too early when it comes to responding to our prayers. Not all the responses to our prayers meet our plans and will. However, we must learn to trust the Lord for the responses we receive. In addition, we must trust in His goodness more than we trust in our knowledge since He created us and He designed each of our lives.

Oh! God give us grace to abide in Your everlasting peace and patience as we wait for our prayers to be answered. Amen.

GOD'S PLAN

Joan Clayton March 2

As a teenager many years ago, I had a serious operation on my sinuses. While under the anesthesia I had an unforgettable experience. I became aware of two angelic beings hovering over me on the operating table. They talked to each other. "We have to send her back. Her work isn't finished yet," one being said.

"Then hurry, because she's about to die," replied the other angel.

I awoke to the sickening smell of ether. I can still remember to this day how sick I felt.

I thought about this event many times. Now that I am older, I look back and see God surely had a plan for my life. A wonderful husband and three marvelous sons, included in that plan, have blessed me beyond measure. A teaching career of 31 years, and now writing for Him, surely have been in His plans for me.

I believe God has a plan for everyone. There are no accidents with God. To me, this life is training ground, a testing place to learn to love, to forgive, and to bless others. "To love the Lord, your God, with all your heart and your neighbor as yourself" is life's highest calling.

It's a wonderful plan for a wonderful life. He has a plan for you, too!

Dear precious Lord, thank You for the time we've had to live. May we honor You with every breath we take, walking in the plan You created for us.

TREMBLING JOY

Connie Bretz March 3

The rain fell as thick as borscht soup that night. Focused on sending my latest poem to a Christian magazine and clutching my umbrella, I dashed outside. Gloomy weather conditions couldn't deter me.

Sporadic lightning snapped into the fringes of my space. Then, a boom and shattering crack inches from me caused the blood to thunder through my heart and shoot into my face with a heat I'd never felt before.

I stopped, turned, and saw what looked like a huge oak tree branch on the street and sidewalk inches behind me.

On legs like cooked spaghetti strands, I ran to Mary's house and told her what happened.

The next morning, Mary and I viewed the scene. No, not a branch, but an entire section of tree had collapsed. We couldn't lift the branch—too heavy.

God's intervention saved me from a death blow, and I trembled in joy and relief.

O God, You are my Rock and my Deliverer. I praise You and I am grateful. In Jesus' name. Amen.

PLANS

Lisa Hill   March 4

"Man plans; God laughs." Unknown

My family anticipated a year of change. We looked forward to selling our business, moving to a new area, and going back to school, but I think God was smiling as He had other plans for us.

Every plan we had unraveled, was stopped, and fell through. I tried to stay optimistic, but secretly, I was beginning to wonder what God was doing in our lives.

Then we discovered I was pregnant! With one hand on my forehead and my eyes rolled back inside my head, I embraced the news. I was thirty-nine years old! Yet, knowing this child was a blessing from God, I began to accept this new plan for my life.

Looking back, I now can smile at the fears and doubts I experienced while waiting for our new little boy to arrive. Seconds after delivering our son, I knew just how wonderful God's plan for our family truly was. I was given the greatest gift.

Now, I enjoy just watching our newborn son revel swaddled tightly in his blanket, his belly full of milk. My heart warms as I watch his father sigh as he holds him close. This was not the plan we had made. I should be back in school, pursuing my degree in some unknown town as my husband heads off to his new job. But God had other plans. What plans has God for you?

"For I know the plans I have for you," declares the Lord,
"plans to give you hope and a future."
                                                                        Jeremiah 29:11 (NIV)

PSALM 118
Tune of *While By Our Sheep*

Glenda Joy Race   **March 5**

Let us give thanks unto the Lord.
His mercy endures forever.
For He is good (He is good.)
And merciful. (Merciful.)
He answered my call of distress.
        (He answered my call of distress.)

With the Lord at my side, I will not fear
What man may do against me.
Oh I will trust (I will trust.)
In the Lord (In the Lord.)
Rather than put my trust in men.(I will put my trust in the Lord.)

The Lord is my strength and my song.
He is my salvation.
How great His works! (Great his works.)
Praise His name! (Praise His name.)
The right hand of God does valiantly.
        (The right hand of God does valiantly.)

This is the day the Lord has made.
We will rejoice and be glad.
How great our Lord, (Great our Lord.)
Who shows us light. (Shows us light.)
We will exalt and give Him thanks.
        (We will exalt and give Him thanks.)

NOT FORGOTTEN

Jana Carman   **March 6**

I will not forget you! See, I have engraved you on the palms of my hands.

(Isaiah 49:15-16 NIV)

We each have our own ways to keep from forgetting important things. You may write yourself a note, or tie a string around a finger, or turn a ring inside to your palm, put your hat on backwards, or write on your hand.

Knowing how easily we forget, God gives us divine "strings around our finger." The rainbow reminds us of His promise not to destroy the whole earth by water again. The Sabbath and the tithe remind us that part of our time and our possessions are His by right. The Communion service reminds us of Christ's love and sacrifice.

I am glad that God forgets some things. Jeremiah 31:34 says that He "remembers their sins no more." But He also remembers, and Isaiah wrote that He uses my favorite method—writing on one's hand. Jesus looks at the marks on His palm and remembers me for whom He died.

Dear Lord, may I always remember what You have done for me, and be truly grateful! Amen.

THE VISUAL PRESENCE OF GOD
Charles E. Harrel **March 7**

And the LORD went before them by day in a pillar of cloud to lead the way, and by night in a pillar of fire to give them light, so as to go by day and night. He did not take away the pillar of cloud by day or the pillar of fire by night from before the people.

(Exodus 13:21-22 NKJ)

The San Gabriel foothills of Southern California, though picturesque, have a dangerous side, especially for the inexperienced. Temperatures, which are hot during the day, chill down quickly after sundown. Hypothermia is a common concern, not to mention the rattlesnakes, coyotes, and mountain lions. No wonder the two lost hikers were afraid.

As I listened to my Sunday school teacher tell the story, I realized why these young boys were ill-prepared to spend a night on the mountain. With no overnight gear or water, they were already in serious peril. Nevertheless, the next morning, the boys were found alive, huddled beneath a stained-glass window at a church in LaCanada.

The lost hikers said they had followed a bright light through the night, leading them to safety. The search party found a small burning candle inside the church's windowsill, hardly visible a mile away, let alone from where the boys were lost.

Sometimes we need the visual presence of God to lead us. Whether it's a supernatural fire, a miraculous cloud, or spiritual direction from a devotional, we should always trust in God's divine guidance.

FINDING DELIGHT IN DETOURS
Margaret Steinacker March 8

> Elisha said to them, "This is not the way, and this is not the city; follow me, and I will bring you to the man whom you seek." And he led them to Samaria.
> (2 Kings 6:19 NRS)

We had not been on vacation for two hours when the first detour sign appeared. We all greeted it with a sigh and then proceeded to decide which path to take.

Road construction and detours attach themselves to summer. Detours allow workmen to make needed repairs or fix dangerous spots in the road, but they bring temporary irritation to most motorists. We have two choices when we encounter them. We can either follow the highway department's outlined detour or ask a local resident about the closest way around. The local route may be narrow, rough, or gravel-coated. It is often shorter, allowing us to reach our destination by the expected time.

In life, we may also experience detours. In God's infinite wisdom, they occur in our lives to provide the path to a closer walk with God. As with road detours, we have two choices. We can choose the way of the world and "enjoy sin for a season," or we can ask God for His directions, knowing we'll be back on the main road with speed. Following God's will brings us to the correct destination at the perfect time.

Proverb: *The detours in our lives may become unexpected blessings.*

A KIND FATHER
Ruth Baldwin March 9

> Be imitators of God, therefore, as dearly loved children.
> (Ephesians 5:1 NIV)

Part of my job on our farm was to gather the eggs. I didn't enjoy being pecked by the hens as I robbed their nests, but I understood their concern.

After high school, I went to Chicago for further education, living in a rooming house run by retired nurses. They offered no cooking facilities, so I ate out. The first day I ordered eggs and bacon. The eggs were cold storage eggs, so old we would have thrown them away at home. They tasted *awful.* I never ordered them again. After graduating, I told my father about those eggs, saying I'd never appreciated what he supplied so much before.

One day, I received a notice from the post office that I had a package. My father had purchased a wooden 12-dozen egg crate and had sent it full of eggs! When I thanked him, he said to return the crate when the eggs were gone. This I did, and soon another crate of eggs arrived. Until then, I had no cooking privileges, but when I shared the eggs with my landlady, she was more than happy to allow me to cook. My father sent them until I left Chicago. What a blessing they were!

I've thought many times about my kind father. He provided so much. How many times does the Lord provide for us? I'll always feel grateful for such a kind human father who emulated a dear heavenly Father.

A ROCKY UNEVEN PATH

Lanette Kissel　　　　　　　　　　　　　　　　　　　March 10

And the LORD said unto Satan, Behold, all that he hath is in thy power; only upon himself put not forth thine hand.
(Job 1:12 KJV)

On a recent camping trip at an Indiana State Park, as I read a trail map, I noticed that most of the trails were rated "moderate" to "rugged." We were hiking on a trail that never seemed to level off. We were constantly either making our way down the trail or climbing our way back up, with rocky uneven ground beneath our feet at all times.

We see from the scriptures about Job that having faith does not mean that our path will always be an easy one. But even during severe testing, God had no intention of abandoning Job. God watched over Job through every step of the ordeal. So you, too, may rest assured that when your foot falls upon rocky, uneven ground, God will be right beside you every step of the way.

Dear Lord, help us to call upon You to help us when the road beneath us gets rough and rocky. Amen.

I WILL TRUST IN YOU
Linda Mae Richardson   March 11

Sometimes I feel so overwhelmed, Lord.
My problems seem to loom before me—
Like towering mountains I have no strength to climb.
They obscure my vision from seeing anything else.
My eyes are fixed on them and I find myself
Feeling discouraged and hopeless.

How many times I have asked you to remove the mountains,
Or at least to show me a way around them.
I know You have the power to do this and
Sometimes in Your great mercy and sovereignty, You do,
But I am also learning that You give me the strength to endure
And the courage to start climbing.

Would I have chosen this path if I could?
No! I would pick one smooth and easy and without suffering.
But would I have learned these many great lessons
Or have known Your love and care in troubles?
No! I doubt I would.

And so I thank You, Lord, that my struggle has not been in vain.
That I am stronger now because of it...
Knowing You are with me, always, through all things!

What time I am afraid, I will trust in thee. In God I will praise his word, in God I have put my trust.
(Psalm 56:3-4 KJV)

HIS PROVISION
Barbara J. Myler   March 12

A deep orange sunrise cast a glow against the rugged bark of trees outside my window. The glowing bark resembled burning logs, which have reached the ember stage.

Contemplating this striking comparison, I realized that this is one way our merciful God provides for our needs. The blessing of energy from sunlight warms the earth and stores its energy in the plants of God's creation.

As we need fire for light, heat, or to prepare food for the

preservation of our bodies, we draw on the provision of our Father. We are His; He knows our every need and has promised to fill them.

I am so grateful that He shows me these things in His creation, to buoy my faith and bolster my fickle human soul.

PREPARE YOURSELF

Flavia Crowner March 13

He who works his land will have abundant food, but the one who chases fantasies will have his fill of poverty.
(Proverbs 28:19 NIV)

When I attended collage, I planned to graduate in four years with a Bachelors degree in Art Education and with a minor in Elementary Education. I knew I had to study. To get my assignments in on time and make good grades, I couldn't party.

I prayed and asked for God's guidance to help me to prepare for my studies for the next four years. I listened for His inner voice and let Him speak to me. He instructed me how to research my assignments and hand in my best work.

God reminded me that I am to be like a farmer planting seeds. He plants his seeds in prepared soil and it will produce plenty of food. As a college student, I needed to acquire good study skills to get ready for my courses and pass them. I joined study groups, used the library, and stayed up late typing assignments to hand in on time.

I'm happy to say that I graduated and I earned my degree in education.

Lord, thank You for granting me wisdom and the perseverance to reach my goal. For showing me that, if I'd chosen to chase fantasies instead of studying, I would be like the farmer who plants his seeds in unprepared soil. Now, Father, help each of us prepare for the next goal. Amen.

GOD AS YOUR SOURCE

Theresa V. Wilson March 14

With God as your source,
you will learn to understand
that the prosperity you seek,
will not come from man.

You'll meet every challenge,
with all might and speed,
and avoid the pitfalls
of unwholesome greed.

You will shake off your cares
and have confidence
that the trials you bear
will reap heaven's recompense.

Our God is the source;
He's reigned through the years
as Key to all resources,
and Savior from fears.

GOD IS OUR STRENGTH

Marie DisBrow   **March 15**

The LORD is my strength and my shield; my heart trusts in him, and I am helped.

(Psalm 28:7 NIV)

My husband and I care for his 96-year-old mother at home. She is now bedridden and completely dependent on us for all her needs. Caregiving is a God-given privilege, but it can also be stressful, both physically and emotionally. If I rely on my own strength to perform my duties, I can easily become frustrated and overwhelmed. It is only when I look to God for guidance that I receive power to care for my mother-in-law—and power to be patient and loving.

We all have stressful moments in life, but we are not alone. Whatever problems and responsibilities we may face each day, the Lord has promised to give us the strength to meet them. The Bible says that "your strength will equal your days" (Deuteronomy 33:25) and "The joy of the Lord is your strength" (Nehemiah 8:10). His joy within gives contentment and the ability to face problems, stresses, and surprises.

As I learned to sing as a child, so long ago: "Jesus loves me...I am weak, but He is strong."

Thank You, Lord Jesus, for giving me strength day by day.
[First published in the Winter 2004-2005 issue of *The Secret Place*.]

THOU ART THE POTTER
Tiffany Schlichter   **March 16**

> *But now, LORD, thou art our father; we are the clay, and thou our potter; and we all are the work of thy hand.*
> (Isaiah 64:8 KJV)

A couple of years ago I had the opportunity to watch a potter at work. It was amazing! He could take a lump of clay that was ugly—it looked worthless—and make it into something beautiful and useful. The time it took for him to make something, and the way it came out, however, all depended on the flexibility of the clay. If it was obstinate, he would continue to work with it. However, if it refused to cooperate, he would throw it to the side. Accordingly, the flexible clay became beautiful pieces of pottery that honored and glorified the potter.

What kind of clay are you? Right now you may feel useless, but yield to God and be willing to do whatever He sets before you. He will use you in ways you can't begin to imagine.

We all need to remember that the Lord is the Potter, and we are the clay. If we truly yield our lives, wills, and desires to Him, we will be amazed at the ways He uses us and the paths He takes us on.

> *Delight thyself also in the LORD; and he shall give thee the desires of thine heart.*
> (Psalm 37:4 KJV)

MAKING A PATHWAY
Lorena Estep   **March 17**

> *The Lord is my strength and my song; he has become my salvation.*
> (Exodus 15:2 NIV)

Circumstances beyond my control were troubling me. Then I read Exodus, chapter fifteen.

The children of Israel were miraculously crossing the Red Sea on dry ground. As they walked through, carrying supplies on their shoulders and children in their arms, they must have gazed up in astonishment at the high walls of water on both sides of the large pathway God had cleared for them.

Their Egyptian captors followed close behind, desiring to return them to slavery. When the last of God's people stepped foot on the other side, God closed the water over their enemies. They were free at last!

I could feel their excitement and sense of triumph as they sang their praises to God with joy.

What a marvelous and miraculous God and Father, who is still the same yesterday, today and forever. I realized He could make a pathway through my troubles too, conquering my fears, if I would only believe and trust in Him. A God who could part the Red Sea can certainly make a pathway through any difficulty.

THE HOLY SPIRIT POWER
Gloria Hall Troup March 18

As Christians filled with the Holy Spirit, we should use His guidance to resist the devil. The devil comes "in the still of the night," ever vengeful, always looking for his prey. But we know that all things are possible because nothing is impossible with God.

Be aware of this great Holy Spirit who is waiting for our call to help us. Sometimes if we don't "ask, seek, and knock," the door will not be opened to us. He is all powerful, ever present, and all knowing. He is waiting for us to ask for His help. So keep seeking Him because He is our Helper and our Comforter. He is our "ever present help in trouble," and He will never leave us or forsake us. Praise God! Amen and amen.

LOST AND FOUND HORIZONS OF FAITH
Janet R. Sady March 19

We ask you to push back the horizons of our hope, and to push into the future in strength, courage, hope and love.
—Sir Frances Drake

The horizons of my faith shattered during a time of great grief in my life. In less than a year, my four-year-old brother died unexpectedly due to a blood clot after breaking his leg, my mother lost her battle with pancreatic cancer, and my father succumbed to a heart attack.

My parents and brother (who lived at home) lacked life insurance, wills, or funeral arrangements. None of my five siblings volunteered to handle these problems, so the burdens fell to me. Where was my hope? I felt as though I were drowning in a sea of despair. "Why did the Lord allow this to happen to me?" I asked.

No one had an answer.

In the midst of my pain, I cried to the Lord, and it was His Spirit who gave me hope and consolation. His love was evident through neighbors bringing food, and my church and friends donating money, sending cards, and most of all, praying for me.

The faith and wisdom to handle this situation came not from myself, but directly from the One who formed the horizon.

Thank You, heavenly Father.

LATE MARCH ANTHEM
Charles A. Waugaman   March 20

> Spring brings God's loving back to flower
> > as snows retreat
> > and greens aspire
>
> from every muddy bed of soil.
> > Each bare-branched tower
> > and barren twig
>
> ignites the land with verdant fire.
>
> Faith fuels the growth of vibrant jade
> > through frosty nights
> > and weeping days,
>
> till hope and patience swell with bloom.
> > Doubts can't invade
> > or fears remain,
>
> when Truth rolls wide the empty tomb.

PRAYER FOR THE POOR IN SPIRIT
Joy C. Bradford   March 21

Dear Lord,

You are such a great God. I know You are in control of all things and I am grateful. You tell us in the Scripture that those who belong to Christ Jesus have given up their sinful nature with its passions and desires. But, Lord, sometimes we slip back into old habits. We need Your constant help.

Today I especially pray for those who call themselves children of God, yet do not demonstrate they are indwelled of the Holy Spirit. Often they show acts of a sinful nature like hatred, fits of rage, selfish discord, and attempts to create factions that are disruptive within the body of believers.

Lord, what are they thinking? Joy seems to be gone from their hearts. Help me to understand and continue to love them as Christ would have me to do. In Galatians 5:22 we find that the fruit of the Spirit is "love, joy, peace, patience, kindness, goodness, faithfulness, gentleness and self-control." It is so hard to care for church members when they do not demonstrate even a few of these attributes.

Keep me from growing weary in this situation. It is so easy to be judgmental when I know that is not how You want me to be. Help me to stay focused on Your Word and keep me from being self-righteous. Show me the wrongness of my own ways so I can serve You better.

When I observe bad behavior, keep me from adding my sin to the problem. Show me how to leave the situation up to You. Galatians 6:7 tells us that "A man reaps what he sows." This is Your business not mine.

Gladly, I am reminded that You, O Lord, will reign forever. Your truth has endured through the generations. Restore us as a people and forgive our sins. We need You in our lives.

In Jesus' holy name we pray. Amen.

BUG WARFARE

CJ Hitz   March 22

Therefore put on the full armor of God.
(Ephesians 6:13 NIV)

We have some missionary friends in Paraguay, South America, who've been bombarded with some interesting tropical ailments. They've gotten scabies, tick bites, and the latest...piques (PEEKS). Piques are tick-like creatures found on stray dogs and live in the sand. They like to embed in your feet and develop their families in your toes! As you can imagine, they really get under the skin! Every night, our friends do a pique check to make sure their feet are clean. When they spot the microscopic black dot under the surface of the epidermis, they go in with their pique artillery...a needle, alcohol, and a cotton swab. If a pique is not discovered within a day, it starts to infect the entire area, causing lots of pain and major walking discomfort. Worse, they are contagious!

They told us that during one pique cleaning session, (their

record is eight at one time) the analogy came to them that we need to perform a daily inspection of spiritual piques. That is, we need to be analyzing our lives constantly to make sure we are living with integrity (the Bible uses the word "Holy") that's pleasing to God. One small sin left unchecked will wound not only us, but also those around us. It will also affect our relationship with God and will hinder our prayer life.

With our spiritual pique artillery (the Bible, prayer, and the conviction of the Holy Spirit) let's get in the habit of doing regular "spiritual pique checks."

KINGDOMS IN CONFLICT
Penny Deary March 23

My heart, His throne
   a humble kingdom
   ablaze with divine light
peace offered in the mystery of meekness

A fallen world, rebellion reigns
   empty hearts fueled by pride
   adrift in darkness
warfare cloaked in deception of grandeur

Clothed in white, dipped in blood
Prince of Peace awaits the word:
"Ride through the clouds in fire and light;
   explode the heavens, shake the earth,
   claim the victory won at the cross."

The kingdom of the world has become the kingdom of our Lord and of his Christ, and he will reign for ever and ever.
(Revelation 11:15 NIV)

THANKS BE TO GOD
Anne Siegrist March 24

Each time I see a cardinal perched on a branch of our giant Norway Spruce tree, or spot one snacking at our bird cafeteria, I say, "Thank You, Lord!"

Cardinals have been special to me since the day many years ago when I was complaining bitterly to God about our long, drab, cold winter. "Nothing ever changes!" I told Him. "Weeks, months go by and there isn't even anything pretty outside to look at." Just then a brilliant male cardinal flew to the brown bush, turning the scene into an artist's painting.

Now I try to develop more fully an attitude of gratefulness for everything. What luxury to snuggle under warm blankets in the winter! How refreshing to drink a glass of pure water! I thank God for a good night's sleep, for a conversation with a friend, an encouraging e-mail, for opportunities to do volunteer work.

I thank Him when the car starts and when I return safely from my errands. I thank Him when I am able to pay a bill as soon as it is due, and when I make a good find at the Salvation Army. I thank Him over and over for my loving family.

Each prayer of thanksgiving makes me think again of all that God has done, and all that He will do in the future. Thanksgiving gives me hope. Thanks be to God!

SNUGGLE TIME
Angela Dilmore   March 25

I long to dwell in your tent forever and take refuge in the shelter of your wings.
(Psalms 61:4 NIV)

Ever since my twin sons were toddlers and able to climb into my lap, we have enjoyed "snuggle time." During snuggle time, we read, sing, pray, or just rock. It is a special time of closeness.

Sometimes I wish I could be the child, and snuggle up close to God. When days are stressful, and life is coming at me from all directions, I imagine myself nestled "in the shelter of his wing," soft, downy feathers tickling my nose. There I can read His word, pray, or just listen. It's a warm, comforting place.

Indeed, we are God's children. The Holy Spirit comforts us when we are sad, scared, stressed-out, or just want to feel close to Him. He is with us always, and I imagine He loves to snuggle, too.

Thank You, Father, for granting us the privilege to experience Your love and comfort through the Holy Spirit. Amen.

JESUS, MY SAVIOR AND MY GOD
Marjorie K. Evans   March 26

I thank You, Lord,

for loving me
enough to die for me.

It was Your blood
You shed for me
alone on Calvary.

And now my sins
are washed away,
and I am free in Thee.

I praise You, Lord,
You rose again,
and wait in Heaven for me.

You have prepared
a mansion there,
and it is just for me.

Then I will spend
Eternity
praising Your Holy Name.

I praise Your Holy Name,
Oh Lord,
my Savior and my God.

Alleluia,
Alleluia,
I praise Your Holy Name.

> For God so loved the world that he gave his one and only Son, that whoever believes in him shall not perish but have eternal life.
>
> (John 3:16 NIV)

NO GREATER LOVE

Joseph M. Hopkins   **March 27**

> Greater love has no one than this, that he lay down his life for his friends.
>
> (John 15:13, NIV)

These words were spoken by Jesus to His disciples in the

Upper Room on the eve of His crucifixion. They were His friends for whom He was soon to die. For them—and for His friends across the centuries—there could be "no greater love."

But what about Romans 5:8? In this verse Paul tells us, "But God demonstrates his own love for us in this: While we were still sinners, Christ died for us." Is this not an even greater love? Perhaps the meaning is that Jesus' love is unconditional. It takes two to make a friendship. God's forgiveness and salvation is offered to all. But only those who accept Jesus' offer of friendship are numbered among the friends for whom He laid down His life on the altar of the Cross.

Dear Jesus, thank You for dying for us helpless sinners so that we can be privileged to know You, not only as our personal Lord and Savior, but as our Friend.

AND WHO IS MY NEIGHBOR?
Shirley S. Stevens   **March 28**

Thou shalt love the Lord thy God with all thy heart, and with all thy soul, and with all thy strength, and with all thy mind; and thy neighbor as thyself.
(Luke 10:27 KJV)

Carl Erskine, the Brooklyn Dodger ace pitcher back in the fifties, struck out 14 Yankees in a World Series game. But he says that as a teammate of Jackie Robinson, he learned a lot more than baseball skills. He discovered how to look beyond race at people's souls, to plumb the depths of what made them human.

Erskine believes that Jackie taught him to deal with his anger about society's lack of acceptance of people who are different. After Carl Erskine's fourth child, Jimmy, was born with Down's syndrome, Carl became involved in the Special Olympics program in Anderson, Indiana. Together father and son attended Dodger fantasy camps. Carl also became involved in his community's program for hiring those with handicaps.

Today Jimmy works for Applebee's Restaurant. His manager reports that his staff is better for Jimmy's working there. He says, "They love him and interact better when he's here."

Carl says that both Jackie and Jimmy have made us a more caring society, as we have been enriched by not rejecting but including those who seem different. Erskine says that they remind us we all need to be treated with dignity.

Lord, help me to treat all people with dignity, to look beyond differences and recognize my neighbor. Amen.

HANDS

Helen Kammerdiener   **March 29**

Thank You, Lord, for hands.
Thank You for hands
    to give a frightened child courage
        in a daunting situation,
    to shake another hand in friendship,
    and to give a gentle touch that says,
        "I love you," without words.
Thank You for hands that have become
    worn and scarred in serving others.
Thank You for nail-scarred hands
    reaching out to say, "I love you,"
    and to give us courage in a daunting world.
Thank You, Lord, for hands.

THE FULLNESS OF HIS GRACE

Martha Rogers   **March 30**

From the fullness of his grace we have all received one blessing after another.

(John 1:16 NIV)

Each day is a blessing, a gift from God. We know yesterday is gone, tomorrow is uncertain, but today is here. On birthdays and other special occasions, we look forward to receiving gifts. Sometimes those gifts are just what we want and love. Other times we wonder what the giver could have been thinking.

We open God's gift for us, and some days it may be beautiful with blessings of family unity, happiness and joy of good health, and a feeling of contentment. Other days we look at the gift and wonder, "God, what are You doing to me? What could You be thinking?" I call it my "box of dirty socks" gift.

We can take the gift of life, mourn, complain, wonder why God is allowing us or a loved one to suffer, or we can take it and thank Him for the opportunity to completely trust in Him.

If we truly believe in His saving grace and love, we trust Him to take care of our days no matter how difficult they may be. The answers don't always come when we wish they would, and they don't always come in the form we would like, but God does hear and answer. He gave the day to us; He knows what it will hold. He knows what we can bear.

What will you do with your gift today? God will break us, melt us, mold us, and fill us if we are completely in His will and seeking Him to guide our way.

Lord, give me strength to rejoice in the day You have made and be joyful despite what Satan seems to be hurling at me.

PREPARED SOIL

Martha K. Weaver   **March 31**

He who conceals his sins does not prosper, but whoever confesses and renounces them finds mercy.
(Proverbs 28:13 NIV)

I weeded my garden to prepare the soil for mulching. The smallest weeds would get choked, but anything larger than an inch might get air and grow through the mulch. I noticed a tiny blade of grass. Was it worth my extra energy to stoop to pull it? Rather than take a chance, I pulled it. To my surprise, its root curled about eight inches below the ground.

I asked myself if this isn't the way "little" hidden sins will get rooted in our minds and attitudes. They will eventually affect our lives. We may appear to be covered with fancy clothes that make us look right. Our façade will not be sufficient to keep the seeds of sin from growing. Until we stoop and confess the root of our problem, the "grass" will spread in our garden of hope and choke the tender plants.

Dear Lord, help me to keep my spiritual garden clean, so that I can be my best for You every day. Amen.

A LIFE OF WORSHIP

Cheryl Wyatt   **April 1**

Let my life be like a velvet rose placed at Your feet.
May the fragrance of my worship be not bitter, Lord, but sweet,
Spilling mercy, help, and truth on every hungry soul I meet.
Let my awe esteem You to the very highest place,
And hold You there by faith in love's unwavering embrace,
Until the day we stand eye to eye and I can give it face to face.

EMITTING A SPARKLE

Connie Bretz   **April 2**

Happy shalt thou be, and it shall be well with thee.
(Psalm 128:2 KJV)

Sammy was ecstatic at his birthday party. He popped caps on the sidewalk and slyly captured a lick of the chocolate frosting atop a tempting cupcake without mother noticing. Sam wholeheartedly played his turn pinning the nose on the clown. The best event: opening presents!

Many times Christians are somewhat glum and prone to complain about circumstances. If we could remember more often to express joy and emit the sparkle of a 'Sammy" at a birthday party, how many might find the Christian walk desirable?

We would cause non-Christians to be desirous of the enthusiasm marking our personalities—the God-given personalities.

Dear God, help us to be living demonstrations of the joy and gladness you have given to us. In Jesus' name. Amen.

UNFRIENDLY SNAPPERS

Lorena M. Estep   **April 3**

My dear brothers, take note of this: Everyone should be quick to listen, slow to speak and slow to become angry, for man's anger does not bring about the righteous life that God desires.
(James 1:19-20 NIV)

"There's a turtle on the road!" my daughter stated as she braked and pulled over.

She got out and approached the large turtle that was in no hurry to get to the other side and safety. She leaned down and took hold of both sides of the shell, only to have the whole body twist and a large strong neck swivel back to try to grasp one of her hands in its jaws.

Dropping it, she jumped away. Determined not to leave it there to a possible death, she tried another approach. That, too, didn't work. The turtle again made a lunge for her hand and moved rather quickly to attempt an attack on her. She turned and ran, the snapper chasing her across the road, which at least accomplished the goal of getting it to safety.

This brought to mind the disgruntled people we know and

want to help, only to have them snap at us and insist they can do it themselves, in their own way.

Snapping and backbiting have no place in a Christian church family. James 4:11 says: "Brothers, do not slander one another." And Galatians 5:14-15 says: "Love your neighbor as yourself. If you keep on biting and devouring each other, watch out or you will be destroyed by each other."

LOVE OVERFLOWING
Linda Mae Richardson   **April 4**

Today, I caught my reflection in the mirror and marveled at the stranger looking back. I reached out with trembling hands to touch my furrowed brow, my graying hair, and to gaze upon my body, which is no longer as young or as quick or as strong as it once was. Then slowly, I looked into my eyes—beyond the creases surrounding them—and I discovered that sparkle of joy that never seems to age, but grows only brighter each day as I walk with my Lord. And as I thought about God's gift of joy, I noticed a smile upon my lips and my face seemed transfigured and made beautiful by God's love.

> *But though our outward man perish, yet the inward man is renewed day by day. For our light affliction, which is but for a moment, worketh for us a far more exceeding and eternal weight of glory; while we look not at the things which are seen, but at the things which are not seen: for the things which are seen are temporal; but the things which are not seen are eternal.*
>
> (2 Corinthians 4:16-18 KJV)

I thank You, Lord, for teaching me to look beyond my physical body (a temporary vessel) and its many troubles to within my very soul. And lo, I find myself so filled with Your Holy Spirit, that in thankfulness, I reach out my two hands to share with others. I find them cupped and overflowing with Your great love for me and for them!

BROKEN PIECES
Evelyn Minshull   **April 5**

> *(While) He was reclining at the table, there came a woman with an alabaster vial of very costly perfume of pure nard; and*

she broke the vial and poured it over His head.
(Mark 14:3 NAS)

Often materials must be cut or broken, pruned, shaped, or sanded—before they can do the task for which they were created.

Quilts require that fabric be cut to specified sizes and shapes. Mosaics are designed from bits of glass, ceramic, stone and other durable materials. Sculpture occurs only when wood or marble is carved away.

Trees and shrubs flourish when pruning occurs. Even in baking, ingredients must lose their identity before the desired product can develop.

The woman who anointed Christ's feet with the precious spikenard first broke the vial. She could have set it on a shelf—waiting for some later, perhaps larger event. But by breaking the vial then, by spilling out its contents at that moment, she gave an example of worship that lives even today.

And when God and Gideon worked together to confound the Midianites, the pitchers had to be broken—both to add to the noise and to release the light.

Is it possible that we may sometimes have to be "broken"—our plans shattered, our dreams in shambles—before we can be shaped and fitted for the work God has designed for us alone?

Must we be prepared by brokenness before we can reflect His light?

GOLDEN GATE

Debbie Rempel April 6

I heard a knock and
ran to the door.
I paused for a
moment when I saw
Who it was.

        Jesus came
        to visit me today.
        What should I say?
        I stood there in awe of
        what I saw:
        a man in a robe of white,

with a heart of gold,
a Man named Jesus.
I took the time
to visit with Him
and learned a lot.
I am glad I opened
the door and spent time
with Jesus, the Master
of my life.

MIRACULOUS MAKEOVER
Marion E. Gorman   April 7

Therefore, if anyone is in Christ, he is a new creation; old things have passed away; behold, all things have become new.
(2 Corinthians 5:17 NKJ)

When I see large, older homes, I often daydream about restoring them to their original grandeur. I love their individual personalities and potential. I think of the stories they could tell. Realistically, I will not accomplish such a project in my lifetime, so instead I contemplate about how people can rebuild their lives.

Like a home, life needs to have a solid foundation. Cementing the crumbling foundation of a person's life begins when one accepts Christ and commits to following Him.

Anger, lying, and jealousy strip away like peeling paint with God's forgiveness. Old thought patterns are rewired so God's love can flow freely. Broken hearts, like shattered window panes, are mended and given hope. Guilt, hidden under old shingles that leak with regret, is covered by the blood of Jesus.

Daily upkeep and needed repair are necessary by staying in God's word. Changed lives are not daydreams. The stories they tell glorify God.

Lord, help me be a carpenter in the miracle of building people's lives for Your glory.

A PSALM OF DAILY MIRACLES
Judy Barron   April 8

See a yellow drop of joy in the redbud tree and hear a goldfinch song.
Watch an oriole and a hummingbird vie for the same drop of nectar.
Witness an old dog struggle to his feet and then run to catch his master.

The air is full of bird song as God's creatures prepare for new life.

The world is awake and bursting with new growth and songs of joy
To the One who is responsible for it all.
And, once again, I am renewed and revitalized and thankfully aware
That I am alive in the beautiful creation made by the Father,
Saved by the Son, and cared for by the Spirit.

Father, all praise to Your Holy Name and Your miracle called Spring.

BEAUTIFUL FEET

Janet R. Sady   **April 9**

And how shall they preach, except they be sent? As it is written, How beautiful are the feet of them that preach the gospel of peace, and bring glad tidings of good things!
(Romans 10:15 KJV)

Feet come in all sizes and shapes. Some people have short stubby feet while others may wear size 15 shoes. Feet with bunions, corns, and calluses can be just plain ugly. (Sorry, but it's true.)

We can have beautiful feet, however. No, I'm not talking about going for a pedicure—having our toenails painted, etc. What I refer to is in a spiritual sense. If we are willing to share the good news of the Gospel of Jesus Christ, and take our feet where God wants us to go, then we will truly have "beautiful feet" in the sight of God.

Father, may I be willing to have You give me beautiful feet as I witness for You wherever You send me. Amen.

THE SPIKES

Catherine Szymanski   **April 10**

God made everything with a place and a purpose.
(Proverbs 16:4 MESSAGE)

The Roman soldier selected three spikes. His left hand clenched the three nails.

Spike One said to his fellow nails, "I hoped to nail a cradle to rock a baby."

Spike Two responded, "I hoped to nail a house where a family would laugh and play."

Spike Three added, "I wanted to nail a barn to house

donkeys and sheep like the one that housed the manger."

The soldier, who didn't hear this conversation, set about his assigned task of nailing the spikes to the cross. For centuries the spikes would be remembered for their role in nailing the Savior to the cross.

Jesus, the Son of God who became a human carpenter, would say to Thomas, "Put your finger here in my side. Feel the place where the spikes penetrated my flesh."

O Lord, when things don't go as we have planned, help us to see the larger picture and to trust that Your plan for us is far greater than we imagine. You are the One who can bring good out of evil and forgiveness out of suffering.

NOT EMPTY AFTER ALL

Charles A. Waugaman April 11

As Easter nears
My heart is full of trumpets:
Fanfares and flourishes and faith
Invade my thought,
Reverberate desires,
Dance like choirs of golden jonquils
Through my mind,
Galaxy in royal violets
Across the greening lawn of hope.

Come, run with me
To that grand garden
Where at dawn
Love finds not the empty tomb of ritual,
But our useless grave clothes
Of fear and sin
Faithfully folded and abandoned
For the radiance of Life.

FROM DEATH TO LIFE

Joan Clayton April 12

I started crying long before it was time to cry. I had seen the Pageant on previous occasions, so I knew the part by heart. Jesus would be coming down the aisle bearing a heavy wooden cross.

The crack of whips by Roman soldiers wrenched my soul. I had to tell myself, "This is a play." Our son portraying Jesus made me hurt even more. I thought of Mary and how her pain had to be searing.

The world will never know the depths of love Jesus had for all of mankind to make such a sacrifice. John 3:16 is still the truth of the ages. Jesus' love is extended to everyone who will receive him.

The future of the child of God is always "the best is yet to be." Even in death there is victory. My grandmother sang about heaven on her deathbed. My mother's last words echo in my ear, "I see the heavenly lights."

Those in Christ Jesus pass from death to life.
Precious Lord, thank You for everlasting life.

MAUNDY THURSDAY
Joseph Hopkins April 13

Now that I, your Lord and Teacher, have washed your feet, you also should wash one another's feet.
(John 13:14 NIV)

Since this is Jesus' mandate (Maundy), why is it obeyed by only a few of the many Christian churches? The key is the word example in the following sentence. Jesus explained, "I have set you an example that you should do as I have done for you."

An example of what? Humble, loving service. That's what Jesus demonstrated when He took towel and basin and washed the disciples' feet. He didn't institute a sacrament, He set an example. Washing the feet of guests who arrive in sandals from the dusty streets was a custom in Bible days. It is not in our 21st century culture. But there are other ways of keeping the spirit of this commandment. If the love of Jesus is in our hearts, we will respond as Jesus did to opportunities to reach out in love to bless those we meet in the course of each day.

Lord, help me to be gracious and loving to everyone You bring into my life today and every day. Amen.

Dave Evans April 14

Images from Calvary's hill,
so long ago:

three crosses,
two sinners,
one Savior—
the sacrifice for sin's
penalty paid

Three men,
two decisions—
(One rejected, one repented),
One redeemed

Three crosses,
two choices,
one message—
God showed His love;
Christ died
for sinners.

But God shows his love for us in that while we were yet sinners Christ died for us.
(Romans 5:8 RSV)

He who believes in him is not condemned; he who does not believe is condemned already, because he has not believed in the name of the only Son of God.
(John 3:18 RSV)

JOSEPH OF ARIMATHAEA

Jana Carman　　　　　　　　　　　　　　　　　　　　**April 15**

I gave him my tomb.
What more could I do?
My voice in the council
was weak, shouted down
when I tried to counter
their passion with reason.

I tried.
Really, I tried.
What more could I do?

So I gave him my tomb,

and spices enough to embalm a king.
I did what I could:
I gave him my tomb.

But even the tomb
was only a loan,
although I thought it was more.
I'll use it myself,
but now I see
any tomb is only a door.

UNEXPECTED MAIL

Helene Burgess   **April 16**

I opened the back door to a gray, cold, very early Easter morning. Many Christians would be at Sonrise Service and here I was, scurrying to feed and water the outside cats. As I did, I noticed the wind had blown some old papers into our huge rose bush.

A tinge of annoyance crept over me as I reached into the bush to pick out the trash. Resentfully I gathered up the litter and then stopped abruptly—one piece had my name and address on it. My annoyance gave way to curiosity. As I turned it over, I saw a picture of a rabbit standing in a doorway. It was a postcard! Somehow a piece of my mail had blown out of my mailbox and landed here. The postcard was from a friend who had visited the actor Jimmy Stewart's museum in PA. "Harvey," the rabbit, was one of the characters Stewart portrayed.

A coincidence that I found it on Easter Day when it had been mailed three weeks earlier? Harvey, Easter, Christ's resurrection, my friend—all these thoughts swirled.

"Oh, Lord." I laughed. "It's tough being human, but You lighten up our moods in such creative ways. Sometimes the thing we least want to do will turn frustration into joy. Thank You that my friend thought of me. Thank You, Lord, for Your resurrection. Thank You, God, for Your Sonshine reigning all around us, even on gray days."

A cheerful disposition is good for your health; gloom and doom leave you bone-tired.

(*Proverbs* 17:22 MESSAGE)

STANDING TALL

Mary A. Koepke   **April 17**

I shall not die, but live, and declare the works of the LORD.
(Psalm 118:17 KJV)

      The long awaited week of warm sunny days gifted us with April blessings. It seemed spring had finally arrived and we were enjoying a celebration. We were free to open windows and doors and spend time on the back porch. We could welcome our bird friends' return to their feeders. Our tulips practically shot up over night; buds exploded to full bloom. Their bold scarlet brought delight to all who viewed them.

      Then, after hearing reports of unexpected snow, we woke to find green lawns and rooftops wearing the winter white that had worn out its welcome. But to our relief the tulips stood tall—heads held high and proud. Blood red blooms tight, they swayed in defiant dance with the forceful gusts.

      I found solace in their fiery courage at a time when our lives were ravaged by the blasts of my husband's death threatening disease. We had only to turn our eyes upon Jesus. His sacrificial blood shed at Easter will always give us courage to stand tall through whatever menaces life might bring.

Father, we praise You for the beauty of Your creation. For the tulips that color our souls and remind us of Your undying love. Amen.

HE IS

Joe LoBello   **April 18**

Great and marvelous are thy works, Lord God Almighty;
just and true are thy ways.
(Revelation 15:3 KJV)

      The society of ours has been blessed by the Lord with so much, freedom and bounty and openness of thought. Many have chosen to erase the traces of God from our backbone and framework. But I can tell you with certainty:

      Jesus was God and man
      He was anointed by God
      Not appointed by man
      He is special in all aspects
      Not flawed in any way

He is Emmanuel with much to give
Not empty-handed
He is not bondage
But our ultimate Salvation
He is our Hope
He is our Redeemer
He is our Shepherd
He is our Messiah
He is our Comfort
He is our light
He is Everlasting
He is everything to all who call upon Him.

A NEW LIFE IN CHRIST JESUS
Connie A. Ansong　　　　　　　　　　　　　　　　　　**April 19**

Because He lives, we live! He conquered death!

Lord Jesus, we are committed to live in God's will. Teach us to know You that we may find grace in Your presence. Certainly Your grace is sufficient for our needs. Please direct our paths to stay focused on Your plan for our lives that we receive the fulfilled life in Jesus Christ. We pray with thanksgiving. Amen.

A CHANGED PERSON
Pat Collins　　　　　　　　　　　　　　　　　　　　　**April 20**

When we give our hearts and lives to Jesus and accept Him as our Lord and Savior, we shed the old life and put on the new. Getting a new start, becoming a new person, we let old habits and resentments drift away, no longer wanted. We are filled with the Lord. We want to share His love, make amends, and live a different life, all for Him. And the angels rejoice when He saves us.

> *Therefore if any man be in Christ, he is a new creature: old things are passed away; behold, all things are become new.*
> *(2 Corinthians 5:17 KJV)*

Father, I confess I've lost the freshness and zeal I had when You first changed my heart. Create in me a pure heart today, Lord, that I would live like the new person I am. In Jesus' name. Amen.

BREAD
Helen Kammerdiener   **April 21**

    Thank You, Lord, for bread—
    Warm, crusty, homemade bread
        fresh from the oven,
    Convenient sliced bread from the store,
    The multitude of choices:
        white bread, raisin bread, rye bread,
            whole wheat, pumpernickel—
        so many I don't know even half of them.
    Thank You for bread toasted in the morning,
        made into sandwiches at noon,
        wrapped in a linen napkin in the evening.
    Most of all, thank You, Lord,
        for the bread that speaks of Your love—
    Your body given for us, Your blood shed for us—
    Remembering how You were crushed,
        and praising You, The Bread of Life.
    Thank You, Lord, for bread.

THERE'S A RAINBOW IN EVERY CLOUD
Louise Sutherland   **April 22**

Genesis 9:13-17

From the story of Noah and the flood, we know that God made a covenant never to destroy creation in that manner again. God also sealed His promise with the physical reminder of a rainbow.

Rainbows are interesting because they consist of two in one, a primary and a secondary rainbow. Between the bows the sky is darker than otherwise. The Bible speaks of a rainbow being in the cloud.

Dark clouds remind us of storms and rain. Every life has times of difficulty and rain. As we go through these wet times, we need to remember God's covenant with us through His Son. If situations come in life that bring clouds of discouragement, hurt, anger, or pain, hold tight to the promise that the Son will shine again. Look to the rainbow for assurance that God will bring life back to your situation, and remember that in every cloud there is a rainbow.

Father, we trust You in clear and stormy days. You are the Light of all the world.

AFTER TRIALS
Ruth Baldwin   **April 23**

The storm is over
God's truth prevails.
Winds blew
Showers—rain—deep darkness.
But through it all
God's steady presence
Guiding—harboring—urging me on.
The storm is over
God's truth prevails,
More precious than before!

BREAKING THE CYCLE OF UNGRACE
Shirley S. Stevens   **April 24**

Moreover he kissed all his brethren, and wept upon them: and after that his brethren talked with him.
(Genesis 45:15 KJV)

In Yancey's book "What's So Amazing About Grace?" he admits that grace is unfair. When I recently taught a seminar in memoir writing, I invited participants to write a letter to a family member, living or dead. When I wrote my own letter, I thanked my mother for being a giver. I remember how she sacrificed for me, sending a five dollar bill in a weekly letter when I was in college. Since she earned only fifty cents an hour, that gift represented ten hours of baby sitting. I also remember her putting her birthday presents in her cedar chest. When I asked if I could wear her new plaid blouse to my school picnic, she let me be the first to wear her special gift.

Sometimes I focus on resentment because of the years when Mother battled alcoholism. Writing this letter helped me to realize that breaking the cycle of ungrace means taking the initiative to forgive as the father did in running to meet the prodigal son or the landlord in canceling a debt too large for his servant to reimburse. Jesus taught parables of grace. When I think of Joseph's forgiving his brothers who had sold him into slavery, I realize that it was painful and took time for him to forgive them. He had to make the first move, but when grace finally broke through, the sound of his grief and love echoed throughout the palace.

Remind us, Lord, that Your forgiveness makes it possible for us to forgive others. It is in grieving and forgiving that we break the cycle of ungrace and open ourselves to Your healing.

THINK ON THESE THINGS

Micki Roberts   **April 25**

Have you ever thought, "I'm a great big failure"? How can we as Christians—children of the King—think of ourselves any less than what God thinks of us?

Did He not make Himself of no reputation? Taking upon Himself the form of a servant and being made in the likeness of man? And being found in fashion as a man, did He not humble Himself, becoming obedient unto death? Even the death of the cross! [Philippians 2:7-8]

This Scripture is speaking of God, the Creator of the universe, who Himself took the form of man to shoulder sin (that's our sin) and then died, the blameless, unblemished Lamb of God, to secure for us eternal life.

Just knowing how much Jehovah God loves us should keep us from thinking of ourselves as failures. Yet, we do.

However, our loving God understands and He forgives. He knows the troubles that we face and the temptations the enemy places before us.

Meditate upon Philippians 4:8 and take it to heart. Then, think upon these things and never again allow yourself to believe the enemy's lie that you are a failure!

CALL TO PRAYER

Bonnie J. Manion   **April 26**

When I hear in my being
His sound of welcoming,
at the voice of my King
my heart's called to sing.

He comes like a flood
over my flesh and blood,

stirs a joy in my soul
that puts Him in control

I just feel, just exist
to experience the bliss,
the glow of His presence
taking hold of my essence

When I want but His will
for my life, to my fill
what He gives is His grace,
peace to my inner space

INNER URGINGS
Joy C. Bradford — April 27

As the special day approached, Stephanie prayerfully considered how she could remember Christina's mother who had recently and unexpectedly passed away. Someone warned her against invading Christina's privacy. However, an inner urging prompted Stephanie to inquire at the cemetery office for directions to the grave site. There, she quietly placed flowers and a card.

The next morning, Mother's Day, Christina and her father sadly visited the plot and found what Stephanie had left. They were surprised and comforted by the thoughtfulness of her gesture. Somehow this lessened the heartache of their visit. Christina expressed her gratitude to Stephanie.

We should follow our inner urgings from the Holy Spirit. No one wants to be misunderstood by their actions, so prayer should be the first step of good deeds.

Commit to the Lord whatever you do, and your plans will succeed.

(Proverbs 16:3 NIV)

LONGING FOR GENTLENESS
Margaret Steinacker — April 28

But the fruit of the Spirit is love, joy, peace, patience, kindness, goodness, faithfulness, gentleness, self-control; against such things there is no law.

(Galatians 5:22-23 RSV)

Can you describe gentleness? The question came up in our first semester Bible class. These thoughts jockeyed for position in my mind.

Gentleness is a mother cradling a newborn in the crook of her arm as she rocks her babe to sleep.

Shakespeare said, "The quality of mercy is not strained. It droppeth as the *gentle* dew from heaven upon the earth beneath. It is twice blest. It blesses him who gives and him who receives."

Gentleness is a soft rain reviving sun-baked plants.

Gentleness is a breeze blowing newly unfurled leaves on a spring day.

Gentleness is one of the fruits of the Spirit.

The next time you encounter a delicate situation where gentleness is required, remind yourself that Jesus taught us by His example. He gently folded the children in His arms. He admonished us to care for others as a shepherd would care for a lost sheep. He said, "Take my yoke upon you, and learn from me; for I am gentle and lowly in heart, and you will find rest for your souls" (Matthew 11:29 RSV). We read, "The Lord's servant must not be quarrelsome but kindly to every one, an apt teacher, forbearing, correcting his opponents with gentleness" (2 Timothy 2:24-25 RSV).

How I long for all Christians to learn from these examples.

Lord, help us to remember to yearn for Proverbs 15:1 in our lives. "A gentle answer turns away wrath."

REJOICE IN TODAY

Martha Rogers   **April 29**

This is the day the Lord has made; let us rejoice and be glad in it.

(Psalm 118:24 NIV)

Recently I attended our cancer support group and listened to the stories of those going through treatment now. I prayed for the wife of one of our members who passed on a few weeks ago. I thought about them as I wrote in my prayer journal and prayed for them. Then this verse began to run through my mind as a still quiet voice, reminding me who He is.

Today is His Day. Yesterday is gone; tomorrow is uncertain, but we have today. Despite my trials and troubles, I can rejoice and be glad in today because He's on His throne and in control of my life.

A friend once reminded me that Satan is a great manipulator. He will use fear, depression, rejection, or whatever he can to fill our hearts with a deep mistrust of who and what our God is. He loves to fill us with unrest and indecision. She also said that whenever my thoughts begin to fill with hopelessness, worthlessness, or despair, I can chase them away with His truths and thoughts of what is pure and holy in God's eyes.

I can rejoice and be thankful for the wonderful world He has given me, or I can sit with my thoughts dwelling on my failures and my shortcomings. I choose to dwell on Him and His merciful love for me.

Which will you choose today? Will this be a day of rejoicing for God's great love and the beauty of the day He made? Turn your thoughts away from all that distracts and turn your eyes to Jesus. He is the source of all joy.

Heavenly Father, bless these wonderful brothers and sisters who read these words today and give them the joy of Your love and devotion.

SHARPENING OUR SKILLS

Flavia Crowner April 30

As iron sharpens iron, so one man sharpens another.
(Proverbs 27:17 NIV)

Iron sharpens iron to bring about and maintain its shape, character, and longevity. God sends others to help us to learn more about Him, His character and ways. He knows we all learn differently, and He is a God of variety. He has provided for everyone who is willing to learn His ways.

God uses Christians to expand our characters as children of God. He gives us many opportunities to learn about Him through the talents of other Christians. We learn at conferences, Church retreats, and Bible studies. Daily, we learn by living in love and serving with our fellow Christians to give God honor.

God wants whatever we learn about Him to maintain longevity. We should never retire from telling of His love, mercy, and the way to everlasting life. Living in humility and submission to others is one of God's ways to teach us to fine-tune our spirit to

His.

Thank You, Lord, for providing a variety of people, with different personalities, spiritual gifts, and natural talents. Thank You that we all learn different lessons at different speeds, that we all can be both mentor and disciple, learning and teaching, useful and growing in Your Kingdom each day. Amen.

GOD'S ABUNDANCE

Barbara J. Myler   **May 1**

I thought I had finished planting flowers this year, when I discovered a large, unplanted area, which I had neglected. I decided to utilize the "volunteers" that were popping up in other places.

Realizing that God had given me these seedlings as a gift, I set about planting a garden of abundance. I had many more plants than I could use. Seemingly, the more I planted, the more seedlings I discovered!

Finally, I stopped planting and left the rest where God had chosen to germinate them. The garden was full, lush and truly a gift of abundance from the hand of God. He is the ultimate Gardener!

SEEDS OF TOMORROW

Cheryl Wyatt   **May 2**

His love will plant seeds
Of joy in your heart
That will choke out
The weeds of sorrow.
One day you'll be healed
From the hurts of your past
And dwell in the hope of tomorrow.

PEACE

Micki Roberts   **May 3**

Be anxious for nothing, but in everything by prayer and supplication with thanksgiving let your requests be made known to God. And the peace of God, which surpasses all comprehension, shall guard your hearts and your minds in Christ Jesus.

(Philippians 4:6-7 NAS)

Peace. Wonderful, glorious, God-breathed peace. At long

last, the peace for which I had so long been seeking settled over me.

It had been some time since I'd felt the peace of God. My life, my heart, my spiritual walk had been stagnant. I'd even begun to doubt my salvation. But God promises in His Word that He will never forsake His children. [Hebrews 13:5] I clung desperately to that promise. And now, at last, I once again "felt" the truth of His promise.

You may find you are in just such a place right now, wondering if God has abandoned you, feeling as though you were never truly saved. You long for God's peace to soothe your troubled mind. Hang on, fellow believer! His peace will come to you in His time.

He will never leave you nor forsake you. Though you may not feel as though it's true, you *are* safe in your Father's arms.

THE GOOD SHEPHERD

Tiffany Schlichter May 4

Fear not, little flock; for it is your Father's good pleasure to give you the kingdom.
(Luke 12:32 KJV)

A shepherd cares for his sheep and looks after them. When the sheep go astray, he brings them back where they belong. Although sheep are foolish and unknowing, the shepherd is wise and caring.

Jesus said, "I am the good shepherd: the good shepherd giveth his life for the sheep" (John 10:11 KJV). He did just that, and continues to care for us and bring us back when we foolishly wander. He is merciful and forgiving; His tender mercies endure even our sinful lives.

Dear Lord, thank You for being my good Shepherd. Even when I am faithless, You are faithful. Even when I forget You, You find me. So often I am like a little lamb who continues to wander away from my Shepherd, yet You always pick me up and lovingly place me in Your strong, steady, and certain arms. Though the world is not certain and the ground below me may shift, my Savior—my Shepherd—is strong and certain. You protect and comfort me. What an awesome God I serve! Thank You for Your goodness!

Some trust in chariots, and some in horses: but we will remember the name of the LORD our God.
(Psalm 20:7 KJV)

WE HAVE AN ANCHOR
Joan Clayton   May 5

We have this hope as an anchor for the soul, sure and strong. It enters behind the curtain in the Most Holy Place in heaven.
(Hebrews 6:19 NCV)

"Mrs. Clayton, we have your husband in the emergency room."

I must admit I felt terrified. I could only pray, "Lord, You are my anchor. Whatever I have to face, You will be with me."

God's presence gave me peace during the long sleepless nights at the hospital. I thought of all the good things. The car accident didn't take Emmitt's life. Things could have been worse.

It takes faith and courage to stay in the heat of life's battles. During life's journey, stress does attack. Hope seems to fade and shadows block the sunshine, but God's Word hidden in our hearts brings great dividends. Each one of us can look back over our lives and see God's faithfulness.

So we do not lose heart. Life has problems, we cannot deny. For trials, we are never ready. We have an answer we can live by. Jesus whispers, "Hold Steady!"

Jesus is the anchor in any storm.

MAYFLY MENTALITY
J. Douglas Patterson   May 6

The mayfly lives only one day; and sometimes it rains. That was the quote on my desk calendar. I read it and mused. But later on I got it. This little insect has a life expectancy of 24 hours; its life is limited to what that one day brings. If it's a beautiful day then it might think that life is fabulous. But what if it's raining? You get the picture—to a mayfly the limited perception of one day determines the reality of a life lived.

Sadly, many people absorb the "mayfly mentality" as their own. One relationship sours, so they keep all people at a distance. "All *those* people are the same" or "I'll never marry again" becomes the mantra of fear, isolation, and prejudice. Bad experiences taint or prevent all future endeavors, leading to wasted lives marked by cynicism and bitterness. It doesn't have to be that way.

Our faith teaches that life is not based on one image glimpsed through a *dirty* window. Rather, it is lived out in a total spectrum of disappointment, failure, success, happiness, joy, sadness, tears, smiles...the whole nine yards. Every day was not Easter to Jesus: He had to suffer through Good Friday. Our moments of sufferings and exaltation, disease and healing, monotony and thrill weave together to form the fabric of life. That's the way Easter has power.

THE TREE
Christi McMath   **May 7**

There is a tree in my yard that has lived longer than I have existed. He who made the tree has cared for it and kept it safe all these years. He made me, too; and I know He will care for me.

I lift my eyes and gaze into His face for help. Am I not dearer in His sight than that tree? Isn't my fragile flesh more precious than its bark? The branching arms of the tree reach heavenward, but my arms that reach out to Him in supplication can touch the Throne of Grace. The wind sways the tree, but it holds fast. It bows, but doesn't break. With God's help, I will hold fast and not break by the winds of life today. The roots of the tree go deep into the earth, while the roots of my faith grow deeper into my Lord, my family, and my friends.

He who made the entire universe won't forsake that single tree, and I know He won't forsake me. He is my source of survival, power, and faith. It is with this faith that I claim His strength, His love, and His help. He is closer and more real to me than that tree. No matter what comes, He is already there, waiting for me.

> *He is like a tree planted by streams of water, which yields its fruit in season and whose leaf does not wither. Whatever he does prospers.*
>
> (*Psalm* 1:3 *NIV*)

ONLY TRUST HIM
Cindy Hawkins   **May 8**

I was driving to church one morning when a car pulled out

in front of me. Three young people had packed themselves in the two-seater. A teenager, her head out the window, sat on the passenger's lap. To top it all off, the car bore battle scars in the form of dents and scratches on the bumper and passenger door. By getting into the car that morning, the passengers were placing their lives in the hands of the driver, in spite of his less than stellar driving record. Talk about misplaced trust!

I wonder what I place my trust in that may be unwise. Occasionally I have sought the counsel of someone who touts a non-Christian point of view. Other times I've followed my fluctuating feelings. Should I always rely on news reports? All too quickly I've given credence to an "expert." I've often struggled over trusting my gut instincts when tackling a thorny problem. Like the passengers in the wrecked car, I am guilty of errors in judgment.

On the other hand, I never err when I place my faith in the Bible. Its promises are true and its Author trustworthy. I'd stake my life on it.

> That is why we have a great High Priest who has gone to heaven, Jesus the Son of God. Let us cling to him and never stop trusting him.
> (Hebrews 4:14 NLT)

YOU ARE MY ONLY HOPE
Della Ray   May 9

> I cry out, God, call out: "You're my last chance, my only hope for life!"
> (Psalm 142:5 MESSAGE)

When I first read the above verse, a smile came to my face when I remembered a similar line from *Star Wars*. Princess Leia sent a message to Ben where she said, "Help me, Obi-Wan Kenobi. You're my only hope."

After the smile, I was saddened by the fact that so many people today are like Princess Leia. Their only hope rests on a person, a mere man, someone with possible strength, but with definite limitations.

However, when David wrote, "You're my only hope," he was speaking of God. God is the One who with all wisdom, strength, and knowledge created the universe, holds it in His hands, and watches over us as a Father watches over His children. We have God, our Father, who loves and cares for us. "We love Him because He first loved us," (1 John 4:19). "For I know the plans I have for you," declares the LORD, "plans for welfare and not for calamities" (Jeremiah 29:11).

Therefore, when we cry out to God with the same words that David spoke, "You're my last chance, my only hope for life!" we can expect our Father to move on our behalf. So, the next time that things are looking poorly, reach out to God. He is your only hope.

LIGHT BETWEEN THE LINKS
Shirley S. Stevens **May 10**

The righteous cry, and the LORD heareth, and delivereth them out of all their troubles.
(Psalm 34:17 KJV)

My gold chains often become horribly tangled. When I tug, the knots grow worse. Sometimes, if I put the chain on a flat surface and work slowly with a needle, the knot loosens. At other times, I impatiently tug and poke, poke and tug. If I am too impatient, I break the chain.

Before this happens, I have learned to hand over the knot to my more patient friend Carol. She says a prayer, then finds the spot where the chain will give and release. She tells me that she looks for light between the links.

Help me, Lord, to practice patience in my time of troubles. Remind me to turn to You for the light which will enable me to escape the snare.

A PARENT'S FAITHFULNESS
Joy C. Bradford **May 11**

Hannah was married to a good man, Elkanah, who loved her. However, he could not meet all her needs. Hannah looked directly to the Lord God through worship and prayer to find hope.

Hannah longed to have a baby. Her rival constantly mocked and upset her. Eventually, Hannah quit eating and fell into a period of bitterness and despair.

When her family traveled to the temple at Shiloh, Hannah broke away from the others and went to the synagogue alone. She poured out her heart in prayer. She asked God for a baby and promised to give the child back to His service, if she was granted her request. After overhearing and then listening to her story, the priest Eli gave Hannah encouragement that her request would be granted.

We know that Hannah was a believer who struggled. She prayed and worshiped God at home and in a house of worship. She asked God for what she wanted, and she trusted Him as she had been taught to do.

When her prayer was answered and Samuel, "asked of God," was born, Hannah was thankful and remembered from where her gift had come. She praised God for His goodness and when her son was old enough, she took him to the temple to live with Eli. There, Samuel worshiped and ministered to the Lord.

Hannah kept her promise as God honored her.

Lord, help us look for the wisdom in Your Word and to apply it to our lives. As we learn more about You, may we look to the Bible for inspiration, guidance, and hope. Amen.

WISDOM

Linda Mae Richardson   May 12
At the end of my days, I hope to look back,
Not to number my days or simply keep track.

Though we hope for a life which is healthy and strong,
It is sad if we see just a life that was long.

For our number of days, short or long was a gift—
Did I use them with wisdom to help and uplift?

A life filled with meaning adds width to its days—
Years filled with love—lived by faith and with praise.

Lord, teach me to measure—Your thoughts as my guide
Then I'll look back on life and thank God mine was "wide"!

> *So teach us to number our days, that we may apply our hearts unto wisdom.*
>
> (*Psalm 90:12 KJV*)

TAKING CHANCES

Connie Bretz   May 13

He leadeth me beside the still waters.
(Psalm 23:2 KJV)

Crystal Lake, Illinois is a welcome haven of calm water to people who are looking for a smooth boat trip.

One day, as I sat on the weathered, gray pier, my friends urged me to jump into their boat alongside the gray planks.

I hesitated. The space spread to three feet. Then I decided to chance it. With my left leg on the pier, I jumped on my right leg—into the boat. As the boat lurched away, I did the splits and splashed into the lake. Funny! But I could have been hurt.

How often we take chances that harm us. I could have waded safely to the boat from the shore.

Dear Father, help me to pray before I leap into a situation or decision that creates harm. In Jesus' Name. Amen.

INTO ME SEE

Bonnie J. Manion   May 14

    Intimacy means
    Sharing me,
    Caring about you.

    Intimacy says
    Into me see,
    I want to know you.

LOVE LETTER

Jana Carman   May 15

The prayer of the upright is His delight.
(Proverbs 15:8 KJV)

Beloved,
    I missed you today.
    Although I waited long, expecting you,
    you never came.
    My dear one, don't you know
    how sweet your presence is to me?
    Your secrets and your sorrows shared,
    Your overflowing joys, and even

your requests for help are precious to me,
eloquent of your love and trust.
I'm sad when you don't come,
and jealous of the things which push
between us, taking time I'd rather spend with you.
I long to share your life. That's why
I wait each day,
hoping that I'll hear you say,
    "Dear Lord—"

MY SHEPHERD

Pat Collins   May 16

Lord, You are my shepherd. I am one of Your sheep. One who keeps going astray. Yet, You always come after me and bring me back to where I belong. Time and again I wander off. You take my hand and lead me back to You.

Oh, such love! To care and come after one of Your lost children when You have many who are faithful. I'm so thankful, Lord, that You hold onto me and keep me close. I need a little more guidance. Thank You, Lord Jesus, for not giving up on me when I go the wrong way. Thank You for showing me the way back home, home to You.

> But now, thus says the LORD, who created you, O Jacob, and He who formed you, O Israel: "Fear not, for I have redeemed you; I have called you by your name; you are Mine."
>
> (Isaiah 43:1 NKJ)

LITTLE BY LITTLE

Marion E. Gorman   May 17

> And the Lord your God will drive out those nations before you little by little; you will be unable to destroy them at once, lest the beasts of the field become too numerous for you.
>
> (Deuteronomy 7:22 NKJ)

The warm spring morning filled me with enthusiasm. New growth peeking up through the soggy soil filled me with anticipation, encouraging me to extend my flower beds considerably. However, my excitement subsided when the new beds became impossible to maintain. Soon they were overtaken with weeds, and I lost my struggle to manage them properly.

When the Israelites were ready to go into Canaan and conquer the nations the Lord had given them, He told them to do it little by little. He knew if they destroyed it rapidly, they would be unable to keep up with the work required to rebuild, and it would become wilderness.

So it is as we enter life with Christ. We cannot possibly absorb all God has for us immediately. If we try to grow too fast, we cannot properly sort out truth. Our lives will become tangled, and spiritual growth will be stunted. We need to mature as Christians slowly, letting each truth change us a little at a time. As you meditate on His word and respond in obedience, "... then you will make your way prosperous, and then you will have good success" (Joshua 1:8, NKJ).

GOD SINGS OVER YOU
Janet R. Sady   **May 18**

The LORD your God is with you, he is mighty to save. He will take great delight in you, he will quiet you with his love, he will rejoice over you with singing.

(Zephaniah 3:17 NIV)

Sometimes when my husband and I take a trip, I sing in the car. I sing for the joy of a chance to travel away from the pressures of daily drudgery. I sing for the joy of seeing new sights and sounds that God has provided. I sing for the joy of having my husband's undivided attention.

Did you ever think about God singing? Why would God have cause to sing over us? He has great joy in seeing us come through His Son for salvation. He takes delight when we praise His name, pray to Him, and show His love to others.

Our heavenly Father, thank You for a voice to sing Your praises. May everything I say and do cause You to sing over me with joy. Amen.

ALL TO WORSHIP AND HONOR OUR GOD
Carol Cleal   **May 19**

Golden rays of sun shine down to warm the earth.
Soft gentle rain falls to refresh God's world.
Various shades of green stretch across the countryside.

Splashes of color interrupt the span as flowers raise their delicate heads.
Reminders of God.
All to worship and honor Him.

Dark heavy clouds fill the sky
as bolts of lightning dart across.
Then the torrents of fresh clear rain come to cleanse the earth.
Reminders of God.
All to worship and honor Him.

Leaves rustle with a gentle breeze.
Birds chirp a good morning song
Squirrels play tag as rabbits taunt the dogs.
Reminders of God.
All to worship and honor Him.

Church bells ring through the air.
People dress in fine array.
Voices raised to heaven.
Reminders of God.
All to worship and honor Him.

WE ARE HIS REFLECTION

Martha Rogers   **May 20**

Praise the LORD, all you nations; extol him, all you peoples. For great is his love toward us, and the faithfulness of the LORD endures forever. Praise the LORD.
(Psalm 117 NIV)

Despite the troubled times facing our nation and our President, we have a blessed hope in our God. His faithfulness endures forever. God has a place for every creature. He knows the name and path of every star. Not a river flows that He doesn't know its source.

Even more so, He knows our hearts. He knows each of us by name. Not a tear falls He doesn't know and comes to wipe away. He knows our every joy and triumph, our every sorrow and fear.

Whether we stand in a crowd of applauding admirers, or sit

alone with our tears, He is there. We trust Him to see us through illness, death of loved ones, family problems, rejections, heartaches and more. Praise Him for these things and become as refined as silver in the fire. Praise Him and trust Him, and He will be reflected so others may see Him in you.

Heavenly Father, I pray today Your love and beauty will be reflected in me.

NONE LIKE YOU

Charles E. Harrel   **May 21**

Lift your eyes and look to the heavens: Who created all these? He who brings out the starry host one by one, and calls them each by name. Because of his great power and mighty strength, not one of them is missing.

(Isaiah 40:26 NIV)

Have you ever watched the midnight sky on a cloudless night? It's dazzling, as countless stars shine against a backdrop of total blackness. These specks of light glisten in bold patterns when unhindered by the glare from the city. It is easy to be drawn in and sit quietly transfixed, watching the twinkling horizon for hours.

Through the years, many have attempted to count and name these lights. Early astronomers identified them by using actual names, while today's astronomers use their coordinates instead. Even after thousands of years of observation, the total number of stars in the heavens remains unknown.

While humanity can only guess, God knows the exact number of stars in His universe. He gives each one a specific name because He doesn't need coordinates to keep track of them. God's power and strength are clearly unmatched in the universe. Our God has no equal.

Most High God, our best efforts can never compare to Your handiwork. Your might and ability are unequaled. Your glory is matchless. Every time we scan the horizon, we realize there is no one like You. Amen.

PSALM 19
Tune of *The First Noel*

Glenda Joy Race   **May 22**

The heavens declare, the glory of God

And the earth and sky show his wondrous handiwork.
Day to day it pronounces speech
And by night it shows its knowledge.
It is good, it is good
For it is all made by the Lord

The law of the Lord is Perfect.
It converts the soul with a sure testimony.
It makes the simple wise with right statutes .
And the commands of the Lord open eyes.
Trust the Lord, Trust the Lord
For his truth endures forever.

The words of the Lord are finer than gold
And much sweeter than honey from out of the comb.
So let my words and thoughts
Be acceptable in Your sight, O Lord.
You are my strength, and redeemer.
I must declare your great glory.

MAKING HEARTS FEEL GOOD

Lorena Estep   **May 23**

"Lord, why do we do all this hard work?" I grumbled one spring day, feeling especially tired and weary. My husband and I were doing a cleanup of our more than two acres of flower gardens. It had been fun creating the theme gardens several years before, but now keeping them up sometimes felt like drudgery. Just hours later, the Lord answered my question.

An older couple stopped to look at a truck we had for sale. While the men talked business, the woman asked if she could look at my flowers. As I took her around the gardens, she kept exclaiming about how lovely it was. Then she put her hand on her chest and said, "Oh, it just makes my heart feel so good!"

Okay, Lord, if it makes even one person's heart feel good, then it's worth the hard work. Forgive me for grumbling. I also thought of the groups who came each year to picnic and tour the gardens, plus friends who came to relax and paint. Suddenly I had renewed energy, and the cleanup no longer seemed like hard work because I viewed it as serving God by serving others.

Offer hospitality to one another without grumbling. Each one should use whatever gift he has received to serve others, faithfully administering God's grace in its various forms.
(1 Peter 4:9-10 NIV)

CRY OF HIS HEART
Cheryl Wyatt   **May 24**

The cry of Your heart is an orphan's tear,
A beaten child wrapped in loveless fear,
The lonely man on the crowded pier.
Do they know You see; do they know You hear?

A widow's memory of happy days,
A user's desperate fog of haze,
The sacred given to lust that pays.
Don't they know there's hope, and a better way?

A mother's empty arms and shattered dreams,
The mangled car and the lifeless teens,
The broken vows and forgotten rings.
Do they run to You when life wields these things?

Can they know You're drawn to the broken-hearted?
That You cried tears of blood in a starlit garden—
That You carried their sin to a cross of shame?
Jesus, You died; we don't need to be the same.

MEDITATION ON ACCEPTING LOVE
Charles A. Waugaman   **May 25**

      Mary Keith was one of those precious people one loved to visit. Although unrelated, she lived with the grandmother of Sonja, one of our Sunday School children. There she had one room in a crowded little house made spacious with caring.

      But I first met Mary in the hospital. She was then approaching ninety and had been semi-invalid for some time. After visiting her, I always left refreshed and walking high. No gift was too small to be greeted with deep, honest thanks. No time spent with her was ever wasted.

      When Mary returned home, I decided to visit her again.

That decision was almost the downfall of our friendship.

Sonja's grandmother could not have loved Mary more if she had been Mary's own daughter. And her love overflowed on any person who showed Mary kindness. I left after my first visit with a dozen eggs. The next visit closed the same way. Then raspberries were given, smelts, rhubarb—whatever was at hand was gifted upon me.

Much as I knew the visits were expected and longed for, much as I wanted to go, I felt as if I were being paid. It bothered me. My visits grew farther and farther apart.

It was some time before I silenced my pride enough to know I had misunderstood their love. Love is certainly selfless giving. Love is even sacrifice. But it also requires selfless acceptance.

I think there are moments when acceptance and sacrifice are almost identical.

Dear Loving Father, please forgive the many times I selfishly try to do things for myself, the great lengths to which I go in evading You simply because I don't want to feel indebted. Help me to see that any refusal of love is a refusal of You. For Jesus' sake, Amen.

EIGHT SECOND RIDE

Dave Evans   **May 26**

He has set a day when He will say in the right way if the people of the world are guilty. This will be done by Jesus Christ, the One He has chosen. God has proven this to all men by raising Jesus Christ from the dead.

(Acts 17:31 NLT)

This is the word He spoke: God gave us life that lasts forever, and this life is in His son. He that has the Son has life. He that does not have the Son of God does not have life.

(1 John 5:11-12 NLT)

You fork your bronc
for a wild ride through this life;
holding on tight, hoping to make it
to the eight-second buzzer

Now your ride is over—
and the buzzer has yet to sound:

some would say you've gone
to the big rodeo in the sky
to collect a gold buckle,
but the Judge only scores
on who was your sponsor—
His Son, and you've won
or some other trail, and you fail—
and there are no re-rides.

OLYMPIC TRAINING
Anita Estes May 27

Fixing our eyes on Jesus, the author and perfecter of faith.
(Hebrews 12:2 NAS)

Watching the gymnastic Olympic competition is inspiring, especially the balance beam maneuvers. It's amazing what concentration and strength these young athletes possess to twirl in the air and land perfectly upright on a piece of wood.

The life of a Christian is similar. Great concentration and determination are needed to walk the narrow path while the crowds shout to go the broad way. Though we might not twist and twirl, we need to focus our strength to achieve the goal—to walk like Jesus. This takes focus and commitment in order to succeed in building spiritual prowess.

Like any other Olympic hopeful, we have a coach showing us the way, encouraging and leading us on. We need to listen to what He says by reading His Word and talking to Him through daily prayer. When we spend time in training, we will know what to do in our Christian walk. With our eyes fixed on Jesus, we can achieve Olympic heights of faith!

Dear Lord, guide us in all we do and keep us focused. Help us to push aside the many distractions in this life and look to You.

SEEDS OF THOUGHT
Betty Redmon May 28

Tis a very tiny seed
    Of thought that brings forth fruit or weed.
It all depends on how we plant
    The things that we would have Him grant.
So stand on guard through act and deed,

Thoughtful ways to always heed.
For as the tree grows from the soil,
    With no false notion does it toil.
But in its honest, faithful way
    Springs anew each passing day.
To bring forth beauty for our eyes
    With fruit and shade that glorifies.
The wondrous ways God's work is done
    When we commune with the Holy One.

For whatever a man sows, that he will also reap.
(Galatians 6:7 NKJ)

REMEMBERING DEAR FRIENDS

Joseph Hopkins　　　　　　　　　　　　　　　　　　**May 29**

I thank my God every time I remember you.
(Philippians 1:3 NIV)

Paul, a prisoner in Rome, wrote these words to his Christian friends in Philippi. But they are appropriate as we remember our dear friends, whether living or ascended to Glory.

Art Garrett was my fishing buddy. He departed this life in 1994, and the end of Arthur was the end of fishing for me. In the fall of 1987, I broke the news to Art that I would be leaving for Malawi in January to serve as a missionary in that southeast Africa country.

He said sadly, "Well, we wet a lot of lines together over the years."

I'll never forget those words. It was Arthur's way of saying that there would be no more wetting of lines, no more fishing trips to Canada, Lake Erie, or our favorite fishing haunts in the lakes and streams of Western Pennsylvania. And the remembrance brings tears to my eyes.

I am comforted by the sure hope of reunion at God's appointed time. For Art was a devoted Christian, an elder in the Neshannock Presbyterian Church in our hometown of New Wilmington. It was our custom to pray together before making the first cast of the day. No fishing trips were made on Sunday. The Lord's Day was reserved for church and family. Art was an excellent fisherman and a gifted craftsman. Although he had only a one-room schoolhouse education, he was a skilled carpenter, electrician, plumber, and mechanic. He left a legacy of many beautiful houses, one of which he restored after it was severely damaged by fire.

But to me he will always be remembered with admiration and affection as my fishing buddy. Thanks for the memories, Art. I thank my God every time I remember you.

Why not pause and thank God for the dear friends whose memory you cherish?

LIGHT

Janice Harris May 30

In nakedness, Lord,
I hid from You,
cowering, unaware
that trees are not made
to hide behind.

You called, You searched,
and suddenly, ashamedly,
I was standing,
without excuse,
before Your gaze.

You
reached down
and lovingly offered me,
bathed in Your light,
no fig leaf,
but a robe of white.

JUMPING IN RHYTHM

Fara Linn Reed May 31

And we know that in all things God works for the good of those who love him, who have been called according to his purpose.

(Romans 8:28 NIV)

"Cinderella dressed in yellow/ went upstairs to kiss a fellow/ made a mistake and kissed a snake . . ." This sing-song verse used to echo on the school playground. I can remember longing to be able to jump into the spinning rope like the older girls and keep the song going. At first, I often failed to time my entry and would feel the rope's sting across my leg. Once I learned to watch and time my entrance with the rope's highest upward movement, the rope would not wrap around my legs. The song would continue its rhythm. What a wonderful feeling to join the song with my jumping.

"How many doctors would it take. 1,2,3 . . ."

Similarly, when I am not in God's will, I feel the sting of my selfish choices as they trip me. Romans 8:28 reminds us that when we love God and are working toward His purposes "all things work for the good." How do I know God's will in my life? I watch and wait for His timing, just like the jump rope. What joy I know when I join with His rhythm and song!

BREAK TIME

Barbara Peer   June 1

My soul finds rest in God alone.
(Psalm 62:1 NIV)

"C'mon, Barbara, it's break-time!" said Nancy, heading for the break-room. I grabbed my purse, digging for change for the vending machine. Today we got treated to a large box of homemade cupcakes. My favorite!

Anyone who's ever been in the break-room of a workplace can plainly see the evidence of what people do to relax: overfilled ash trays, candy wrappers, empty soda cans and coffee cups, along with half-filled boxes of pastries—all indicative of what people do on break. Such a variety of commodities for consumption are available for our refreshment. But are we refreshed? Are we restored? More likely we're momentarily stimulated only to feel even more depleted after the effects wear off.

For the long term, rest and restoration must come from our connection with Jesus. He is the way, the truth, and the life. [John 14:6] "Your love, O LORD, reaches to the heavens...with you is the fountain of life" (Psalm 36:5,9 NIV). Time spent in the Word is life-giving and restorative.

We can take aspirin one day for a headache, then on another day for a sore back. How does the body know where to send it? It's a mystery. Just as mysterious is the working of the

Word in our lives, but it works. Meditating on the Word of God is revitalizing. It's life to us—not only for our eternal salvation, but also for every day, right here, right now.

STARVE A FEVER; FEED A COLD

Joe LoBello June 2

Feed them also and lift them up for ever.
(Psalm 28:9 KJV)

Maybe some of you will remember the saying: *Feed a cold. Starve a fever.* I remember my mother saying that many times in my childhood. Today many people are intent on feeding their bodies with vitamins, health foods, low carbs, and less fats.

So, too, with our spiritual lives, we must feed our spiritual selves mostly with the Word of God. Reading the scriptures can lift us spiritually and uncover the answers to the problems of the day. In fact, the more spiritual we are the stronger we are in Christ. Our doubts and fears are starved to death, as our reliance on Christ grows stronger.

The colds and the fevers of life grow strangely dim in the hands of the great Physician—Christ, the Lord.

So then faith cometh by hearing, and hearing by the word of God.
(Romans 10:17 KJV)

TASTE AND SEE

Marjorie K. Evans June 3

O taste and see that the LORD is good.
(Psalm 34:8 KJV)

It was wintertime. The Kansas wheat harvest had been very poor, and the farmers were unable to pay Daddy for repairing their machinery. He and Mama struggled to provide for my sister, my brother, and me.

One evening all Mama had to prepare for supper were potatoes, onions, and milk. So she made a big pot of potato soup. As she lifted the lid and added the milk, I peered into the pot. The soup was white and unappetizing-looking. "I don't want any of that soup. It doesn't look good," I said.

Little sister Mary said, "But Mahwe, maybe it tastes good. When I taste it, I'll see."

Later Mama added browned onions, salt, and pepper to the soup. When she ladled it into our bowls it looked good. We tasted it, and it was delicious.

Isn't that sometimes the way we are as we begin to read certain portions of the Bible? We think, "That doesn't look interesting" or "That doesn't apply to me." But when we really taste God's Word—study and meditate upon it—we find it is "delicious." It nourishes us and enables us to grow as Christians.

May our prayer be that the Lord Jesus Christ will help us each day—not just to look at, but to truly "taste" His Word, that it may strengthen us in faith and love.

GREEN PASTURES

Dave Evans June 4

> *I love them that love me; and those that seek me early shall find me.*
>
> *(Proverbs 8:17 KJV)*

The sun rolls over
for a few more moments' rest,
before slowly climbing over the hill
where, below, a small herd of horses,
gray silhouettes against the
higher hill, placidly stand
'mid verdant green pastures,
caring for nothing, merely
waiting to be fed a morning serving
of alfalfa hay...
In the oaks, birds awaken
and begin their morning
song of gratitude

After I roll over
for a few more moments' rest,
may I rise to repose
in the verdant green pastures
of Your Word, caring for nothing
but to be fed by Your hand.

> *And early in the morning he came again into the temple, and all the people came unto him; and he sat down, and taught them.*
>
> *(John 8:2 KJV)*

ROCK OF AGES LIGHTHOUSE

Kathy Johnson   **June 5**

Your word is a lamp to my feet and a light for my path.
(Psalm 119:105 NIV)

Growing up in Michigan, I had always hoped to step foot on Isle Royale. A wilderness National Park located closer to Minnesota than Michigan in Lake Superior. Finally the time presented itself, but the weather didn't cooperate. The season for traveling by boat over to Isle Royale was fast drawing to a close, only four days left. The first two days, gale force winds and the repercussions from the winds canceled the boat. On the third day we were able to travel over to the island. The day spent on the island was enjoyable, and soon it was time to head back to the mainland. After leaving the island, we passed by the Rock of Ages Lighthouse. Even with the light, three ships had been lost on the rocks at the base of the lighthouse.

God's Word is like the lighthouse, in providing never ending light to guide us along life's way. The difference is, God's light will never fail us. Even though our paths may cross rocky shoals, we will never go down.

The Word of God testifies to the forgiveness we receive by the blood of Christ's suffering and death, and the gift of eternal life prepared in advance for us.

WHAT A PITY

Helen Kammerdiener   **June 6**

He was in the world, and the world was made by him, and the world knew him not.
(John 1:10 KJV)

How could the religious authorities of Jesus' day know Someone they refused to hear? Am I like them? How many times have I been deaf when Jesus spoke to me? How often has He spoken with a voice I didn't want to recognize? How often have I been too busy "serving God" to see His hand reaching to guide me? In all the clamor of things that call for attention, how can I focus on His still, small voice in the depths of my soul?

I must take time to read His word, to pray, and to listen. Listening needn't take a lot of time. I can listen for His voice as the washer gurgles, focus on His goodness while the vacuum sweeper hums, and meditate on His word while the mower growls. I will hear His voice in the turmoil of life as long as I focus my thoughts on seeing Him, hearing Him, and serving Him.

What a pity that many of those who saw Jesus never actually saw Him. What a pity that many who heard Him speak never really heard Him. What a pity if I don't see and hear any better than they did.

Dear Jesus, please open my eyes that I may see and follow You, open my ears that I may hear and obey You, and plant Your love in my heart that I may willingly serve You. Amen.

STORMS

Micki Roberts June 7

He maketh the storm a calm, so that the waves thereof are still.

(Psalm 107:29 KJV)

I once heard a pastor remark that you are about to go into a storm, you are in the midst of a storm, or you have just come out of a storm. Sounds pretty accurate, doesn't it? How well you come through a storm depends upon how well you prepare for it. Since I've lived in Florida all of my life, I've learned several lessons about how to "ride out" storms:
1) Monitor the weather at all times;
2) Always take storm warnings seriously;
3) When storm warnings are given, stay alert;
4) When storm tracks are given, make protective preparations;
5) As the storm approaches, take shelter;
6) As the storm rages, remain inside and monitor weather reports;
7) When the storm has passed, begin anew;
8) *Always* remain alert for the next storm.

These same lessons can be applied to our spiritual walk.
1) Be prepared by immersing yourself in God's Word;
2) Take His Word seriously;
3) Stay on guard (in His Word) watching for storms;
4) Protect your spiritual life using God's Word;
5) When the storms of life are raging, take shelter in the arms of the Master of all storms;
6) As the storms are raging, stay tuned to God's Word for His direction;
7) When storms pass, begin anew with the lessons you've learned;
8) Finally, *always* remain alert for the next storm by diligent study of God's Word.

SITTING AT THE FEET OF JESUS
Debbie Rempel June 8

> I'm sitting at His feet,
> drinking from
> the well of His
> Word, which
> never runs dry.
>
> When I am thirsty
> and in need of living
> water, I go to the Word
> and drink freely.
>
> I know that by
> reading His Word daily,
> I will be satisfied
> and my cup will
> be filled to overflowing.
>
> It's a joy
> to know I can
> drink from the never-ending
> well of God's Word.

STAYING ON TRACK
Leigh DeLozier June 9

Sow for yourselves righteousness...for it is time to seek the LORD.

(Hosea 10:12 NIV)

A friend of mine laughs that she needs to have company for dinner more often because it makes her really clean the house. I can relate to that all too well, knowing how prone I am to letting housekeeping slide in favor of other things.

The same can be true of my spiritual life. It's much easier for me to stay on track if I'm involved in a weekly Bible study. But once the study ends and I no longer have "homework," it's easy to let other things get in the way of my quiet time. Whether it's a deadline for work, the pile of laundry in the hamper, or my children wanting to play, distractions are everywhere.

Sometimes it seems like finding time for a five-minute devotional is hard enough, let alone preparing for and attending a weekly Bible study. But Jesus repeatedly taught His followers about the importance of daily prayer and study time, whether with a group or alone. I've found that any amount of time during the day is sufficient, and that even an on-the-go devotional reading or prayer can help keep my spiritual house in order—whether the house I live in is neat or not.

Lord, help me always find time for You so my spiritual house is in order and my relationship with You is on track.

A TEACHING TIME
Connie Bretz   **June 10**

I set My bow in the cloud, and it shall be for a sign of a covenant between Me and the earth.
(Genesis 9:13 NAS)

The glass prisms hang from my east kitchen window, and the sun shines through them. What a delight to see the refracted light here and there on my white linoleum in the form of mini rainbows.

I shook the prism gently and Rachel, my five-year-old friend, and I jumped over the jiggling color bands, trying to step on them while singing at the same time.

"What makes rainbows?" Rachel asked.

"It's the sun shining through the prism," I explained.

Later, after Rachel went home, I thought of a Biblical answer I might have made: rainbows are God's promise not to flood the earth again, and a golden one, too.

Heavenly Father, please help me to be ready with a Biblical answer instead of a secular or theoretical one. In Jesus' name. Amen.

CHOOSING THE BETTER THING
Lorena Estep   **June 11**

"Martha, Martha," the Lord answered, "you are worried and upset about many things, but only one thing is needed. Mary has chosen what is better."
(Luke 10:41-42 NIV)

Once more I had overextended myself preparing for a

ladies' Christmas tea. For weeks I worked, sending out invitations, decorating, baking, and buying gifts. Stressed over it all, I became irritable with my husband, who was trying to help.

In Luke, when Martha was weighed down with the serving of Jesus and the others who were gathered at her home, she became irritated with her sister, Mary, who sat at Jesus feet instead of helping with the serving. Martha complained to Jesus about it. He lovingly pointed out that Mary had chosen the better thing.

I could hear Him substituting my name for "Martha." I realized, though serving is important, when we take it to extremes and become angry with others, it's time to stop and review the most important part of serving the Lord: worship and fellowship with Him.

> And our fellowship is with the Father and with his Son, Jesus Christ.
>
> (1 John 1:3 NIV)

LETTING GO

Marion E. Gorman June 12

> But Jesus said to him, "No one, having put his hand to the plow, and looking back, is fit for the kingdom of God."
> (Luke 9:62, NKJ)

A hurtful situation caused separation from my spiritual family. In my heart I knew God's desire was for me to let go of the past and people whom I loved. However, I was reluctant to make the necessary break, causing more heartache for myself and others. As I went forward, God provided a wonderful spiritual family, but I still continued to nurse my hurt.

We moved from the area for a few years and when we came back, I once again attempted to restore the past. I could not accept that I should be estranged for any reason from brothers and sisters in Christ. My stubbornness caused a great deal of additional pain.

I questioned experiencing so much agony as a child of God. A mental picture of Jesus, as He agonized in the Garden of Gethsemane, passed through my thoughts. He let go of His life so I could be forgiven and thus able to forgive. I was finally able to let go of the past completely and was filled with relief and peace. I followed Jesus out of the garden and laid my burden at the foot of the cross.

Lord, help me not to carry burdens that You desire to carry for me.

THIS IS THE WAY
Linda Mae Richardson June 13

As I awoke this morning
And I thought about my day,
I felt weighed down by problems
And it seemed I couldn't pray.

But then I heard God's gentle voice,
My Shepherd calling me
To take His hand and let Him guide
O'er paths that frighten me.

And when in doubt, I cannot see
Which path will lead to You,
I hear a word behind me say,
"This is the path to choose."

And, oh the joy, as step by step
I let You lead the way,
And learn to trust in You alone
To bring me peace today.

So when my day is at an end
My prayer of praise will be,
To thank You that You came to save
A sinner such as me!

Thine ears shall hear a word behind thee, saying, This is the way, walk ye in it, when ye turn to the right hand, and when ye turn to the left.
(Isaiah 30:21 KJV)

TRY A LITTLE PATIENCE
Betty Jane Hewitt June 14

Be still before the LORD, and wait patiently for him.
(Psalm 37:7 NIV)

Of all the fruits of the spirit, patience is a thorny one for me to receive.

I strain to hear God's word within the din of my daily comings and goings. There is much too much noise. My hypertensive personality causes me to hurtle through the day chattering away in meaningless conversations with anyone who will listen. I am so pre-occupied by own immediate concerns I can't wait for answers either from God or other people.

Today is an exception. My family are off on their own pursuits, and I choose to stay home alone, forcing myself to simmer down, relax and appreciate the solitude. So, on a bright brassy June morning I am resting on our backyard swing beneath the grape arbor and gazing down upon the river that meanders along our back pasture. A book lies open on my lap and I am blissfully sipping a cup of Lemon Lift tea. Our black Lab lies at my feet. I am content.

In the hush of this moment it seems so elemental, so simple. In order to hear God speaking to me, all I have to do is to be still and listen. Why am I so impatient?

Here, I am aware of God's world. My calmed mind centers in this soundless second of time, and I am still. God whispers to me. I am blessed.

BE PATIENT

Pat Collins   **June 15**

Be patient, oh please, be patient. Please don't give up. Dig in, get stubborn, or whatever it takes, but don't let go. When things seem at their worst, the answer is closer than you think. That is when you need to hold tight and wait, because God couldn't be closer.

God never breaks His promises and He never will. If the answer is different than you may have been looking for, then you know it was God's way and not yours. God's way is always so much better. Rejoice! He loves you. He gave you His best.

For God so loved the world that He gave His only begotten Son, that whoever believes in Him should not perish but have everlasting life.

(John 3:16 NKJ)

IMPATIENT EMILY, IMPATIENT ME
Fara Linn Reed   **June 16**

      Four-year-old Emily danced around excitedly as I dug into the dirt of the flowerbed. She clutched the seed packet we had picked out. On the cover, bright yellow sunflowers waved against a bright-blue sky. She gently placed each seed in the small hole I had made, and we covered each one with soil. After watering them, we stood back to take in our work.

      "Can I see the flowers tomorrow, Mama?" Emily asked expectantly.

      Her impatience made me chuckle and I gently corrected her, "Oh no, honey, we have to wait. It will take awhile."

      I experience a similar impatience each time I want growth in my spiritual life and see only mud. Paul says, "Neither he who plants nor he who waters is anything, but only God, who makes things grow" (1 Corinthians 3:7 NIV). No matter how much I yearn for the fruit of God's Spirit blooming in my life right now, I must remember, I cannot bring about the growth by myself. I can prepare the soil of my heart, plant the seeds of truth and water them. But God is ultimately in control of the growth. Instead of being impatient with myself as Emily was impatient with her seeds, I must hear God's voice gently correcting me, "No, my child, wait, it will take awhile."

A DAD'S VOW
Peter Paulson   **June 17**

      My dad contracted polio when I was around two. The doctors told him he had the worst case in the state's history. In those days, polio meant death, iron lungs, or paralysis. Dad prayed and made a vow. The virus dropped dramatically overnight, but only after it had permanently weakened his leg muscles. Working at a cabinet shop, he would hitch his wide leather belt to the saw so he could continue working and feed his family. The years passed.

      Twenty-two years later on a beautiful, blue-sky June afternoon, Dad stood before a packed-to-the-rafters church and placed a fire-red yoke over my head, carefully adjusting it to hang straight. The yoke is called a stole and it symbolizes the consecration or setting aside of one to the ordained ministry. The vow had been fulfilled. I was to do what he could not.

Centuries ago, another Dad made a vow. Most books of the Old Testament tell of it. Then at the right time, He placed a cross on His Son's shoulder. A vow had been fulfilled. Jesus did what God could not. The Almighty, Eternal God could not die. God's Son did.

A vow is a vow. God has made one for you as well.

ONE FATHER'S LEGACY

Joy C. Bradford   June 18

You were always my rock and never once did you forget the emotional needs of your youngest child. Thank you for always finding time for me. You were a person I could always talk to and you listened without judgment. Often, you pointed out another way to approach a problem. Sometimes you had no solution, but heard what I had to say. When I was wrong, you lovingly corrected.

You were the best granddaddy to my two young children. I hope you knew they loved you dearly and you left a void in our lives that no one could fill. When you died of prostate cancer, we were not ready to give you up. You made the holidays so special that they were never the same after you left.

You raised me to believe that marriage was forever and that I had better be careful of my choice. Since I was Daddy's little girl, you could have been critical of my husband. Thank you for accepting and respecting him. Know that the feelings were mutual. I was always surprised, but later understood, why you always took his side. That was your way of supporting my marriage. Now, all three of your children have stayed in marriages of over 40 years' endurance.

Because I respected you as a man of honor, I can trust my husband to be honorable. Lastly, because of your wonderful example as a father, I can unconditionally love my heavenly Father. Thank you.

For the grace of God that brings salvation has appeared to all men. It teaches us to say "No" to ungodliness and worldly passions, and to live self-controlled, upright and godly lives in this present age.

(Titus 2:11-12 NIV)

ADOPTION
Janet R. Sady   **June 19**

He came unto his own, and his own received him not. But as many as received him, to them gave he power to become the sons of God, even to them that believe on his name.
(John 1:11-12 KJV)

I have a delightful adopted nephew. He has all the same rights and privileges to an inheritance from his parents as my natural children do.

God sent Christ to the Jews, His chosen people. When they refused Him, He offered salvation as adopted sons to the Gentiles.

The same offer is open to all today. If we will receive Him and believe on His name, we are adopted into His family to become His children.

Heavenly Father, we thank You for the opportunity to come into Your family through Your Son, Jesus Christ. Amen.

TREE OF LIFE
Joan Clayton   **June 20**

In the midst of the street of it, and on either side of the river, was there the tree of life, which bare twelve manner of fruits, and yielded her fruit ever month: and the leaves of the tree were for the healing of the nations.
(Revelation 22:2 KJV)

From my yard, I viewed this small but strong evergreen tree every time I took refuge in my swing. Whenever problems mounted, I found myself in the swing. Maybe I thought I could swing the troubles away. My children were leaving the nest. I prayed protection for them. My husband's serious surgery plagued my thoughts, and I prayed.

In my swing time, I noticed something different about my young evergreen. It didn't mind the forest of trees around it. No matter how much the larger trees grew and brushed against it, my little tree determined to grow anyway. It refused to give up. The larger trees crowded and outgrew this tree, but it stood its ground. It has grown with patience and persistence.

Now it is the tallest tree in our yard. Through the years, this tree didn't look at its surroundings. It didn't mind the problems. I love to look at this champion tree from my vantage point while swinging. It is tall and lush, growing to maturity.

I learned a lesson from that tree and its determination.

I will "stand fast in the Lord and in the power of his might." I will press "toward the mark" in spite of hardships and grow to maturity, too. My goal is "The Tree of Life on either side of the river!"

I'll meet you there.

DEALING WITH FEAR
Caitlin O'Conner, age 13   **June 21**

Fear. It's a part of human nature. To be afraid is normal, although unhealthy. [Proverbs 29:25] But as children of the Most High God, we do not have to be afraid. For if we are in the care of the Almighty, who by words alone spoke everything we see and everything we cannot see into existence, what enemy can touch us? [Psalm 27:1] Surely *no one*. [Psalm 56:3-4]

I've been in many a situation where I have been afraid. Some times it's too hard not to be afraid. I know; I've been afraid. Afraid of things that I thought may happen, afraid of things happening at that instant. But no matter the problem, no matter the trial, God is always there to help and to comfort. Trust in His ability to deliver you. If you but trust in the Lord to deliver you, whatever you fear will be handled by His Hand.

WHAT YOU SEE MAY NOT BE WHAT YOU GET
Evelyn Minshull   **June 22**

We were at a yard sale, Mother and I, when she hurried over to show me her treasure. It was not pottery, but china—a fragile cup and saucer, intricate blue floral and gold on white as gleaming as bridal satin.

"Only fifty cents," she gushed, holding it carefully cradled in crumpled tissue. "Isn't it lovely?"

"Lovely," I agreed.

She wouldn't trust it to the trunk of the car—where some of the more plebeian purchases might crush it—nor consign it to the back seat, where who knows what might befall it. Instead, she held it on her lap.

I drove with extreme caution.

"I can't believe it" became her litany. "Only fifty cents. Why, you'd think it would be a prized heirloom!"

It was only when she gently unswathed it for display that she recognized the truth—and the true value. Someone had painstakingly glued together its many broken pieces. The cup was even glued to the saucer.

"Whoever—" Mother began, then laughed. "Why, it must have taken more than fifty cents worth of glue!"

Lord, so often the world fools us. But we know that Your promises represent "Truth in advertising." When You offer love, it is unconditional. When You give guidance, there are no detours, no missed intersections. And when You promise eternal life—we rest in the assurance that it will be Life beyond anything we have ever imagined...and that it will, indeed, be everlasting. Amen.

NO NEED FOR DELETION
Charles A. Waugaman June 23

    Found is the source of evening music
    (cool and smooth as wind-dried sheets)
    That teases up the summer window
    Till midnight lullaby's enchantment,
    Soothes turbulence to peace.

    Here the granite where I'm lying
    (weather-smoothed and ribbed with quartz)
    And the lithe, insistent water,
    Spilling hungrily to ocean,
    Free relentless melody.

    Which, I ask, is most substantial—
    Ceaseless brook, ubiquitous rock
    Or the harmonies they loose,
    Laser sharp and deeply healing,
    Overcoming lethargy?

    Stream without its stones runs silent;
    Rocks in drought dull and corrode;
    Thought of life devoid of music
    Suggests that nothing dare be squandered
    Nothing wasted, nothing scorned.

Lord, water in a mossy bed spills little music. Help me not assume retirement is meant for ease. Help me to sing through every circumstance and cherish the boulders. For Jesus' sake. Amen.

THE PATHWAY OF THE RIGHTEOUS
(Celebrating 65 years of marriage)

Mary Rose Pearson   **June 24**

The path of the righteous is like the first gleam of dawn, shining ever brighter till the full light of day.
(Proverbs 4:18 NIV)

We have journeyed down life's pathway hand in hand a long, long time;
We have climbed a-top some mountains and have known the desert's clime;
But our journey's also led us through a flow'ry garden nook,
In the pastures green and shady, and beside a quiet brook.
Our great Guide along this journey has been Jesus Christ, our Lord.
He has led in righteous pathways and has kept us by His Word.
We are happy when we follow ev'ry day and ev'ry night
In the path of His commandments, for they've taught us what is right.
We can say with firm assurance that we're glad we've come this way,
For the mountains brought us beauty, and the deserts made us pray.
Even clouds that hovered o'er us brought the blessed showers of rain.
If our way were just now starting, we would go with Christ again.

PLANTING YOUR GARDEN

Ida Jancso   **June 25**

Cultivate the soil. It has to be ready to accept the seeds. First, you plant seeds of faith. Plant them deep. Faith needs strong roots. "And the prayer offered in faith will make the sick person well; the Lord will raise him up. If he has sinned, he will be forgiven" (James 5:15 NIV). Scatter seeds of love. Without love, weeds of hate will take over. Plant seeds of wisdom. "Now listen, you who say, 'Today or tomorrow we will go to this or that city, spend a year there, carry on business and make money'" (James 4:13 NIV). Every garden needs seeds of patience. "A patient man has great understanding" (Proverbs 14:29 NIV). Finally sow seeds of trust. Your garden will be productive if you have patience and trust in the Lord.

SEEDS OF RIGHTEOUSNESS
Rhonda Hodge   June 26

Every year my husband and I plant a huge garden which includes a large variety of vegetables. Both of us share in the planting, but for one reason or another, every year I seem to get the responsibility of being the caretaker of the garden. Actually, I don't mind. I'm on a mission.

As I pull one weed out at a time, I'm reminded of all the nasty little bad things that are still a part of me that aren't pleasing to God, and I ask Him to make sure that He plucks them out so they don't grow into huge ugly weeds in my mind and character. After I've spent a full day in the garden pulling weeds, I'm a little tired and sore, but I feel so good.

I imagine this is how the Lord will feel when He comes back at the end of the age to harvest His crop...seeds of righteousness...that He's planted. Just as I discard all the weeds before it's time to harvest our crop, Jesus will do the same thing with the bad seeds that are sown by the evil one.

> *The Son of Man will send out his angels, and they will weed out of his kingdom everything that causes sin and all who do evil. They will throw them into the fiery furnace, where there will be weeping and gnashing of teeth. Then the righteous will shine like the sun in the kingdom of their Father.*
> *(Matthew 13: 42-43 NIV)*

I'm thankful that Jesus is the Master Gardener of my life.

GOLDFINCH GIFTS
Mary A. Koepke   June 27

Settled in my porch rocker,
I anticipate company.
From back woods, you bounce
to your feeder with burst
of chirps and twitters.

Claws cling to the perch,
flip gold and jet upside down
in peerless performance.
From port below you peck
each thistle seed.

Mate in olive drab soon comes
to bob a feeding dance.
Heads cock now and again.
In fear of raptor.

You teach clumsy fledglings
avian acrobatics—but when
some sassy sparrow
flutters mimicry, he retreats defeated.

Lifted from our topsy-turvy world—
I praise God for goldfinch gifts.

UNCLENCHED FISTS

Dolores Fruth June 28

I clenched my fists and said a prayer.
I questioned, are You really there?
You surely know that when he died
I lost my love, my life, my pride.

The hurt is deeper and so strong.
I want to know what I did wrong.
I could strike out to friend and foe.
I am so lost, where can I go?

Then slowly I unclench my hands.
I am so tired, You understand.
Release me, Lord, so I can be
A better person. Set me free!

The Lord then placed His hand on mine.
He told me of His plan divine.
That fists will threaten to destroy,
While open hands give others joy.

I put the hurt and pain aside.
I felt the warmth of love inside.
Now I will try to serve and give
With open arms to those who live!

SAM

Elizabeth M. Van Hook　　　　　　　　　　　　　　　　　　**June 29**

> *Praise be to the God and Father of our Lord Jesus Christ, the Father of compassion and the God of all comfort, who comforts us in all our troubles.*
>
> *(2 Corinthians 1:3-4 NIV)*

Teddy bears are chubby, furry, cuddly, endearing, and always bring a smile.

My friend, Sue, was diagnosed with an aggressive cancer and within a few months had lost nearly a hundred pounds. While undergoing chemotherapy and radiation, she went back to attending church again. She pleaded with God to take her pain away and heal her. The pain only increased.

I prayed for Sue's healing, too. Living four hundred miles away, I could not visit her, hug her, or tell her that God would be with her through this ordeal. Instead, I sent Sam, a curly-haired, caramel-colored bear dressed in a sky blue bathrobe printed with white and gold stars and moons on it. Sam was to be my "bearer" of smiles to Sue. He wore blue suede fringed moccasins on his chubby feet. I placed in the box a copy of a meditation that I had written called *Bear Hugs*.

My niece, Carol, Sue's daughter, called to tell me that Sue hugged and kissed Sam whenever she felt pain. He was never more than an arm's length away from her. Despite her weakness, her last task at night was to remove Sam's slippers to get him ready for bed.

Teddy bears always seem to bring comfort and a calmness. I had agonized on whether I should mail Sam to Sue. She did not seem the teddy bear type. She was an attractive, sophisticated, independent woman. However, I knew Sam was just what she needed now.

Sue died two weeks later on Christmas morning. Sam was at her side. She was only fifty years old. Both Carol and I felt at peace knowing that Sam had provided comfort and laughter in those last days.

Father, thank You for helping me to realize that everyone is a teddy type and that we can bring comfort to those who are hurting. Amen.

BE OF GOOD COURAGE

Shirley S. Stevens   **June 30**

Wait on the LORD: be of good courage, and he shall strengthen thine heart.

(Psalm 27:14 KJV)

As I looked around the room in the chemotherapy suite at Magee Hospital, I saw a woman holding a lamb and stroking it. I could tell that she took comfort from that stuffed animal, a gift from her daughter. Two women who had lost their hair wore pink and white knit caps with Big Ben's insignia on them. Ben, the rookie quarterback of the Steelers, was a hero to many Pittsburghers.

Today, however, I wasn't thinking of the Steelers and their feats at Heinz Field. Instead, I admired the courage of these women who were fighting their battle with cancer as they came for their hour-long IV infusions.

I prayed: *Lord, help these women to know that You will be with them, both as they receive these treatments and as they deal with the side-effects at home. Reassure them that You will travel with them through the Valley of the Shadow and that You will strengthen their bodies and spirits. Amen.*

LIKE A GOOD NEIGHBOR

Cindy Hawkins   **July 1**

"Love your neighbor as yourself." Love does no harm to its neighbor. Therefore love is the fulfillment of the law.

(Romans 13:9-10 NIV)

A recent poll showed that some people don't trust Christians. How can we restore people's trust in us as followers of Christ? The best way to change public opinion begins next door. In the parable of the Good Samaritan, Jesus teaches us to reach out to our neighbors. His desire is that we exemplify the "love your neighbor as yourself" principle. [Luke 10:27-28 NIV]

While we may not encounter a person robbed, injured, and abandoned by the side of the road, we probably know someone who is hurting on the inside. A young, overwhelmed mother may be hungry for morsels of wise advice from an experienced mother. A lonely widow yearns for an invitation to tea. Next door a marriage is crumbling. A co-worker in a nearby cubicle just wants someone to talk to. The man in the corner house needs help with errands until the leg cast comes off. Showing mercy and being a good neighbor are one and the same.

The saying goes that no one cares how much you know until they know how much you care. When we stop and meet someone's needs, we are demonstrating love toward the neighbors God puts in our path. Who are your neighbors that need a touch of God's love today?

Show me, Lord, the person who needs a brush with Your loving, life-giving presence. Help me to follow Your example and reach out to those who are in desperate need of You.

KIND GESTURES
Annettee Budzban July 2

As it is written, He [the benevolent person] scatters abroad, He gives to the poor; His deeds of justice and goodness and kindness and benevolence will go on and endure forever!
(2 Corinthians 9:9, AMP)

Kind gestures nurture our souls, as well as others.

On a blazing hot day as my friend drove along, she noticed the workers on the road construction site wiping sweat from their foreheads, their T-shirts drenched with perspiration. With a burdened heart, she watched them struggle against the hot sun to complete their tasks.

Once home, she gripped a six-pack of soda, and hurried back to the work site. When she stopped the car and carried these cold drinks to the workers, their tanned faces beamed with relief that someone was kind enough to bring them a refreshing drink. As she drove away from the work site, she was overcome by the good feeling that she had helped someone in need.

The Bible tells us that God will always remember our acts of kindness and love. However, fear that we are being taken advantage of can keep us from showing kindness. But if we get past the fear, we find kind gestures help to nurture our souls when we need refreshment. That's why they must be done with the motivation to bless another.

With the use of our imagination and the leading of the Holy Spirit, the opportunities to be kind to someone are endless. Let's stop along life's path to sow some seeds of kindness.

LOVE REQUIRES UNSELFISHNESS
Joan Clayton   **July 3**

Carry each other's burdens, and in this way you will fulfill the law of Christ.

(Galatians 6:2 NIV)

"Glad to see ya!" With our help Uncle Steve had lived ten good years in his home alone, enjoying life despite his handicaps. After his 91st birthday, his knees began to give way, even on his walker. My husband and I found a wonderful facility, and Uncle Steve is happy there.

His eyes light up when he sees me and when I hug and kiss him he says, "Thank you!" But I'm the one to say, "Thank you." I say "Thank you" to God for the years we were able to help extend his life with our love. I say "Thank you" for answered prayers on Uncle Steve's behalf.

God gave us an opportunity to help a lonely, hurting soul. We learned many lessons from the experience. It hurts to love; it takes sacrifice and unselfishness.

One day Uncle Steve will walk out of that crippled body on two strong knees. He will not need a walker, wheelchair, or crutches.

I know when I meet Uncle Steve in heaven I'll hear him say, "Glad to see ya!"

Dear God, grant us strength to care for others in this journey of life. Amen.

GOD CARES
Linda Mae Richardson   **July 4**

It seems when problems weigh me down
God lays His gentle hands
Upon my heart to let me know
He cares and understands.

And though each problem still remains
I know He'll help me see
The way to conquer every one
Together—God and me!

BARTER: THE GIFT OF LOVE
Shirley S. Stevens   **July 5**

This is my commandment, that ye love one another, as I have loved you.
(John 15:12 KJV)

When my friend Elaine was confined to her bedroom as she battled cancer, she loved to look out the window at the rows of corn. She said that she heard God's soothing voice in the hushing sound from the wind moving through the corn rows.

One day, when she saw the farmer cutting down the stalks, she told her husband how much she would miss the comfort of the corn rows. Her husband, Jack, baked an apple pie that afternoon and took it over to the farmer. He asked that the farmer leave two rows of the corn stalks for Elaine to enjoy. And the farmer did!

Lord, help me to use my talent, whether in baking a pie or in writing a poem, to bring comfort to those who suffer. Amen.

WHAT KIND OF FRIEND AM I?
Janet R. Sady   **July 6**

And when they could not come nigh unto him for the press, they uncovered the roof where he was: and when they had broken it up, they let down the bed wherein the sick of the palsy lay.
(Mark 2:4 KJV)

The demands on our time from everyday shopping, cleaning, banking, paperwork, etc. are numerous. During these busy times, a friend may call us, looking for a shoulder to cry on, or just needing to vent. Are we too busy to listen or help?

The friends of the man sick with palsy, didn't only take time to bring him for help, but when they could not get into the house where Jesus was speaking, they removed the roof and lowered him to the Lord. Jesus not only healed his body, but forgave his sins, as well.

One of my friends shared a personal experience of attending a church with an acquaintance. Another person in the group brought a man from a foreign country, who shared the gospel in his language. After listening to the service, this man made a decision to trust Christ as his Savior. That's the kind of friend I want to be to those around me!

Father, help me to take time to be a friend to others, so that they might catch a glimpse of Jesus in me. Amen.

A CALL IN THE NIGHT
Lorena Estep   July 7

To the Lord I cry aloud, and he answers me from his holy hill. I lie down and sleep; I wake again, because the Lord sustains me.
(Psalm 3:4-5 NIV)

The ringing of the phone was a jarring sound at 2:00 a.m. I awakened and rushed to grab it before a second ring could arouse the children or my husband.

"Hello," I answered softly.

"Is Mabel there?" A quavery older female voice asked.

"I'm sorry," I told the woman. "You have the wrong number."

"Oh. Well, I'll just talk to you, then."

And she did for at least half an hour. I heard all of her physical problems, and finally was asked if I thought she should take one of her sleeping pills. Not knowing anything about her actual physical condition or her medications, I answered, "Maybe you should try going back to bed without it. Since we've talked, you might be able to sleep."

"All right," she agreed, and hung up.

I prayed for her and thanked the Lord that I could be a comfort to a stranger who called in the night.

I realized how thankful we can be as believers that God is always available for a call in the night from His children, and we would never get a wrong number with Him.

"Call to me and I will answer you and tell you great and unsearchable things you do not know."
(Jeremiah 33:3 NIV)

GOD WILL MEET OUR NEEDS
Martha Rogers   July 8

And my God will meet all your needs according to his glorious riches in Christ Jesus.
(Philippians 4:19 NIV)

The greatest test of faith for our family came when our

grandson Mikell needed a liver transplant. Cystic fibrosis had attacked one of the most vital organs in the body.

While waiting for the transplant, Mikell endured many trips to the hospital for platelets to replace those he'd lost with his liver malfunction. One particular week he went in for a minor procedure on his sinuses, and a call went out for blood and platelets to have on hand for the surgery.

Friends and loved ones donated an ample supply of platelets. Mikell didn't need them all, and he went home after successful surgery. A few days later he began bleeding, and his parents again rushed him to the emergency room. They arrived at ten on a Saturday evening.

The doctor immediately knew he needed more platelets. With no time to call for donors, the nurse called the blood center. She learned the platelets left from surgery earlier in the week were still in the cooler, slated for disposal at midnight. At 11:15, those platelets were sent to Mikell's room. They saved his life.

God already knew the need would be there and supplied the extra platelets. He also knew exactly how long they would last and provided them for Mikell when the need arose.

Once again God showered His divine mercy on our family. He is always on time, never too early and never too late.

Father God, may we always put our trust in You. You will never fail us, and will take care of all our needs.

GREAT GAIN
Tiffany Schlichter July 9

But godliness with contentment is great gain. For we brought nothing into this world, and it is certain we can carry nothing out. And having food and raiment let us be therewith content.
(1 Timothy 6:6-8 KJV)

Many people are not content with what they have—and most of them have much more than food and clothing! Yet they feel that they do not have enough. Really, our only need is Jesus Christ, and He graciously provides other things. If we are not content with our present state, we will not easily learn this lesson, regardless of what situation we find ourselves in.

Contentment is satisfaction. The apostle Paul was satisfied with whatever his situation was. He had learned how to be content with little or with more. Can we not learn this as well, especially when we have so much more than this godly man did? "Not that I speak in respect of want: for I have learned, in whatsoever state I am, therewith to be content. I know both how to be abased, and I know how to abound: every where and in all things I am instructed both to be full and to be hungry, both to abound and to suffer need. I can do all things through Christ which strengtheneth me" (Philippians 4:11-13 KJV).

Thank You, Lord, for the many wonderful things You graciously provide. Please help me to learn contentment with the situations I am in and the things in my possession. Amen.

IF IT WERE ONLY FOR ME

Joe LoBello   July 10

In this vast and wonderful creation,
with stars set without number
and the depths of the crystal blue seas,
if I were the only man on earth,
My Lord would have died for me.

If salvation was meant for me alone,
He still would have been the Lamb
and taken the stripes of my transgressions.
If I were the only one to need,
Christ would have died just the same.

My journey on earth has purpose
For He endured the pain.
He rose in glory that I might live.
Yet if I were the only soul to save,
My willing Savior would die for me.

If I were the only one,
God would have still sent His Loving Son.
If it were only me,
Christ would have come for the victory,
If it were only me....

RED AND WHITE CONTRASTS
Kathy Johnson   July 11

>The cardinal at my windowsill
>Shines brightly red with orange bill
>The pure, bright, white snow
>Sets a background show
>
>Train ride through Scotland
>Sheep wandering loose
>Caught on the track
>No place to dash
>
>All this reminds me
>Of the words from Isaiah:
>"Though your sins are like scarlet,
>they shall be white as snow;
>though they are red as crimson,
>they shall be like wool." (Isaiah 1:18 NIV)

RETURN TO HARMONY
Mary A. Koepke   July 12

Restore us to thyself, O LORD, that we may be restored!
(Lamentations 5: 21 RSV)

    A little Pennsylvania town, quiet and quaint, Harmony's roots are deep in the 1800's history of a communal gentle people who anticipated the imminent coming of the Lord. An eclectic mix of then and now, the main street has historical row houses, log houses, restored houses, and a museum stocked with reminders of the past. This pleasant place draws visitors seeking old-fashioned Memorial day parades, fourth of July fireworks in the park, street concerts, and the annual Dankfest and Wienfest Naht festivals.

    Then came relentless rain, an aftermath of hurricanes forcing their way north. Rain breaking records of one hundred years—ground-soaking rain that pushed mud and trees down hills, poured through streets, overflowed streamlets and wide creeks into low places. The owners of the ice cream parlor, gift shops, and lumber yard were caught unprepared. Trying to move possessions, caught in muddy swirls, finally retreating—shocked by loss. In churches, the congregations prayed for the afflicted. The community drew together to clean up debris, repair damage, provide shelter, food, and compassion. Restoration began with hope for the future—trusting that God is always with us.

Heavenly Father, in a world filled with inhumanity, war's devastation, violence and cruelty, where is harmony? The people of Harmony, Pennsylvania and the world beyond will always have times of suffering. And we, like the Harmonites of old, look to the divine harmony of the second coming.

JESUS' NEW COMMANDMENT
Joseph Hopkins July 13

A new commandment I give you: Love one another. As I have loved you, so you must love one another. By this all men will know that you are my disciples, if you love one another.
(John 13:34-35 NIV)

A new commandment? What about Leviticus 19:18, in which we are told, "But love your neighbor as yourself." Is this not what Jesus said to His disciples, then and now? The newness, then, was not in the commandment itself but in the way it was beautifully illustrated by Jesus. "As I have loved you," Jesus said. As He reached out to the poor, to women in that male-dominated society, to prostitutes, the despised Samaritans and tax collectors, to the sick and the demon-possessed, so you and I are called to do likewise. One of the early church fathers observed, "See how these Christians love one another!"

Could this be said of your church, or mine? Could it be said of you, or me?

Father, please forgive our insensitivity to the needs of others, especially the marginalized people of our society. Fill our hearts with the love of Jesus for all of our brothers and sisters in the great family of God. May His love move us to action: feeding the hungry; clothing the naked; and visiting the sick and the imprisoned.

THE RING
Jennifer Kanode July 14

Love is patient, love is kind. It does not envy, it does not boast, it is not proud.
(1 Corinthians 13:4 NIV)

I have a silver thumb ring that I've been wearing for about two or three years now. Imprinted on it are the words "True Love Waits." I got this ring before I was married. It served as a reminder to me not to rush into marriage and to wait until I was married to have sex.

Shortly after I married, a friend asked, "Are you going to take your thumb ring off now?"

I told him that I wasn't. For some reason I felt I needed to continue to wear the ring. Since then, I have lost it several times. I couldn't find it for days, but then it would pop up. One day I was gardening and lost it in an overgrown patch of weeds. I thought it had finally disappeared for good. I prayed, and I found it a few seconds later.

The ring has now taken on a different meaning for me. Even though we are now married, we both must strive to continue to be pure, even in marriage. My love must show respect for my husband and for all people.

Father, help us to show love to all Your children. Help us to remember that You have created every living thing, and You love and care for each of us unconditionally. Thank You. Amen.

MEDITATION ON A TONE POEM

Charles A. Waugaman   **July 15**

Job 38:4-7

Dear, sweet, Jesus, what a change from the island vacation—the symphony! The children are in bed, asleep, and I relax before the TV. I expected You on the island; that is Your world, Your creation. You are at home there.

But here! So at ease with the orchestra, and DON JUAN and Strauss.

And why not, you ask? Is there anything of sin or tragedy I do not know? Did you imagine beauty and harmony and dissonance beyond Me? If you thrill to a quintet of French horns, did you expect Me to be untouched?

Would I have died for you if I had been ignorant of sin? Would the horn have been invented had I not dreamed it before the world began? Would you have throbbed so to music if I had not tuned you to quiver at such sounds?

Oh, dear Child! Dear excited re-creator! Did you not

know I have conducted orchestras since the world began?

Forgive me, Lord, I cannot see the other players. I can seldom hear them, even faintly. Please tune me to harmonize in Your orchestra; to do any solos clearly and well. Make me willing to be blended to Your music. Love through me, Lord. Amen.

PRAYER OF A LIGHTNING BUG
Evelyn Minshull   July 16

Lord,
is it sometimes not enough to *be*—not *do*?
Surely I serve no soaring function in Your world.
I cannot scatter clouds—as breezes do—
Nor—like the birds—fill Your ears with music.
I cannot aerate the soil—as earthworms must—
      to foster growing...
nor do I propagate the trees by ferrying pollen
      from bloom to nodding bloom.
I cannot still the buzz and bite of gnats, mosquitoes...
nor neutralize the blight of beetles' foraging.

But I can *be.*
At night—joined by my fellows—
our flickers create a moving galaxy of minor stars—
      enchanting children.
Even their elders pause in fascination...
remembering, perhaps, a Mason jar,
      harnessing brilliance for a magic bedtime...
 remembering a youthful night at meadow's edge—
      before maturity's demands snuffed buoyant innocence.
My incandescent winking charts the way to wonderment.
Lord, quell my doubting.
Is it enough to be—not do?
AMEN.

It was he who gave some to be apostles, some to be prophets, some to be evangelists, and some to be pastors and teachers.
(Ephesians 4:11 NIV)

BACK TO THE BASICS

CJ Hitz   July 17

If you've practiced a sport for any length of time, you know what it means to go through a "slump." Professional athletes go through slumps. Whether you're talking to an NBA basketball player struggling with his jump shot or a PGA golfer struggling with his swing, they'll tell you the same thing when it comes to working out of a slump. "It's time to get back to the basics." The fundamentals. These are the essentials necessary to play the game correctly. In golf, something as simple as the way you're gripping the club can throw your swing off.

We live in an age of gimmicks, fads, and fancy solutions to many problems we face. Churches are no strangers to these "cool, hip, state of the art" methods. There's only one problem. *They're not working.*

Records show the largest Protestant denominations in the U.S. have reported 0% new growth over the last couple of years. Zero. Even with multi-million dollar building campaigns, the most expensive gadgets, or the hippest youth facilities, churches are seeing little impact. We've been relying on gimmicks over God.

Jesus gave his disciples a key "fundamental" to practice after His resurrection. Are you ready for this? Here it is. *Waiting.*

In Acts 1:4, Jesus tells the disciples to *"<u>wait</u> in Jerusalem until the Father sends you what he promised."* So simple, yet so profound. Many times, we rush to begin a new program in the church, and then we ask God to bless our efforts rather than asking for His direction in the first place. When it doesn't get the desired result, we're left scratching our heads. Ready to come out of your spiritual slump? Get back to the basics.

GOD LOVES A CHEERFUL GIVER
Tune of *Johnny Has Gone for a Soldier*

Glenda Joy Race   July 18

> He who sows seed sparingly,
> Will sparingly a harvest receive.
> There is one thing we should know
> God loves a cheerful giver.
>
> If you sow bountifully,

Bountiful the harvest
Will be for your family.
God loves a cheerful giver.

As a man purposes in his heart,
Not by grudge or necessity,
Let him give to God what he will.
God loves a cheerful giver.

Why rob God; why be cursed?
Give all your tithes and offerings.
So God may pour out a blessing for you.
God loves a cheerful giver.

(2 Corinthians 9:6-7; Malachi 3:8-10)

CLOTHES

Elizabeth M. Van Hook   **July 19**

God made us plain and simple, but we made ourselves very complicated.

(Ecclesiastes 7:29)

The fortune in my cookie at the Chinese restaurant read: *Good clothes open many doors, go shopping!* Kathy, the comic strip character, and I have made that our mantra!

The deep purple dress that I was planning to wear to Jackie, my nephew, and Carol's wedding did not fit. The ceremony was only a week away. Even if I starved myself, the dress would not fit! I was annoyed with myself for indulging in too many midnight snacks of coffee ice cream.

All I could think about was clothes. The next day, I took the bus to the mall to go shopping. Every dress I tried on was either too short, too long, too tight, or the wrong color. I should not have let things go to the last minute.

Our God is wise. He knows how to get His messages to me. On the way home, Julia sat next to me on the bus. As we talked, I explained my dress problem. With the warmest of smiles, she told me, "I am simplifying my life and only doing things that really matter. I have had three bouts of cancer and am now in remission. Betty, what I wear isn't important to me anymore."

Julia's words quieted my panic attack. I resolved that when

I went home, I would look through the dresses in my overflowing wardrobe closet again.

Father, forgive us for making our lives so complicated by being preoccupation with the world. Thank You for giving us people along the way to convey Your message and keep us focused on Your plans for our lives. Amen.

SPENDING TIME

Theresa V. Wilson   July 20

We spend too much time on things that won't last.
We spend too much time on things of the past.
By storing up treasures and worthless artifacts,
We think life's pleasures will keep us on track.
While we spend our moments on frivolous things
And looking for "stuff" to which we can cling,
We forget God has given freedom to choose—
Right or wrong, give or take ...win or lose.
Today I must stop and consider my choice:
Keep "I" on the throne or listen to God's voice.
We're all fender-benders. We all make mistakes.
But it's the one who surrenders, who sees heaven's gate.
By sharing your journey through the stories you tell,
You help others to focus, persevere, and excel.
So get on the stick, don't let yourself fall.
At the turn in the bend, you'll meet the Master of all.

DO IT WHILE YOU CAN

Jana Carman   July 21

Walk while you have the light.
(John 12:35 RSV)

What we can do easily in daylight—work, walk, see—becomes difficult, even impossible, in the dark. Think of trying to find a lost key or, worse yet, a lost child in the dark. That's hard even with artificial lighting. "Walk while you have the light," Jesus said, meaning those listening should believe in Him while He was still with them. We might rephrase it, "Do what you need to do while the circumstances are favorable."

There is no time like the present, because life is uncertain. Another opportunity may not present itself for making that apology, writing that letter, learning that family history, getting right with God. As procrastination pushes today's work into tomorrow's, eventually something important is left undone because there is not enough time to do it or the person is no longer available. The night is coming.

Lord, I have presumed that I "can always do it tomorrow." Forgive my presumption and give me the push I need today. In Jesus' name. Amen.

A LITTLE BIRD SAID
Leigh DeLozier   **July 22**

Ask where the good way is, and walk in it, and you will find rest for your souls.

(Jeremiah 6:16 NIV)

We were preparing to move, so the garage was stacked high with boxes and other things. When we heard something crash one night, the children and I were quick to investigate.
The victim was a small birdbath dish my godmother had given us. Pieces of glazed blue ceramic lay scattered at our feet.

I picked up the pieces, knowing it couldn't be fixed. The little bird that had perched on the bowl's rim had somehow remained intact, so I placed it on the shelf above the kitchen sink.

As silly as it sounds, that little bue bird became an important reminder. It sat watching me with its head tilted to one side, always seeming to ask questions. *So how's your day going? Were you a little tough on the kids just then? Have you asked for patience today?* It almost became an extension of my conscience.

I packed more things each day, but Little Bird remained on the shelf to the very end. And once we moved in the new house, he took up residence on the windowsill above the sink, still asking questions.

It makes me a little sad that the birdbath broke, but I'm thankful that Little Bird didn't. Sometimes God can use the most ordinary things to help keep us on track.

Thank You, Lord, for ordinary reminders that keep us on the right course.

A GOD THING
Margaret Steinacker   **July 23**

The LORD is the Everlasting God, ...He will not grow tired or weary.
(Isaiah 40:28 NIV)

Fifteen months ago, I couldn't have told you about "God Things" in my life. As a Sunday-morning-Christian, I wasn't into Bible study. But when the new music director arrived, his wife and I started a friendship based on her teaching school and my working for a school superintendent. Then mutual love for books became a focus.

A year later my husband Bob, a non-believing retired principal, had 55% of his malignant liver removed. Complications followed. But each week, as I waited in the hospital, God continued to show me His "things." When the cell phone bill came, I received an unexpected check for a few cents less than the total. Best of all, Bob has found the Lord as his Savior! He's witnessing to family, friends, and medical staff. Students from the school where he was principal have surrounded our home and prayed many times. God has worked miracles in the lives of these teens. They've been able to witness to friends who used to make fun of them.

I've learned patience in a way I had never expected. My emotional and physical strength has been in the Lord. The only way I know to express this is to say, "It's a God Thing."

Lord, I thank You for Your strength and immeasurable understanding. Help me always to lean on You.

WATER CHILD
Barbara Ann Yonnotti   **July 24**

Embryo in water
Sea of the womb
Floating for survival
Soul has to abide
Born physically
And drink of the water
Spiritually to know
Him.

Whoever believes in me, as the Scripture has said, streams of living water will flow from within him.
(John 7:38 NIV)

PERSONAL GOD

Micki Roberts   **July 25**

Have you ever meditated upon a scripture and the Holy Spirit opened wide your understanding? So much so that you couldn't wait to share what you'd learned with your spouse or a close friend—only to realize it didn't hold the same meaning for them?

When this happens to me, it serves to remind me that God is a personal God. That my relationship with Him is individual and separate from the relationships He enjoys with others.

Does this mean we should not share our spiritual discoveries with others? Of course not! If you have a spouse or a friend who will rejoice with you over the precepts God is teaching you, by all means, share!

However, let me extend a word of caution. There are those who will downplay or even belittle your excitement. Sometimes they totally ignore what you've shared by beginning to talk about something designed to steer the conversation away from your topic.

Matthew 7:6 tells us: "Do not give what is holy to dogs, and do not throw your pearls before swine, lest they trample them under their feet, and turn and tear you to pieces." [NAS] In other words, know who you're talking with and what you can share with that person.

As always there are exceptions to the rule. If you are certain that God is leading you to share your experience with someone, be obedient. You never know what He may use to open hearts to His truth.

IF

Barbara Peer   **July 26**

When Jesus was baptized by John, God spoke in an audible voice declaring Jesus as His Son. Right after that Christ went into the wilderness to be tempted by Satan, who began with "If you are the Son of God..." When Satan said "If," he was challenging Jesus to doubt that He was the Son of God.

Satan comes to us with the same challenge: If you're really a Christian, why aren't you better than you are? If you're a new creation in Christ Jesus, why do you still have the same old hangups? If you were smarter, more successful, cleaned up your act, then maybe God would love you.

The way Jesus dealt with Satan was by referring back to the Word: "It is written..." We can follow His example by falling back on what is written about us: "You are all sons of God through faith in Christ Jesus" (Galatians 3:26 NIV). It is our faith in Jesus which makes us Christians—not our own ability to perform: "Because of his great love for us, God, who is rich in mercy, made us alive with Christ... It is by grace you have been saved, through faith—not by works" (Ephesians 2:4-9 NIV). "He who loves me will be loved by my Father, and I too will love him and show myself to him" (John 14:21 NIV). The Word assures us of God's love, and there are no "ifs" about it.

REST FOR THE SOUL

Dave Evans July 27

> Tonight my heart,
> heavy with care,
> calls out to You;
> in the darkness
> You seem so far—
> yet as I pray,
> Your Spirit reaches out
> and my soul finds rest.

Return to your rest, O my soul, for the LORD has dealt bountifully with you.

(Psalm 116:7 NAS)

ONE DAY AT A TIME

Pat Collins July 28

Lord, keep me from rushing around so. Help me to slow down, so I may not miss the many blessings you send my way. Help me not to worry about tomorrow, but to enjoy today. To take one day at a time.

There is so much beauty to be seen in each day I don't want to miss it by worrying about tomorrow. You will take care of tomorrow, You always do. Today let me enjoy the sunshine, singing of birds, the small flower that may not be there tomorrow.

There are so many things to be seen, and shared. Help me

not to miss today by rushing about, but really to look at what it holds, and be ever thankful for what You give me. One day at a time.

> *Trust in the LORD with all your heart, and lean not on your own understanding; in all your ways acknowledge Him, and He shall direct your paths.*
>
> *(Proverbs 3:5-6 NKJ)*

CLOUDY WATER

CJ Hitz   **July 29**

> *But Jesus often withdrew to lonely places and prayed.*
>
> *(Luke 5:16 NIV)*

Have you ever seen one of those glass bubble-looking things that you shake and it looks like a blizzard inside? Eventually, after you set it down, all the little flakes settle on the bottom. You can get a similar effect when you take a glass jar, fill it with river water and shake it up. After several minutes, the sediment settles on the bottom.

At times, our lives resemble these shaken containers. The waters become stirred and cloudy to the point where we lack focus and clarity. During these times it becomes necessary to quiet ourselves so we're able to hear the voice of God again. This happens only when we take a break from distractions and activity. Jesus knew the importance of allowing the "water to clear." Luke's Gospel tells us that "Jesus often withdrew to lonely places for prayer." Yes, even His life became cloudy at times. Jesus was, quite possibly, one of the busiest people ever to live, constantly encountering people who wanted something from Him.

Activity in our lives is a good thing. Let's just remember to allow the water to clear from time to time.

THE GIFT OF PEACE

Shirley S. Stevens   **July 30**

> *Grace to you, and peace, from God our Father and the Lord Jesus Christ.*
>
> *(Philemon 3 KJV)*

My friend Rita made me a tee shirt which read: I gave at St. John Laterne's.

The shirt was a reminder of our visit to Rome where we

had strolled through the square in front of St. John Laterne's Church. At two o'clock in the afternoon, when the temperature was 100 degrees, only tourists were out walking. I was between two nuns from Pittsburgh, who were showing me the special sites of The Holy City.

Suddenly I felt a tug and let out a shriek. I had heard the sound of a motorbike, but didn't realize what was happening until I watched two men on a motorbike speed off with my purse.

Earlier that morning, the Italian sister who ran our convent guest house had insisted that we leave our important documents and most of our money with her. I was grateful that I had listened, so I lost only a few thousand lira (about thirty dollars) and my eyeglasses. Yet I was angry and felt violated. That evening I prayed and "offered it up" as my friends encouraged me to do. If I continued to dwell on my rage about having my purse stolen, I would ruin the good memories of my vacation.

Instead I sent up a prayer of thanks.

Thank You, Lord, for keeping me safe in my travels. And thank You for the reminder that a thief can steal my purse, but he can't steal my peace. Although I can't change what has happened, I can choose the attitude that I take toward that event and remember that You are worthy.

REST

Helen Kammerdiener July 31

    Thank You, Lord, for rest.
    Thank You for pillows and sheets,
        and quilts and beds.
    Thank You for chairs and stools
        and sofas and recliners.
    Thank You for Sundays and holidays
        and evenings and nights.
    Thank You for Your warm Presence
        granting me peace in a troubled world.
    Thank You, Lord, for rest.

A HUMMINGBIRD'S TREAT

Tiffany Stuart August 1

Therefore, as we have opportunity, let us do good to all people, especially to those who belong to the family of believers.
(Galatians 6:10 NIV)

One hot afternoon while drinking iced tea with a friend in her backyard, I noticed a bright green hummingbird buzz by. Instead of flying to the sugar feeder, this tiny bird surprised me and flew straight into the swarm of gnats nearby. Jumping about in midair, it frantically swallowed as many gnats as it could. The bird seized the moment and feasted.

I want to be like this hummingbird and see the unexpected opportunities God puts in front of me. Instead, in my tunnel vision, I survive on stale sugar water. I miss those special moments where God provides various ways for me to minister to others. I need to view serving as an opportunity, not as an inconvenience. I long to grasp the benefit of the visiting "gnats" God places in my life.

Almighty God, open our eyes to see the people around us. Give us hearts that eagerly jump at the opportunities to be good to others. We trust You will satisfy our hunger, as we lay aside our desires and meet the needs of others.

ANOTHER DAY IS THROUGH

Pat Collins **August 2**

Dear Lord, another day is ending. I ask myself, how did it go by so fast? How did I use this day? Did I witness for You? Did I speak Your name to anyone? Did I thank You, for all You've done for and given me, or was I too busy doing my own thing?

Lord Jesus, please forgive me for my neglect of You during my busy day. I am so thankful You do not forget me. Help me to be more loving and aware of You during my day, and stop long enough to seek Your love and guidance, and be ever thankful You never neglect me.

> *In all thy ways acknowledge him, and he shall direct thy paths.*
>
> (*Proverbs* 3:6 KJV)

LIFE IN THE FAST LANE

Angela Dilmore **August 3**

> *There is a time for everything, and a season for every activity under heaven.*
>
> (*Ecclesiastes* 3:1 NIV)

It is a typical day. I'm fussing about all the errands to run, things to do, and places to go. I'm a full-time mom with a part-time job. And I am busy. I often long for a little "down time."

Occasionally, though, I do have a day that is less hectic. A day at home, with the kids in school, and nothing to do but housework. It's peaceful and quiet. It occurs to me, on these rare days, that if every day were this peaceful, I'd be bored to death.

I realize now that God provides for me a balance between busyness and boredom. I thank Him for asking me to do just enough to keep life interesting, but not so much that I am overwhelmed.

Dear Lord, thank You for quiet moments in the midst of a brimming schedule. Amen.

WALK WITH ME

Linda Mae Richardson August 4

> If you really want to help me,
> Then come walk with me a mile
> And remind me of the joys of life
> That always make me smile.
>
> You need not know the perfect words,
> Nor special things to do.
> It is enough you walk beside,
> And I'll gain strength from you.
>
> For I've learned my cancer journey
> Is a lonely place to be,
> When I seek to walk its many paths
> With strength from only me.
>
> Then when my journey seems too long
> And coldness fills the night—
> Your friendship warms my heart and soul,
> Renews my will to fight!
>
> So walk beside me for a while;
> It needn't be all the way.
> God molds your love into a gift
> Made perfect for this day.

FEAR NOT
Shirley S. Stevens   **August 5**

> *Are not five sparrows sold for two farthings, and not one of them is forgotten before God? But even the very hairs of your head are all numbered. Fear not therefore: ye are of more value than many sparrows.*
> (Luke 12:6-7 KJV)

As I drove over to my friend Rita's house with a container of homemade soup, I was feeling depressed because her chemotherapy had led to terrible bouts of nausea. I had been praying that God would send a sign that He was watching over her.

Sitting at the light leading to the ramp for the interstate, I looked up at the utility wires, which seemed to form a musical score. Perched on the wires were birds, who seemed to be notes on a musical staff.

I started to sing the spiritual "His Eye is on the Sparrow." In the last line, I inserted my friend's name. "And I know He watches Rita."

Dear Lord, help us to remember that Your eye is always on us, that You value each sparrow and each person.

MEDITATION ON ENTERING FRIENDSHIP
Charles A. Waugaman   **August 6**

Like a cathedral, friendship can be entered or observed. I recall the time I baked a cake for friends who were experiencing bereavement.

"Let's take it out of the pan and wrap it in foil. Then there will be no dishes to return." We were a young family then, with little extra for such things as disposable foil baking pans, and every store was a considerable drive.

We thought we would save our friends bother. But I wonder. Was that really entering friendship or staying on the circumference? Was the comfort we sought theirs or ours?

In Maine we had a friend who responded to every act of kindness. No bowl was returned empty; no visit was made without a telephoned thanks; no thank-you sent that didn't merit response by return mail. It became a game to get one kindness ahead of her. And we always lost. Lost? Never!

But such friendships are rare. Even with the Friend. So many claim Him, yet only circle Him with nods at Bethlehem and Calvary or the garden tomb. "Circumference Christians!" What a loss. To make of the Door a wall—and be content.

Dearest Jesus. Friend. May my human friendships echo Yours for me. May every friendship center in You. Eagerly. Amen.

A FRIEND
Debbie Rempel   **August 7**

As I look at you,
my beautiful friend,
I realize how
wonderful you are
to God and to me.

I see you as a flower
grown in God's garden.
I am blessed because you were
a seed planted by God
to bloom where you are.
I am glad God
planted you
in my garden,
where the colors of
friendship grow.

MAKING WRONG TURNS
Lorena Estep   **August 8**

Your word is a lamp to my feet and a light for my path.
(Psalm 119:105 NIV)

"Did I miss the turn, Lord?" I opened the map and tried to read and drive on I-81 at the same time. "Yep, I surely did!" I had passed the exit to route 66 that would have taken me over to I-95, my ultimate goal on my trip alone to Myrtle Beach, SC. Now I searched for an alternate route.

It looked like route 211 would do it. It soon came up and I exited. Before long, I found myself climbing, making many twists and turns. A sign read that this road traveled through the Shenandoah Mountains.

"Well, Lord, life often does take us down some windy,

winding roads, both literally and figuratively." I only had to look back through the years of my own life to realize how true it was. I also had to admit that all the wrong turns had been my own doing.

But just as the Lord eventually got me back on the right road on this trip, so He did in my life, and I can never thank and praise Him enough for never giving up on me.

> The Lord is my shepherd. ... He guides me in paths of righteousness.
>
> (Psalm 23:1, 3 NIV)

MY PRAYER

Joan Clayton **August 9**

> Lord, I give myself to you.
> (Psalm 25:1 NCV)

I cling to You, O God. I cling with every fiber of my being, for without You I am hopelessly lost. Thank You for Your tender mercies and Your loving kindness. Thank You for delivering me out of the enemy's snare.

Grant me the knowledge and wisdom to recognize the onset of the enemy's strategy and may I boldly resist in the power of Your precious blood.

Make my conversation right, I pray. In the midst of problems, may I boldly declare that through Your Son, I am more than a conqueror.

Cause me to realize moment by moment I want to live in Your divine will for my life. Help me to run to You when I am tempted. May I die to self so You can rise up mightily in me. Empower me to forget those things in the past that I might make a new beginning this very day to "press on toward the mark of the high calling in You."

May I be strong in faith, live in obedience, and glorify You in every word and deed. In that name above all names...Jesus.

INSEPARABLE LOVE

Charles E. Harrel **August 10**

> For I am persuaded that neither death nor life, nor angels nor principalities nor powers, nor things present nor things to come, nor height nor depth, nor any other created thing, shall be able to separate us from the love of God which is in Christ

Jesus our Lord.
(Romans 8:38-39 NKJ)

The love of God is unlimited, unceasing, inexhaustible—and that's just the prelude. No wonder the Apostle Paul believed nothing inside or outside this world would ever separate us from God's love.

Paul's revelation of unconditional love was more than doctrinal; it was also personal. He sensed God's wondrous love at work in his own life, even when he considered himself as the worst sinner of all. Through all his trials, mistakes, and shortcomings, the love of God never cast him away. Paul further discovered that God's love brings believers into unity with Christ, and when individuals are in Christ, their love becomes inseparable.

The things that cause separation can seem powerful, but the love of God is always stronger. There is absolutely nothing that can sever the cords of God's love in your life.

Jesus, I feel so secure when I remember Your love. It gives me strength and encouragement each day. Thank You for loving me, and please know this—I love You, too. Amen.

MY LORD AND GOD

Carol Cleal August 11

My Lord and God,
Praise and glory to You each day.
As the sun rises and sets,
You are there.
My guide, my mentor, my soul.

My Lord and God.
What peace You give as
Each day is filled with Your love.
I need only to look for it.
It may be a thank you,
A comment, the beauty
Of nature or the sweet loving
Song of a bird.

My Lord and God
Unending praise and glory to You.

For You are an awesome God
Who cares for His child.
Your love overflows to me.

THE POOR OLD YARDSTICK'S SON
Joseph Hopkins   **August 12**

Who was the Poor Old Yardstick's son? Why, the Rich Young Ruler, of course! His story is told in Luke 18:18-27. He asked Jesus, "What shall I do to obtain eternal life?" Jesus told him he must obey the Ten Commandments. He replied that he had done so all his life. But had he? In the Sermon on the Mount Jesus explained that the commandments must be obeyed not only in letter (deeds), but in spirit (motives). He used the 6th and 7th commandments as examples. We must not only abstain from murder but from rage; not only from adultery, but from lust. In refusing to give up his wealth to follow Jesus, this young man had broken the very first commandment: "You shall have no other gods before me."

Years ago, as I was riding the B & O from Pittsburgh to Washington, a man got on the crowded train in Harper's Ferry and sat down beside me. When he learned that I was a seminary student, he said, "I like to think that the Rich Young Ruler was Joseph of Arimathea. Because 'he turned away sorrowful.' Perhaps later he made the decision to make Christ the Lord of his life, and then giving away his riches was no longer necessary."

Lord Jesus, help me to put You first in my life today. May I earnestly desire to surrender my imperfect will to Your perfect will and to obey Your commandments not only in what I do and say but in what I treasure in my heart.

A NEW WARDROBE
Elizabeth M. Van Hook   **August 13**

Dress in the wardrobe God picked out for you: compassion, kindness, humility, quiet strength, discipline. And regardless of what else you put on, wear love. It's your basic, all-purpose garment. Never be without it.

(Colossians 3:12-14 MESSAGE)

It was Saturday night, and I was tired from traveling from mall to mall looking for the right dress for Jackie's wedding. I unwillingly resolved to look through my wardrobe closet again.

After our Sunday morning worship service, my friend Patty asked why I seemed so preoccupied. I told her that the next weekend I would be doing the Old and New Testament readings in my nephew's wedding ceremony. I explained to her that I was more concerned about how I looked than what I had to do.

At first, Patty gave me a puzzled look, and then mentioned a shop that I had forgotten. I drove there after church. Entering the store, I saw the perfect dress hanging on the New Arrivals for Fall rack! I tried on the full length cranberry tatted lace dress. It fit perfectly! It was as if it was made for me.

The day of the wedding, I walked up the steps to the podium on the altar with confidence, opened the passage to Genesis, and read about God's creation of man and woman. Then I turned to I Corinthians 13. Before reading that passage often used at weddings, I uttered a prayer that the guests would listen to the message of God's perfect love for their lives.

This from Colossians came to mind as I walked back to my pew, "Dress in the wardrobe picked out for you, and regardless of what you put on, wear love." I smiled to myself and wondered if those who listened to the readings noticed that I wore the "love of the Lord"? Did they want to make His love their newest garment, too?

Father, help me not to be so overly concerned about what I wear today, as long as I wear Your garment of love. I need to trust You more. You take care of the birds and flowers; You surely will take care of me, who is made in Your image. Amen.

DON'T LOOK ON THE OUTWARD APPEARANCE
Janet R. Sady   **August 14**

> *But the LORD said unto Samuel, Look not on his countenance, or on the height of stature, because I have refused him: for the Lord seeth not as a man seeth; for man looketh on the outward appearance, but the LORD looketh on the heart.*
>
> *(I Samuel 16:7 KJV)*

The fourteen-year-old boy on my daughter's school bus was only about five feet tall. The other children teased him. They nicknamed him "book worm." Thirteen years later, this same young man is a surgeon at a major hospital. Some of his former classmates are now patients.

God instructed Samuel to go to the home of Jesse. One of Jesse's sons was to be anointed king over Israel after the death of Saul. Samuel looked at Eliab, the eldest, and was impressed by his appearance. Samuel decided he was the chosen one.

God reminded Samuel not to look on the outward appearance. God looks at a man's thoughts and intentions. We know from reading farther in the Word that God had chosen the youngest boy, David, for the kingship.

This lesson helps to remind us not to judge others by their appearance.

Lord, forgive me for judging others by their appearance. May I strive to be kind and loving to all men so that when they look at me, they may see Christ. Amen.

WHEN OTHERS DON'T AGREE
Theresa V. Wilson   **August 15**

We have choices in this life through blessings, toils, and snares.
At times we'll seek men's voices, not the One who truly cares.
Jesus crossed so many mountains through dissent and argument;
Even those who chose to love Him often questioned His intent.
If you let them, men will challenge your faith, beliefs, your views
Till you find yourself falling out of step, hopeless, confused.
Because of where God's placed you, waste no time on others' cares
For the cross you have to carry is for you alone to bear.
Lift your dreams above life's fracas, so you're reaching heaven's dome,
Knowing Christ and witnesses cheer you from a place that you call home.

MY REFUGE
Marion E. Gorman   **August 16**

In the 1980s the gypsy moths invaded the forested mountains surrounding our Pennsylvania campground. They reached adulthood mid-summer, devoured tree foliage, and hung suspended from the trees on invisible threads.

My imagination grew to nightmarish proportions as I pictured caterpillar covered campers. Our present budget couldn't afford the spraying necessary to fortify us against this assault. During my devotions, the Lord spoke directly to our crisis: "Because you have made the Lord, who is my refuge, even the Most High, your habitation, no evil shall befall you, nor shall any plague come near your dwelling" (Psalm 91:9-10, NKJ). I felt God's protection wrap around our campground and my anxiety dissolved. In spite of the high probability of invasion by the gypsy moths that year, our campground had few moths.

When spiritual plagues of doubt and discouragement infect my faith, there is no need for fear to contaminate my thoughts. "For He shall give His angels charge over you, to keep you in all your ways" (Psalm 91:11 NKJ). My refuge exists when I profess my trust in God's promises of protection. He is waiting to restore my peace.

KNEELING IN BEAUTY
Charles A. Waugaman   August 17

July and August have brought the crest of the year. I climb the gradual curve of White Road, into my neighbors' drive, and continue on past the house into the partly-mown meadows. There, among the riot of plants and vines, summer blossoms profusely and butterflies ramble on the breeze.

Among the matted vegetation, blueberries glow like jewels in the fragrant tangle. Some are deep blue-black as the shadowy stream pools. Others are powdery cerulean as a hazy horizon. Some are succulent azure, shiny as drops of enamel.

As I kneel to pick, I am grateful for such largess, and the agility still to bend in these retirement years. I breathe a prayer for my housebound neighbors and even younger friends who endure limited mobility. My mind is already planning ways to share both bounty and baking.

Mind and fingers add prayer to my activity. Knee deep in mercies, how can I not pray? Surely mercy smiles widest when shared.

Dear Lord, even as I harvest, a butterfly alights upon my knee, tame as friendship. Thank You for all the wings that lift my spirit, my eyes and my aspirations. Help me to wing Your love to others, in Jesus' Name. Amen.

NANIBOUJOU – SOLITUDE
Kathy Johnson   **August 18**

Then Jesus went with his disciples to a place called Gethsemane, and he said to them, "Sit here while I go over there and pray."
(Matthew 26:36 NIV)

There is a lodge along the northern shore of Lake Superior which offers complete solitude. There are no telephones, televisions, radios, or clocks in the rooms or lodge. Guests read books, play board games, knit, listen to the roar of the waves as they crash into the lakeshore, walk along looking for agates, take high tea, meditate, or drop off into a nap as the warm sun shines through the windows of the solarium. The lodge affords peace, quiet, relaxation, solitude, and a time to reflect.

As our Lord approached His final days on earth, He took time to be alone with His Father. Peter, James, and John accompanied Jesus farther into the garden than the rest of the disciples, but were still left behind when Jesus asked them to stay, to watch and to pray. Jesus continued on alone, to seek out His Father's will through prayer and gain strength for the days ahead. Jesus would soon suffer and die in our stead, but rise again on the third day to proclaim victory over sin, death, and the devil.

May we follow Jesus' example and take time to be in solitude with Him through prayer and study of the Bible.

HOLD HANDS WITH JESUS
Joan Clayton   **August 19**

You give me your shield of victory, and your right hand sustains me; you stoop down to make me great.
(Psalm 18:35 NIV)

I have been holding hands with my husband for many years. Those same hands that carried my books at school took my hands in his and pledged all his love to me on our wedding day.

Those same hands built our first home, a house filled with many memories. Three lively boys received training and discipline with hands that prayed a lot. I remember many prayerful nights rocking little boys with fever. The healing hands of Jesus brought them through each siege.

The most precious hands of all are those nail-scarred hands

of our Savior. Because of those loving hands, there is hope, hope for a future. Holding hands with Jesus is what life is all about.

We are engraved in the palm of Jesus' hand and I love to hold His hand.

You can hold hands with Him, too!

GOD IS A GARDENER
Annettee Budzban   **August 20**

A man reaps what he sows.
(Galatians 6:7 NIV)

"I found some wild tomatoes growing in my empty lot. Would you like a few?" Bonnie's neighbor asked.

Bonnie's mind wandered to a year ago when she stood out in her yard, enjoying the flavor of a luscious tomato. With juice dripping over her lips and hands, she ate the ripened fruit down to the core. Then, like a pitcher winding up for his release, she lifted her arm and pitched the core into the vacant lot next door.

As she reached out her hand to receive the small, ripe tomatoes she pondered, "Who would have thought those seeds I carelessly threw away would sprout to produce more tomatoes?"

We need to think about the seeds we are planting. We sow a variety of them daily. Seeds such as kindness and encouragement will better ourselves and others. Seeds of bitterness and jealousy poison our souls, causing us and others to be miserable. Seeds of diligence and perseverance to change our health, finances, career, or relationships can help us reap a blessing in these areas. The seeds of laziness and self-centeredness are sometimes carelessly tossed without a thought and produce an unwanted harvest.

God is our Gardener, instructing us to watch what we are planting. The choice is ours—it helps to remember that harvest time will come.

AND IT WAS GOOD
Shirley S. Stevens   **August 21**

And God said, Let the earth bring forth grass, the herb yielding seed, and the fruit tree yielding fruit after his kind, whose seed is in itself, upon the earth: and it was so.
(Genesis 1:11 KJV)

John Chapman was a Christian who roamed the Northwest

Territories. He had caught a vision of the wilderness with apple trees, orchard after orchard of fragrant blossoms promising a fruitful harvest for the settlers. So he traveled with a bag of seeds, planting as he walked.

On my morning walks, I see hollyhocks in one patch along the road to the school. One August day, I decided to follow in Johnny Appleseed's footsteps by picking the dried seed pods and broadcasting them along the roadsides. Sometimes I simply tossed them into a ditch. In other spots, I scratched the surface with a stick and spilled the seeds into the dirt. I realize that it will take two years for them to bloom, since only foliage appears the first year. But I plant them and dream of pink and rose flowers which will delight hummingbirds and school children. As I walk, I smile at my vision and nickname myself Holly Golightly.

Dear Lord, help us to plant seeds today and trust that You will grow them. Amen.

BEAUTY OF THE EARTH
Ida Jancso   **August 22**

I remember when I was a child living on a small dairy farm. I would stand in the barn door on a nice day and look up at the sky. I was always fascinated by the clouds. I would see different images in them. Perhaps an angel with big white wings.

Even then I thought how wonderful our God is to create such a beautiful world. I think how amazing all the different trees and wild flowers are, the vegetation He put on this earth.

When I see man's greed for material things and riches, destroying so much of this beauty, I fear for this world. But I know that God knows all and sees all, and He will not let this beautiful earth be destroyed before its time.

Dear heavenly Father, grant that from day to day I may keep in mind the excellence of Your love and the greatness of Your power, and with complete confidence, not let fear overtake me.

UNVEILING OF SOUL
Barbara Ann Yonnotti   **August 23**

God's near when the soul cries. Each spectrum of the being is washed with hope. Fear becomes lost to joy.

ROSE-COLORED MORNING
Dave Evans · August 24

Darkness—before dawn,
tired from its overnight vigil,
begins to wane;
silhouetted against the sky
gray of billowy clouds
bleached white
in emerging light,
rose-colored as
the sun peers above
the horizon

touched by the beauty
crafted by Your hands;
may my life
also be rose-colored
this morning.

DIVERSITY IN GOD'S WORLD
Judy Barron · August 25

Nicodemus asked...Our Law does not judge a man, unless it first hears from him and knows what he is doing, does it?
(John 7:51 NAS)

Today's scripture deals with prejudice and discomfort with those different from us. I am reading this while visiting in Hawaii where there are so many different races, lifestyles, and personalities. Each one adds to the flavor of the islands. This great variety of humanity expresses the immense richness of God's heart. Imagine how bland this beautiful place would be if it had only one variety of flower—no matter how beautiful—or only one type of bird—no matter how lovely in color. God has chosen to give us such variety to enjoy in the world around us. Why would He do any less with His beloved children? He has made each one of us unique and special, and we should rejoice in this individuality, not fear it. God loves each of us for ourselves and He has shown us, through the example of His Son, how to love and care for each other.

Father God, I ask for Your help in relating to others who may be different from me. Show me how to see each person as having something unique to offer our world. Let all our strengths benefit the whole and our weaknesses be a chance to reach out in love to one another. In the name of Your dear Son, Amen.

ALLOW JESUS TO SHINE

Micki Roberts   **August 26**

Everything about you and me that is unreal—God hates, and hates it more in His own people than anywhere else.
—*C.H. Spurgeon*

Recently, I heard a pastor make a statement concerning the way Christians should behave in public, stating that many Christians do not pray over their food when dining in a restaurant. I was left with the impression that he believed this to be a serious offense.

Personally, I would rather Christians spent a few seconds silently thanking the Father for their food, instead of making a public display of praying. For many times, these same people treat their server in a manner that belies their claim of being Christians. They arrive at the restaurant during the peak rush and demand to be seated immediately. Once they are seated, they insist upon instant service and expect to receive their food within moments. To make matters worse, they speak unkindly to the server and, many times, make comments to their companions about the incompetence of said server. Finally, they depart, leaving a mere pittance meant to pass as a tip.

Many times I've heard people who work in food service state how much they hate working on Sundays because "church people" are the most difficult of all their customers. What a sad commentary on the world's perception of Christians.

So, by all means, thank God for the food He's provided. But more importantly, allow Jesus to shine.

JOTBAH

Peter Paulson   **August 27**

His mother's name was Meshullemeth daughter of Haruz; she was from Jotbah.
(2 Kings 21:19 NIV)

I grew up in Beaverton, Oregon. Naturally a beaver served as our high school mascot. With a penchant for easily identifiable nicknames, I chose Pacific Lutheran University for college. We were known as ... ready? ... the Lutes! Now I live in Bremerton, named after the Bremers.

Jotbah didn't get by that easily. *Jotbah* itself means *excellent for water*. In a parched part of the world that would normally create instantaneous fame and popularity. The fact is, however, Jotbah is named in the Bible as the hometown of one Meshullemeth, daughter of Haruz. She married the bloodiest tyrant in the Bible and birthed a prince so corrupt that his own officials assassinated him when he became king. Evidently the excellent water did not suffice.

Note that there is no question about the water being excellent. The difficulty is that the excellence of the water was not matched by a similar excellence of life.

The same holds true with baptism, by the way. The water is excellent. The difficulty is when the excellence of the water is not matched by a similar excellence of life.

May my faith fellowship not be shamed or ridiculed because of my conduct. Amen.

FOR IT IS HE

Joe LoBello August 28

> I will lie down in peace and sleep
> For the peace cometh from the Lord.
> I am poured out like water and my bones are out of joint,
> But He is my sustenance and my deliverer.
>
> I cried out unto the Lord in my distress
> And His hand lifted me out of the pit.
> I came to Him as a sinner
> And He redeemed the soul of His servant.
>
> I wait on the Lord, and in His Word do I hope,
> For my feet stand on the truth of my salvation.
> If I do not remember the Lord,
> Let my tongue be forever still.
>
> I am kept from the raging waters,

For it is He.
I am not defeated by my enemies,
For it is He.

The snare is broken; I am not consumed,
For it is He.
I am loved and protected, revived and perfected,
For it is He.

FORGIVENESS

Joy C. Bradford   August 29

> *For if you forgive men when they sin against you, your heavenly Father will also forgive you. But if you do not forgive men their sins, your Father will not forgive your sins.*
> (Matthew 6:14-15 NIV)

Our pastor has been teaching believers the happiness and rewards of living a life forgiven. Matthew tells us that God's forgiveness is conditional. If we have accepted God's son Jesus as our Savior and made Him Lord of our lives, we will obey Him when He says to forgive others.

In 1989, my birth family had an emotional feud that went on for months and resulted in genuine hard feelings. This dramatic memory has haunted me. Although each person involved wears the Christian label and is a leader in his or her individual church, the matter has never been resolved.

The two sides cannot find a way back together. Somehow, we do not have willing spirits and/or the humility to acknowledge another point of view. I am deeply troubled by this. The travesty has hurt the cause of Christ. I pray for reconciliation.

> *"If your brother sins, rebuke him, and if he repents, forgive him. If he sins against you seven times in a day, and seven times comes back to you and says, 'I repent,' forgive him."*
> (Luke 17:3, NIV)

When we have been hurt by others and disappointed by their actions, it is difficult to forgive, especially if they are not repentant. Yet, we must.

RESCUED

Audrey Kletscher Helbling **August 30**

For he has rescued us from the dominion of darkness and brought us into the kingdom of the Son he loves, in whom we have redemption, the forgiveness of sins.
(Colossians 1:13-14 NIV)

I was weeding my flower bed on a sunny, summer Sunday afternoon when I noticed something in the street. It was at the very edge of the driving lane, just outside the path of oncoming traffic. Vehicles whizzed by as I walked toward the road.

Suddenly a robin swooped down in front of me onto the pavement. The object moved, and I saw it was a baby bird, now being fed by its mother.

If I didn't act soon, the baby would be road kill. Just as I was considering my options, a bicyclist peddled toward me down the sidewalk. Perfect timing, I thought.

"Could you get that baby bird out of the street?" I pointed to the chirping fledgling. "It can't fly and it's going to get hit."

For a moment it appeared the rider would pedal past me. But then he suddenly slowed, turned his bike wheel and headed for the street. The young man bent down, gently scooped the feathered creature from danger, rode across the lawn and deposited the baby among my flowers.

"Thank you!" I shouted, as he sped away. The rescue was complete, the bird temporarily safe. Huddled among my pink dianthus, the robin was a vulnerable bundle of quivering feathers.

We are not unlike that baby bird. As fragile, sinful humans, we need constant tending to keep our fledgling feet pointed in the right direction, away from danger. We need God's Word to nourish our souls. We need prayer to keep us close to our heavenly Father, yet able to spread our wings in faith. Most importantly, we need Jesus to scoop us off the highway of death and lead us on the road to heaven.

Thank You, God, for sending Your Son, Jesus, to rescue us from certain death. Like the baby bird, we have been saved. Help us always to remain close to You and to seek nourishment through Your Word continually. Amen.

WAITING ON GOD FOR HIS COMING
Jon Kattenhorn   **August 31**

I will come back and take you to be with me that you also may be where I am.
(John 14:3 NIV)

When I was a boy and my family traveled to our cabin, I was allowed to bring my friend Joe. He told me that he would be at my house by 3:00 in the afternoon. I remembered this and began to look for him. I told my Mom, "He should be coming soon!" I waited, looking out the living room window, hoping he would show up. I said, "Mom, where is he?"

Mom said, "He will be here. Just wait. He will come."

Christians often find themselves waiting at such a window. Waiting for Jesus' return. He promised that He would come back for us. But unlike my friend Joe, He didn't give us a time or date. Sometimes I grow impatient, and like a child, I ask, "Where is He?"

His word gives me the answer. James 5:8 says, "You, too, be patient and stand firm, because the Lord's coming is near." We know He is coming, but we do not know how soon He will come, so we just need to keep looking out the window.

As we wait for His coming, we should be excited that we will see Him.

Lord, may we be watching for Your coming. In Your name. Amen.

CLEANING FRIDGES—AND MY LIFE
Leigh DeLozier   **September 1**

Wash away all my iniquity and cleanse me from my sins.
(Psalm 51:2 NIV)

Something in the fridge doesn't smell too good. Actually, something in there stinks. I can't figure out what it is, despite going through everything. Finally, I resort to super-cleaning it all, set a new box of baking soda in the back and hope for the best.

How many times do I have things in my life that stink without my realizing it? Or what kinds of things should I avoid so my life won't reach that point?

Sometimes the answers are obvious, but sometimes things that might not seem like a big deal can become really ugly over time. Those are the things I have to be more careful about—everyday things like gossip, impatience, or jealousy. They can start out so small and seem so harmless, yet can grow to touch every aspect of my life, like the smell in my fridge.

When I discover these stinky problems, I can't just mask them with a spiritual version of baking soda and go on my way. Instead, I need to go deeper than that—to the source of the problem—and be totally cleaned from the inside out so I can start fresh.

Thank goodness Jesus doesn't mind stinky people or stinky lives that need help. And thank goodness He's the best Cleanser of all!

Thank You, Lord, for cleansing me completely so I can be a fresh breath for You instead of a stinky mess. Amen.

DEVIL'S KETTLE

Kathy Johnson September 2

You will again have compassion on us; you will tread our sins underfoot and hurl all our iniquities into the depths of the sea.
(Micah 7:19 NIV)

In Judge Magney State Park in northern Minnesota, the river, as it cascades over a falls, is divided by a huge rock. Part of the water continues down into the river below, but the other part disappears into a huge boulder which looks like a kettle (named Devil's Kettle). The water which enters the kettle has never been traced; it just disappears.

So it is with our sins when we come before the throne of grace and confess to God. Because Jesus suffered, died, and rose again, we can be assured as repentant sinners that our sins have been cast into the depths of the sea and covered with the redemption purchased by Jesus' blood. Our sins are forgiven and forgotten by God.

Dear Lord, give me the peace which surpasses all understanding, knowing, as a repentant sinner, You have cast my sins into the depths of the sea and will remember them no more. In Jesus Name. Amen.

USE MY LONGINGS

Charles A. Waugaman September 3

Each morning, Lord, when I invest time with You, the many

friends and relatives with whom You have blessed my years come to mind. And I am rich all over again. I long to visit, call, bless, encourage each of them.

I remember helping people of all walks and persuasions of life, who daily stuff my postal box with URGENT and EMERGENCY needs, that my substance must discard or shortchange although I long to respond with swift and substantial assistance.

Ministers and missionaries You have sent through the years to enrich, inspire and comfort me come vividly to mind, and I long to visit, contact, and assist their selfless endeavors. But I am tied by time and resources to "longing."

Surely, God, You, who called into being this amazing world and astounding, expanding universe from nothing, can fashion something from my incessant longings.

In gratitude and faith I place them in your loving hands.

Bless beyond the horizon of my hope.

Keep me longing, and I'll be back. I love You, Father. Amen.

CONSISTENCY WINS THE RACE
Joe LoBello   **September 4**

And let us run with patience the race that is set before us.
(Hebrews 12:1 KJV)

So many of us get bored, tired, and just run down with the day after day routine of life. It all seems so frustrating and it is—when our focus is not on the spiritual, life is a daily challenge.

Today's scripture tells us to run the race with patience and trust. The race for a believer is the path to salvation. We need to walk and follow God's will. Consistency is the key. Daily reliance on the Lord's strength to get over the dull routine, boring daily chores our lives can be without Him.

Remember by perseverance even the snail made it to the ark. Run life's race with the best trainer of all, Jesus our Lord.

UNLESS THE LORD
Tiffany Schlichter   **September 5**

Except the LORD build the house, they labour in vain that build it: except the LORD keep the city, the watchman waketh but in vain.
(Psalm 127:1 KJV)

Without the Lord, we are nothing. One pastor put it this way: "We must get to the humbling point in life where God cannot use us until there is nothing of us, and all of Him." Many times we try to do things in our own flesh, and that is impossible. In ourselves, we can do nothing.

But the good news is that in Christ, we can do anything He calls us to. We have to allow the Lord to work through us. We must go to Him, seek His guidance, and follow His righteous instructions.

Often a tool is used in handwork—whether it is a needle, paintbrush, pencil, hammer, knife, etc. Although you are the artist and creator of your work, you might accomplish it through a tool. Our relationship with God is similar. We are simply tools for His glory. When we try to be virtuous without the truly virtuous One, we are like needles trying to sew without their seamstresses or paintbrushes trying to paint without their artists. Our victory is impossible unless we allow Christ to work through us.

Thank You, Lord, for giving us victory. May we always give You the glory, honor, and praise! Amen.

GRUMBLING AGAINST CIRCUMSTANCES
Lorena Estep   **September 6**

So Moses and Aaron said to all the Israelites, "In the evening you will know that it was the LORD who brought you out of Egypt, and in the morning you will see the glory of the LORD, because he has heard your grumbling against him."

(Exodus 16:6-7 NIV)

Just days after the Israelites experienced the astounding miracle of the parting of the Red Sea, they complained because they had no water. They accused Moses of bringing them into the wilderness to die of thirst. Then God provided water.

Soon their food supplies dwindled. They again grumbled, saying Moses brought them to the wilderness to die of starvation. Then God sent them manna in the morning and quail in the evening. Moses pointed out to them, that when they complained against him, they actually grumbled against God.

How often do we complain against circumstances when good times turn bad? Our grumbling takes on a more serious note when viewed as complaints against God, who has supplied our needs. Let's turn our grumbling into thanksgiving.

Be joyful always; pray continually; give thanks in all circumstances, for this is God's will for you in Christ Jesus.
(1 Thessalonians 5:16-18 NIV)

BURDENS AND TRIALS
Pat Collins September 7

A new commandment I give to you, that you love one another; as I have loved you, that you also love one another.
(John 13:34 NKJ)

Our burdens can make us better than we ever imagined—stronger, gentler, more patient, courageous, loving, and understanding than we would otherwise be. As I asked God to soften a loved one's heart and bring him back, a thought came to me. How much more Jesus wants me to soften my heart and come back to Him.

Lord, without trials and hardship, I would never know the way You turn burdens into blessings with every passing day. Today's burdens can strengthen me for tomorrow. Thank You, Jesus, for such a wonderful lesson.

GROWING IN THE STORM
Jennifer M. Stevenson September 8

When you pass through the waters, I will be with you; and when you pass through the rivers, they will not sweep over you.
(Isaiah 43:2 NIV)

As I walked home one day, I heard a big kaboom! Droplets of water began to fall from the sky. Caught in the unexpected storm, I looked to the left and to the right, but saw no way out. Even people I knew drove past me. Drenched, I thought, "God, please get me out of this." But He popped an old saying of my grandma's into my mind: "Hiccups mean you are growing."

My thoughts turned toward the emotional and spiritual storms of my life. Like the rainstorm, earthly trials come at us unexpectedly from every direction, while people just seem to pass us by. We get drenched in worries. Frozen with fear. Tossed by worldly winds. When we are ready to give up in despair, we need to remember "ain't no river too wide, or valley too low" for the Lord. Nothing is too hard for Him to handle, and He always has our best interests at His heart—even the hiccups for growth—because "God works all things together for the good of those who love Him and are called according to His plan" (Romans 8:28).

Draw close to God and you will grow through the storm.

Heavenly Father, whenever we go through trials, please help us to remember that nothing is too hard for You to bring us through. Amen.

TRUDGING THROUGH ADVERSITY
Margaret Steinacker   **September 9**

With every prayer and request, pray at all times in the Spirit, and stay alert in this, with all perseverance and intercession for all the saints.
(*Ephesians 6:18 HCSB*)

When Grandmother died in 1964, it unexpectedly snowed 24" overnight. We had several houses full of guests from different states. With the funeral on hold for a minimum of three days, the pressing need for a larger food supply became evident. So, Dad and I walked six blocks to the market.

Whenever I consider perseverance, my mind replays this scene. Each step required us to push one leg into the snow to make a hole, and then similarly make a hole for the other leg. The next step required pulling one leg out of the current hole and then pushing to make another. *Exhausting* barely describes it. If we considered the trip to the store difficult, horrendous would have to describe the trip home. Our arms held an extra 10-15 pounds of groceries. Despite the circumstances, we kept going, encouraging each other along the way.

Today's scripture encourages us to persevere at all times, through all adversity, for all saints and in any situation. The message is clear; we dare not relent. As we serve Christ in striving to feed the spiritually hungry, we must persevere. The load we carry may seem exhausting, but as we put on God's armor, we have the strength to stand. We become Christ's hands and feet as we spread the good news of the gospel.

"I'll be His hands to do what I can, because He has loved me, too—I will be Christ to you."
—*Marty Parks*

HERE ME IS, GOD!

Marjorie K. Evans September 10

"Truly David was a man after God's own heart," I said to our teacher as we discussed the Bible study.

She agreed, then told me the following story:

"My friend teaches a Bible class to youngsters ages four to twelve. During the lesson about David, she taught the children that God had been searching for a boy with a heart willing to serve Him. Finally, he found David, a young shepherd boy who truly loved God and faithfully served Him.

"My friend ended her story by saying, 'Children, today God is still looking for boys and girls who will love Him and be willing to serve Him with all their hearts.'

"At that moment a four-year-old boy stood up, pulled open his jacket, pointed to his heart and announced, 'Here me is, God.'"

Oh, that each one of us would be willing to say, "Here me is, God!"

TEARDROPS

Dave Evans September 11

Slowly, almost methodically,
one lone drop spills over
eyelid's edge
and descends downward,
over hot, flushed cheeks
and jutting jaw;

quickly it begins to fall,
just as a flash flood follows
with ferocious force.

The heart of the Father,
compassionate and caring,
reaches out His hand
to catch that first lone tear
and the terrible torrent,
lovingly placing them all
in a bottle labeled
remembrances.

You keep track of all my sorrows. You have collected all my tears in your bottle. You have recorded each one in your book.
(Psalm 56:8 NLT)

A SOLEMN ANNIVERSARY
Angie Kay Dilmore September 12

Romans 12:9-21

It was Thursday morning, September 13, 2001. Our usual group had met at church for Bible study and fellowship. We were all still reeling from the shock of two days prior, still trying to come to grips with the horrific events of that fateful day.

We had intended to study Romans 11 that morning, but for some divine reason, we skipped to chapter 12.

"Love must be sincere. Hate what is evil; cling to what is good. Be devoted to one another in brotherly love. Honor one another above yourselves. Never be lacking in zeal, but keep your spiritual fervor, serving the Lord. Be joyful in hope, patient in affliction, faithful in prayer. Share with God's people who are in need." *We prayed for the victims, their loved ones, the rescue workers.*

"Bless those who persecute you; bless and do not curse." *We prayed for the terrorists.* "Rejoice with those who rejoice; mourn with those who mourn. Live in harmony with one another." *We prayed for the families of those who survived and those who died.*

"Do not repay anyone evil for evil. Be careful to do what is right in the eyes of everybody. If it is possible, as far as it depends on you, live at peace with everyone." *We prayed for our fellow Muslim Americans.*

"Do not take revenge, my friends, but leave room for God's wrath, for it is written: It is mine to revenge; I will repay, says the Lord." *We prayed for President Bush and the leaders of our country, and wondered what they might be planning.*

"Do not be overcome by evil, but overcome evil with good."
The words filled our hearts as tears filled our eyes. God spoke to us that day through His Holy Word.

Heavenly Father, bless us by granting us hearts like Yours. Amen.

EXPERIENCING GRACE

Anne Siegrist — September 13

My husband and I were sitting in a restaurant, watching with amusement as a man snagged one stuffed animal after another from a machine for his little niece. Finally, with a stack of animals piled on the table and chairs, he gave up.

I smiled at the little girl. After a suggestion from her mother, the child picked up one of the toys and walked over to me.

"For me?" I asked in surprise.

She nodded.

I reached out for the gift, amazed at the grace the little girl had shown to me, a stranger.

The Apostle Paul said, "For it is by grace you have been saved, through faith—and this not from yourselves, it is the gift of God" (Ephesians 2:8 NIV).

Once I reached out in faith for the gift of salvation offered to me, a stranger to God. I had done nothing to deserve the gift a small child offered to me, and I had done nothing to deserve God's salvation. But I reached out and took these gifts offered to me in grace, and I have been blessed.

HE HEARD ME
Tune of *Shenandoah*

Glenda Joy Race — September 14

I sought the Lord
And He heard me.
Oh, magnify the Lord.
Exalt His name,
For he delivered
My soul, He found the way,
Through the cross of Calvary.

Oh, Jesus said,
Do not be troubled.
Believe in God and Me.
In my Father's house
Are many places.
Away, I go away
To make a place for you.

I will bless the Lord
At all times.
His praises will continue.
My soul will boast
In the Lord alone.
Oh see, the Lord is good,
So put your trust in Him.

WHERE IS MY BIBLE?

Janet R. Sady September 15

Thy word is a lamp unto my feet, and a light unto my path.
(Psalm 119:105 KJV)

A friend gave me a carved cedar box to hold my Bible. If I would decide to put my Bible in the box, I would know where it is at all times.

I carry my Bible to different rooms where I have devotions. I also use it to look up scriptures for teaching a Sunday School lesson or work on a Bible study. I sometimes forget it at church or in the car. My Bible looks well used. The gold is worn from the edges, and all the compressed pages are pulled apart.

God wants me to read His word and hide it in my heart, not in a box. There are many truths to be learned and used to light my path through this world.

Father, help me not to neglect the reading of Your word. May I be mindful to apply Your truth to my life and to share it with others as You give me opportunity. Amen.

I GO A-FISHING

Jana Carman September 16

In handling boats and nets I know
just how and where to drop the net,
and when to draw it in. One tends
to stick with what one does the best.

But knowledge is no guarantee,
and labor, all night long, may yet
fail to fill a fisher's net.

An old fish may grab the bait

even though he's reached his age
and size because he knows
to leave strange baits alone.
And I, experienced old fisherman,
took the hook He threw me,
and He hauled me in.

I'm learning now a different skil:
with what to bait the hook,
and how and when to draw it in
in order to catch men.

GOD CAN USE ANYONE

Anita Estes   **September 17**

Judges 11

God can use anyone. He chose Jephthah, the son of a harlot, to deliver Israel. Even though his own half brothers drove Jephthah out of Gilead, God did not forget about him. Jepthath became a valiant man. When the Israelites were attacked, they turned to Jepthath and asked him to be their leader. After he recovered from the surprise, he forgave them and agreed to the task. God used him to bring peace to his land.

God can do the same for us. In the eyes of the world we may be rejected and lowly, but God can raise us up. Perhaps the trials that tried to rob you of health or peace of mind are the very things God will use in other people's lives to encourage them—as long as we forgive others and trust God. Jephthah didn't sulk and say to his brothers, "No, I'm not going to help you because you drove me away." Neither should we.

God equips all Christians with everything we need to minister to this dying world which lacks the basics of faith, hope, and love. God isn't contained by your background, your experiences, your job, or your position in life. He can use you. People need Christ today. With crime on the rise, victims of natural disasters, terrorist attacks, and all manner of evil breaking into our homes, people need to hear the gospel message. They need people who will minister to their physical, emotional, and spiritual needs. People who will love them, listen to them, encourage them, and point them to the only One who can defeat their enemy. God needs some more Jepthaths. Are you one?

PRAYER OF THE SQUIRREL

Evelyn Minshull   **September 18**

Lord,
My autumn hoard speaks not of greed—
    rather of prudence.
Once ice encapsulates my caches...
Once hordes of snowflakes camouflage terrains...
I should be fortunate to locate any of my harvest.

Consider, too—
my short-term memory is flawed.
What seemed a sensible repository
    now eludes me.
I scamper here and there,
    but every heap of dirt or pebbles lacks distinction.
If none are found, how shall my family survive
    the winter's horrors?
        How shall I?
And so ... to maximize success, I scatter stockpiles
    in earthen graves,
    in rotted knotholes,
    in leafy niches.

But You, Lord—
You are the One whose providence exceeds
    all understanding,
for You arrange that all those acorns escaping reclamation
    will germinate,
        transforming into oak trees.
What blessing! That my reckless gathering
    contributes to regeneration of Your forests.
Thank You for using me!
Amen.

> *And whoever does not provide for relatives, and especially for family members, has denied the faith and is worse than an unbeliever.*
>
>   (1 Timothy 5:8 NRS)

MACARONI AND CHEESE

Judy Ferrell September 19

Pursue righteousness, faith, love and peace.
(2 Timothy 2:22 NIV)

When they were little, our granddaughters loved macaroni and cheese. It was their favorite food. They could hardly wait for the macaroni to boil so the milk and cheese could be stirred in. They couldn't read the directions on the box, but they knew what needed to be done.

One day their aunt Jill fixed macaroni and cheese for them from a recipe in her cookbook. Since it wasn't from a familiar box, Lauren and Emily wouldn't eat it. Resourcefully, Jill said, "This is the macaroni and cheese that Ariel eats." That is all it took. If Ariel, the mermaid, liked it, they would eat it.

There are people who look at Christianity and want no part of it because it is not what they are used to. However, if we win their respect by pursuing righteousness, faith, love, and peace, they will be more likely to want to "taste and see that the Lord is good" (Psalm 34:8 NIV). It behooves us to live our lives in such a way that others will be drawn to Jesus because of what they see in us.

Father, help me to live my life in such a way that others will want to taste what I have, salvation in Jesus Christ.

TO TED, MY LITTLE MAN

Betty Redmon September 20

Come, little man, stand up and see
These values that so really be:

The sunshine on this our land,
The wide beach with gleaming sand,
Through mountains reaching to the sky,
On which the clouds go rolling by,
The cooing of the gentle dove,
The whole earth filled with mothers, love,
The hand of friendship held so dear,
The joy of having someone near.

So stand, little man, grow up and see
These are the values that really be.

Oh listen, dear child—become wise; point your life in the right direction.
(Proverbs 23:15 MESSAGE)

FRIENDSHIPS OF GOD
Joy C. Bradford September 21

Our good friends from Pennsylvania have just left after a three-night visit in our Texas home. We have known each other about fifteen years and struggled together with many of life's issues along the way. Thankfully, a common belief in God has played a big part in our relationship.

Tonight I celebrate that through the years we have forgiven each other, overlooked differences, and helped each other through hard times. I believe our friendship has been possible because Jesus is our mediator, and we are equally yoked through *His* plan for our lives.

Friendships are demonstrated throughout the Bible. Christ enjoyed the fellowship of His disciples, and they were not perfect men. Paul befriended Timothy and gave him worthy advice in his letters. Young Mary went to Elizabeth to share the news of the pending birth of Christ and probably to seek her counsel and understanding.

Lord, thank You for providing friends who follow Your example by accepting us and forgiving our many faults. Amen.

CALLED TO SUFFERING
Micki Roberts September 22

The Spirit Himself bears witness with our spirit that we are children of God, and if children, heirs also, heirs of God and fellow heirs with Christ, if indeed we suffer with Him in order that we may also be glorified with Him.
(Romans 8:16-17 NAS)

Suffering is a mark of our relationship with Christ. Yet, we do not like to suffer. We beg and we plead with God to remove suffering from our lives. Romans 8:16-17 conveys to us that we suffer with Him (Christ) in order that we may also be glorified with Him. Suffering is ours because it was His.

Perhaps you feel that God is asking too much of you. Consider what Christ our Lord suffered. There is no doubt that He bore cruelty, pain, humiliation, and suffering—even unto death. Does He deserve honor and glory? Most definitely! Therefore, if we are to be glorified with Christ, we must suffer with Him.

When you find yourself in the midst of suffering, read John 18-19 to remind yourself of the suffering Christ endured for you. Take comfort in Psalm 31:14-15: But as for me, I trust in Thee, O Lord, I say, "Thou art God.? My times are in thy hand." Then say with the Psalmist: "Not unto us, O LORD, not unto us, but unto Thy name give glory" (Psalm 115:1 NAS).

FAITH EMPOWERS
Linda Mae Richardson   **September 23**

Faith empowers me to bring the ugly,
Broken pieces of my life—
Shattered by sin and fear, sickness and despair—
And with trust, to place them at Your feet.

Then, as You draw me into Your caring arms,
And wipe away each tear,
I marvel how You pick up the broken pieces
And remold them into a life
Made whole and beautiful by Your love!

EMBRACING OUR BROKENNESS
Shirley S. Stevens   **September 24**

He hath anointed me to preach the gospel to the poor; he hath sent me to heal the brokenhearted.

(Luke 4:18 KJV)

I enjoy visiting museum gift shops because they often offer unusual items. Recently when I stood at the register waiting to make a purchase, I noticed a bowl filled with silver stones. Each had a word etched into its surface. I dug into the bowl and fished out the words "tears," "pain," "trust," "hope," and "love." In the bottom of the bowl I found one stone with the word "forgiveness."

It was obvious that stone had been a popular choice. Debating about which stones to purchase, I started to put back "tears" and "pain." After some thought, I decided to buy them, too, since they are a part of our lives.

I took the stones home and put them in a small crystal dish on my dresser. Each morning when I do my meditation, I pull out one of the stones. I pray for family and friends who are dealing with situations related to the word of the day.

Dear God, thank you for allowing your Son to experience all aspects of life here on Earth. Because He embraced our brokenness at Calvary, we can find hope, trust, and love to bear our burdens each day.

A RAINBOW OF COLORS

Debbie Rempel September 25

A quilt made of many colors—
red, yellow, blue and more.
The colors of a quilt made by a
grandma I adore.

She hand-stitched the pieces together
for this work of art on my wall.
And the picture of us beside it
reminds me of her and
the beauty she
created with her hands.

A friend quilted
the pieces to
finish the masterpiece,
making it a beautiful rainbow of colors
crafted with love from
the heart.

MY SISTER'S QUILT

Penny Deary September 26

Come to Me, all you who labor and are heavy laden, and I will give you rest.
(Matthew 11:28 NKJ)

A river of blue
flows between
patches of soft yellow.
Flowering hopes border

the patchwork of sorrow and joy.
Layers of comfort and warmth
To cover you tenderly.
Quilted together
with threads of love and
bound with prayers
to the Lord above.

NEVER SAY GOOD-BYE

Joan Clayton September 27

Precious in the sight of the LORD is the death of his saints.
(Psalm 116:15 NIV)

Our beloved friend died in a bicycle accident. The whole community mourned. He meant so much to so many. His example and influence upon lives cannot be numbered. Although he had a business of his own, he managed to minister to others. His sermons and Sunday school lessons will be long remembered as a life displaying love for his fellow man.

The funeral portrayed a celebration of life, a tribute to a man of God. In the "twinkling of an eye" our friend went from death to life... eternal life.

The child of God never says good-bye for the last time. For the Christian, death is a reward.

I shall know "Him" when I see him. I shall look upon his face.

His eyes so filled with love, compassion, and such grace.
I shall know him when I see him, for there will be no tears.
All the trials and heartaches will be of yesteryears.
I shall know him when I see him, this lifelong friend of mine.
His love cannot be measured. It endures the test of time."

Thank You, Lord, for heaven, a place of pure delight where we never say good-bye for the last time.

LIFE'S ROAD

Helene Burgess September 28

For as long as I can remember, I always thought that as I grew older, life would all fall into place and make sense. How could I have been so wrong! Just really paying attention to Jesus' life should have set me straight. His ministry began at age 30—His life became more difficult after that. As we age, our lives become harder too, more complicated.

God, help us grow as Jesus did by listening to Your Word and following Your way daily. That's where our stability is. That's where our future is. Amen.

THE CHOICE

Gloria Hall Troup September 29

I can't believe autumn is here. I think the seasons are all mixed up. I wonder if the war being fought in the heavenlies against powers and principalities effects the weather. Perhaps it's another way of telling us the end times are approaching. There are "wars and rumors of wars."

Have you made your most important decision? It's not too late to take Jesus Christ as your Lord and Savior. You know He's the only way to escape hell when you die, don't you? Think. If a living hell from pain is bad, how will being confined to real hell for all eternity be?

But remember that it isn't too late, no matter how old you are, to accept Christ. In heaven there is no pain, only perfect peace in the presence of God.

What is your choice?

REBEL

Mary A. Koepke September 30

A stubborn medium—
wet and willful
stain unforgiving—
watercolor's rainbow hues
marry pristine rag
fluid and free
when tamed by an artful hand.

Let me, like watercolor,
surrender happily under
the Master Painter's
tender brush—
compliant
luminous conception
expressing His glory.

BE STILL

Linda Mae Richardson   **October 1**

The night can be my friend or foe, when fears may fade or sometimes grow.
A restful time from daily stress—a kiss goodnight, a sweet caress.
A gentle sleep I long to find, to strengthen body, soul, and mind.
But often it's beyond my grasp—a few short hours that never last.

I seek to quiet thoughts and fears, to hide my worries and my tears.
But on those nights I find it strange—I can't control or rearrange.
A simple truth, that sleep still finds a resting place on quiet minds.
It seeks the soul and spirit, still, which—though imperfect—seeks God's will.

I'll lay my burdens at His feet, a restless night we'll then defeat.
For worry will not change one thing—to God's great mercy I must cling.
He gently rocks me as He speaks of promises I know He'll keep.
"Fear not, for I am with thee now." His gentle kiss upon my brow.

And though I walk through waters deep, my soul is calmed and I find sleep.
His promise, "Though the storms may come ... be still, my child, I'll calm each one!"

WORRIES AND FEARS

Pat Collins   **October 2**

> *The LORD is my light and my salvation; whom shall I fear?*
> *The LORD is the strength of my life; of whom shall I be afraid?*
>
> *(Psalm 27:1 NKJ)*

I face so many worries and fears in this world today. If I sit around, moan and complain, I hardly make it through today. How can I even think about tomorrow? Then, when tomorrow comes, I wonder about yesterday. STOP! This will get me nowhere.

I turn to Jesus; He has control over my worries and fears. I leave them with Him. Yesterday is gone; I need not fret it. I won't worry about tomorrow; God is already there and has it under His control. I'll trust Him. He will bring me through.

Jesus, I thank You for always being there and taking care of my yesterday, today, and tomorrow. Help me always to remember that You have everything under control.

WHEN LIFE SEEMS EMPTY
Sharon Parrett October 3

Sometimes life seems to be unbearable. Nothing goes the way we'd hoped. Depressed, we feel as if life has no meaning. Under the weight of our burdens, we cannot see how to lighten our loads.

Some of us might admit that we asked the Lord to take our burden and the load is still heavy. Can you hear the Father whisper, "Trust me"? He is able. Release your troubles to Him.

Father, we are weak and You are strong. Lift us up in Your arms and hold us close. Help us to turn to You with our problems and let You take care of them. Ease our tortured souls that we may once again be whole. Amen.

FIELD TRIP
Charles A. Waugaman October 4

And does a violet ever doubt,
A daisy dabble with despair?
Do blue-eyed grasses ever shout
That shortness keeps them from God's care?

Yet I, who wear God's image, cower
In thankless anguish, shrinking fear.
Wasting my precious little hour
As if He cannot know or hear.

(I *Peter* 5:7)

A LIFE OF LUXURY
Mary Rose Pearson October 5

My husband and I, with our son, David, had completed a week's evangelistic campaign. Although exhausted, we needed to travel part of that night in order to begin our next campaign the following night, about four hundred miles away. We loaded our equipment, hitched up the travel trailer, and started out. David lay in the back seat of the car, very sick with the flu.

Soon, on a country road, a trailer tire blew out. After putting on the spare, we drove to a service station and parked, intending to buy a tire in the morning. Several problems pressed on our minds. Would David be all right? Did we have enough cash for a new tire, plus traveling expenses? Could we reach our appointment on time? Still, we prayed, cast our cares on the Lord, and slept peacefully.

The next morning, we overheard two station employees talking. One man said, "Hey, that's living! Maybe someday I'll be rich enough to own a trailer and enjoy a life of luxury, too!" Luxury? What a joke! He wouldn't have been envious if he had known our real circumstances.

Actually, we did have a luxurious life. Our heavenly Father, with His limitless resources, could meet every need. Having His peace gave us a wealth this world cannot offer—an undisturbed mind and a tranquil spirit in spite of our troubles. "LORD, you establish peace for us" (Isaiah 26:12 NIV). What God establishes, He means to accomplish, if we will let Him.

LIFE IS PRECIOUS

Joy C. Bradford   October 6

While babysitting during my daughter's day surgery, I answered the door to a stranger, and asked. "Can I take a message for Stephanie?"

"Yes, please tell her that her neighbor Donna Ryan, from the second house down, passed away yesterday. I am Donna's father, and I know she and Stephanie were friends."

Twelve years ago at 30, with three children under the age of seven, Donna was diagnosed with cancer. She prayed to raise her children and now the oldest child was graduating from high school. This week she'd seen her firstborn n his cap and gown.

I had just heard the beautiful word "benign" associated with our daughter and, almost immediately, looked into the grieving face of a parent who had faced the worst. The newspaper said Donna "fought a courageous battle." These seem like empty words when three children were left without a mother.

I remembered a verse from our Sunday class the week before.

> *Though he brings grief, he will show compassion, so great is his unfailing love.*
>
> *(Lamentations 3:32 NIV)*

I claimed this promise for Donna's family.

ONE OBSTACLE AT A TIME
Lorena Estep October 7

Be strong and courageous. Do not be afraid or terrified because of them, for the LORD your God goes with you; he will never leave you nor forsake you.
(Deuteronomy 31:6 NIV)

I was driving alone from Pennsylvania to Kansas to visit my son, who's a chaplain in the U.S. Army. My worst fear was dealing with tractor-trailers I would encounter on the road.

When I passed a semi, I gripped the wheel tightly and prayed until the passing was completed. Soon I relaxed and decided traveling on my own wasn't so bad. I began to notice there was a rhythm to the driving rather like life. Two or three semis would loom up ahead. Taking a deep breath and praying, I'd pass them one at a time, then get back in the right lane and relax again with a clear road before me. Soon several more would be spied, and the whole process repeated.

In life, problems appear, we take a deep breath, pray, and set about dealing with them. Then, hopefully, we enjoy a short breathing space before something else comes along. Jesus says we can cast all our cares on Him. That should be encouraging, even if our problems loom as large as semis.

NO MATTER HOW I FEEL
Theresa V. Wilson October 8

No matter how I feel on any given day,
I choose to kneel and let God's Spirit have sway.
I've received my call and choose to intercede
For God's beloved children and their every need.
It doesn't matter if I like the person, you see.
I must accept the assignment given to me.
Prayer is not the question—our charge is to follow Him.
Give glory, praise, and honor—by rejoicing—we win.
When the early morning command is to arise and pray,
In the Spirit we'll be fighting evil spirits away.
So no matter how it looks, keep praying and pressing through.
Remember, faithful intercessors, our victory is due.

SO GREAT A GOD AS OUR GOD

Micki Roberts October 9

I cried unto God with my voice, even unto God with my voice; and he gave ear unto me.

(Psalm 77:1 KJV)

The psalmist speaks of trouble and calling out to God. He is so troubled that he asks: Will the Lord cast off for ever? And will he be favorable no more? Is his mercy clean gone for ever?

(Psalm 77:7-8 KJV)

Have you ever found yourself in such a place? Calling out to God, yet finding no comfort. Do you find yourself asking, "Is His mercy gone forever? Does His promise fail forevermore? Has God forgotten to be gracious? Hath His anger shut up His tender mercies?" [Psalm 77:8-9]

Take heart and hope in verses 10-13: "And I said, This is my infirmity: but I will remember the years of the right hand of the most High. I will remember the works of the LORD: surely I will remember thy wonders of old. I will meditate also of all thy work, and talk of thy doings. Thy way, O God, is in the sanctuary: who is so great a God as our God?"

See the grace and mercy of God and take comfort in Him. Indeed, who is so great a God as our God?

ASSURANCE OF FAITH

Martha Rogers October 10

Now faith is being sure of what we hope for and certain of what we do not see.

(Hebrews 11:1 NIV)

While I was studying to teach a lesson on faith from the book of James, this verse was among those I used as a cross reference. I know what I hope for in the future, and I have faith God will be with me every step of the way.

Faith is such an important part of our lives. Is your faith one that is alive and working, or is it lifeless and idle? You know it's there, but you're not really doing anything with it. A strong faith relies on God to accomplish what He promised to do for those who trust in Him and follow Him.

Sometimes my faith is weakest when I'm waiting to hear from a doctor about tests and is the strongest when I am faced with a problem or difficulty. Why isn't it the same all the time? I have asked myself this many, many times, but admit I don't really have any answer—other than I am human with all my imperfections.

One thing of which I am sure, God is faithful. He continues to love me even when I haven't trusted Him completely. He stands with open arms to welcome me back whenever I stray. I am still His child even when I fail Him. What a wonderful thought. When my faith is weak, He holds me and gives me comfort. When my flesh is weak, He wraps me in His love and makes me strong. No matter where we go or what we do, we can never escape God's love and concern for us.

Heavenly Father, strengthen our faith today. May we lean on You and fully trust You with every aspect of our lives. Guard and protect us today and guide our footsteps.

THE BURNING BUSH

Mary A. Koepke   **October 11**

And the angel of the Lord spoke to Moses from out of the burning bush.

(Exodus 3:2 RSV)

Answering a knock on our cottage door, we found Doug, a landscaper for the retirement community. "Hi! A lady didn't want this burning bush. My boss said to take it up to Hankey Court for their back slope." We gratefully accepted this lush green shrub—especially when he dug the hole and planted it.

We have struggled to beautify the long slope to the woods. A clutter of weeds, bushes, and leftover flowers, this neglected eyesore bugged my gardener husband. Since we moved in four years ago, we realized the potential of joining with nature to create a lovely landscape. A mixture of wild flowers worked well, with added domestics delighting us with their variety of shapes, sizes, and colors through the seasons. And our cardinals, titmice, and goldfinches find shelter from the hawk in its jumble.

We are humbled to think that out of just such a bush God spoke to Moses. Full in the spring, its foliage is a lovely feathery green. But in autumn its leaves flame with scarlet. Whoever named it saw a synchronicity to the biblical encounter of Moses. We see it as a symbol of God's fiery presence. And since it was given to us as we battled my husband's cancer, it has become an affirmation. We must "turn aside" from the struggles of the world, trusting that God is always with us. We are assured of His shelter and protection.

EPIPHANY

Mary Donovan Vish   October 12

My 80th birthday was a jubilant celebration, hosted by my family. In pure pleasure, I realized all six of my children, some of whom now live out of state, were present. They worked in united fashion to honor me with a glorious get together. To feel hugs and kisses from my children, their spouses, and my grandchildren was a gift unto itself.

Today, life for our young people can be very chaotic. However, as we age, our priorities shift into a different gear. Most changes then are dictated by health status. Often, it is tempting to wallow in self pity as we struggle to accept our new limitations.

I now know it is wise to realize acceptance is very much the order of the day. I think I am spiritually and physically strong enough to make decisions that would benefit all of us. To do so without complaint, to put my burdens at ease by prayer and confidence in a gracious God, to understand—because I am a retired nurse—that I must persevere when given medical advice and instructions...this would be a valuable gift to my family.

I have untold, numerous blessings which include an extraordinary husband of 58 years. Of course, I confess I often seek validation and reassurance. For today, and days to come, I have found it in His Word:

> *When I said, "My foot is slipping," your love, O Lord, supported me. When anxiety was great within me, your consolation brought joy to my soul.*
>
> *(Psalm 94:18-19 NIV)*

PRAYER FROM THE HARVEST FIELD

Kathleen Wolford   October 13

God of all creation, you are my strength and shield,
And I could surely use some help here in the harvest field.
This ministry needs volunteers; that project needs a chair;
The head of Backyard Bible Club has asked if I'll be there.
The choir is short of altos, and I really love to sing,
But I'm heading up the potluck, and that's another thing;

I know I should cut back, and there are others they could ask,
But I'm flattered when they tell me I'm just perfect for the task.
Lately, though, I'm finding that the joy's begun to wane.
I'm preoccupied and grouchy; what was fun is now a pain.
I want to be like Mary, sitting rapt at Jesus' feet;
Instead, I'm more like Martha—preparations incomplete.
I've grown weary in well-doing, irritated, unfulfilled;
I need the calm and quiet of the tempest that You stilled.
Forgive me, guide me, help me, O Lord, my strength and shield;
Make me a better worker in my Master's harvest field.

THE LESSON OF THE LEAVES

Judy Ferrell   **October 14**

Ye shall be witnesses unto me.
(Acts 1:8 KJV)

While my husband was on a mission trip I did some of the things around the house that he normally does. One of those jobs was raking leaves. I knew I could make only a dent in the accumulation, but I didn't want to leave them all for him to do upon his return. I was determined to rake as many leaves as possible. While working I thought about John's soon return and how it would please him to know that I had raked some of the leaves for him.

Then I thought about Jesus' soon return. When he ascended to heaven he commissioned me to "Go ye therefore ..." (Matthew 28:19). He said, "...ye shall be witnesses unto me..." (Acts 1:8). I looked at the leaves and thought of all the opportunities I had had to tell someone about Jesus. Some of those opportunities I seized, just as I stuffed *some* of the leaves in a bag. Others, I let pass by, leaving them for someone else to "pick up."

John didn't expect me to rake, but Jesus does expect me to be about His work. I must not leave it for someone else to do.

Father, help me to be obedient and to seize the opportunities that you give me to tell someone about Jesus. In Jesus' Name, Amen.

JESUS' PURPOSE AND MINE

Joseph M. Hopkins   **October 15**

At last count, Rick Warren's book *The Purpose Driven Life*

had sold 22 million copies, evidence that this is a topic of interest and concern to millions of Americans. As Christians, Jesus should be our model. How did He view His purpose?

Jesus said, "I came down from heaven, not to do my own will, but the will of him that sent me" (John 6:38 KJV). Jesus surrendered Himself to the Father's will. In the Garden of Gethsemane He prayed that the cup of suffering might be removed from Him; but then He added, "Nevertheless not my will, but thine, be done" (Luke 22:42 KJV).

Should not this be our prayers as we begin each day?

Dear Father, help me to seek, find, follow, obey, perform, and submit to Your perfect will for my life today. May all that I do, say, and think reflect the light and love of Jesus to everyone I meet along the way. In His holy name I pray. Amen.

WHEN DAY IS DONE

Betty Redmon October 16

When day is done, 'tis then I see
The gifts that God has given me.
In quiet times, 'tis then I know
That God will always make it so.

The mountains will stand evermore,
As they have always stood before.
The lakes, rivers, onward flow
And on their way, they merrily go.

When on us all, the night descends
And gives us time to make amends,
'Tis then we stop to realize
The blessings right before our eyes.
And thank the Lord, in Heaven above,
For the many ways He's shown His love.

Every good gift and every perfect gift is from above, coming down from the Father of the heavenly lights.
(James 1:17 NIV)

THE ULTIMATE GUIDE TO RELAXATION
Barbara Peer   **October 17**

Printed in large letters, I have a subtitle taped onto the cover of my Bible. It reads: The Ultimate Guide To Relaxation.

One of the primary ingredients for a good day—for many good days, in fact—is peace. But peace is something which must be sought after. [Psalm 34:14] It doesn't come automatically. What does come automatically is rushing around, filling up every minute of every day, multitasking whenever possible, heaping up accomplishments by the dozens. We're rewarded for it. People who do a lot are respected and admired while those who achieve peace and harmony are seldom noticed. They might even be considered by some to be boring.

When I first started reading the Bible, I thought it was pretty boring. It put me right to sleep. I wasn't looking for peace; I was looking for fun and excitement. Life wasn't going to pass *me* by! After a while I discovered just how deadly boring "fun" can be. The thrill was gone, replaced by frustration and discontentment.

Around that time, I began to notice the multitude of scripture references to peace, such as: "Peace I leave with you; my peace I give you" (John 14:27 NIV) and "the peace of God, which transcends all understanding, will guard your hearts and your minds in Christ Jesus" (Philippians 4:7 NIV). Peace is God's gift to us. Receiving His peace gives deep-down, glad-to-be-alive contentment.

A MORNING PRAYER
Joan Clayton   **October 18**

The LORD has heard my cry for help, the LORD will answer my prayer.

(Psalm 6:9 NCV)

Grant me wisdom, Lord, to know when to speak and when to be silent. Forgive my pride and selfishness. Help me to see the good in others and to build upon their strengths.

Please make me aware of every transgression, and may I be quick to repent. May I be sensitive to the leading of Your Spirit.

I ask for wisdom in every thought, word, and deed. May I encourage others in their journey of life. Fill me with compassion, forgiveness, and mercy. May I impart those same qualities to everyone I meet.

Teach me to sing through the storms of life, with my focus on You alone, my anchor holding fast and secure. Help me to know I am not walking blindly, but with You I can do all things. I walk upon the high places of the earth because You guide my every step. May I know the height, depth, and breadth of Your love for me, the everlasting joy of my life.

When my earthly time is ended, may I be found faithful, meeting the dawn of Your glory with wondrous praise throughout eternity for Your extravagant love for me!

In that beautiful name of the King of Kings and Lord of Lords. His name is Jesus. Amen.

WAITING FOR ANSWERS

Leigh DeLozier **October 19**

I wait for the LORD, my soul waits, and in his word I put my hope.

(Psalm 130:5 NIV)

The seagull stands a few feet from us, hoping my husband will throw some snacks toward him. The gull preens a bit and wanders off a few steps, but returns to his original post. My husband has no intention of sharing anything, but the bird still hopes that his patience will be rewarded.

How patiently do we wait for things? For me, the answer sometimes depends on whether I'm waiting for something that's my own idea or waiting for God to reveal Himself or His plan for me. I tend to have a lot more patience waiting for my own desires, rather than the unseen answers or unknown timing of God.

While I'm waiting, I need to ask myself an important question. Am I waiting on the right thing? Or am I waiting uselessly like the seagull, hoping for something that will never—or possibly *should* never—occur?

Only God knows the answers to these questions, and only God will share them with us in His perfect time. All we can do in the meantime is pray and open ourselves to Him so we'll be ready for the answer when it comes.

Father, waiting for answers can be difficult, but only You know what's best for me. Please help me be patient as I wait for Your perfect timing and answers.

DELEGATING WORK

Connie Bretz　　　　　　　　　　　　　　　October 20

God never gives us a job we cannot do.

Our family had planned to meet my son, who had a temporary job in San Raphael, CA. Our arrival was early, and so we waited outside the huge warehouse for Ben.

A deafening crash alerted us to an accident that had occurred inside the warehouse. For no reason that I understood, I said, "It's Ben!"

It was Ben. While driving a fork lift, he knocked down a wall and an entire shelf attached to it. He came out of the warehouse looking frightened and pale.

During a quiet family lunch, Ben said, "My boss said that anyone who could drive a car could drive a fork lift. I didn't want to do it because I had never had that experience."

How wise that God never gives Christians a job for which they are unsuited.

Heavenly Father, thank You for giving us jobs and gifts that are appropriate for our needs and talents.

MY PART

Mary Herron　　　　　　　　　　　　　　　October 21

Train up a child in the way he should go: and when he is old, he will not depart from it.
　　　　　　　(Proverbs 22:6 KJV)

When my children were young I loved to tuck them in at night, especially on wash day. The sheets had hung in the sun and fresh breezes all day, bringing a comforting aroma in with them. I would read to the children, pray with them, then give each an extra kiss. I'd return to my husband downstairs feeling that my family was safe and God would watch over us through the night.

Now, my family is grown, their beds empty, and they are scattered near and far. I miss that contented feeling, but then I remember God is watching over them still. Though we feel our children are not as close to Him as we had intended, I repeat Proverbs 22:6 to remind myself that we trained them and did our part.

Cutting remarks and sour attitudes do not bring us closer, but add a gulf between us. It is hard to leave things in God's hands and remember He doesn't need all our helpful hints. We are His prayer warriors, still interceding for those precious children.

Oh, Lord, help me to realize You are in control and do not need my input. Give me the patience to let You do Your job and obedience for me to do mine.

PRAYER OF THE ARTICHOKE

Kay J. Clark October 22

> Creator,
> purge my life.
> Peel
> away the leaves
> of pride.
> Strip
> away the spines
> of selfishness.
> Break
> away the bracts
> of boorishness.
> Bare my heart.
> Anoint me
> with the oil of Your love.
> Salt it
> with the essence of Your grace.
> Then I shall be
> full of Your flavor.

IN HIS IMAGE

Della Ray October 23

Then God said, "Let Us make man in Our image, according to Our likeness."
(Genesis 1:26 NAS)

We know that we have been created in the image of God. No believer would argue that we are like God in form. But sometimes we forget that we are like Him in our desires.

John and Staci Eldredge addressed this in chapter two of their book *Captivating*. In short, it talked of how women, in the likeness of God, are ones who desire to be pursued. What a thought provoking idea! God wants to be pursued!

One of my favorite Bible verses is Jeremiah 29:13: *"You will seek Me and find Me when you search for Me with all of your heart."* God not only wants to be pursued; He wants to be found. He does not play hide-and-seek with us and wonder how long it will take for us to give up. He desires our pursuit of Him. Our actions of pursuing Him tell of the great value that we put on His presence in our lives.

Have you pursued God lately?

GOD, IT IS YOU

Caitlin O'Conner   **October 24**

God, it is You who fills the sky with clouds.
Silent, they move and never seem to make any sounds.
God, it is You who causes the river to flow.
You've created and blessed me with all that I know.
God, it is You who makes the leaves fall.
God, my needs, You satisfy them all.
Almighty Creator, I thank You for all You've given to me,
Especially for Your Son dying, though perfect was He.

THE WOLF AND THE LAMB

Janet R. Sady   **October 25**

The wolf also shall dwell with the lamb, and the leopard shall lie down with the kid; and the calf and the young lion and the fatling together; and a little child shall lead them.
(Isaiah 11:6 KJV)

A curse has been upon the earth since Adam and Eve disobeyed. Enmity exists between animals and man, and among the animals themselves.

When I toured Yellowstone National Park, I witnessed some unusual behavior. Wild donkeys, white-tailed deer, buffalo and even black bear came up to the cars to be fed. This is unnatural. Prolonged violation of the "Do Not Feed" policy has produced a dangerous situation. Tourists and wild animals do not fear each other. Park officials warn of wild animals that have turned aggressive toward humans when hungry.

One day, the curse will be lifted, and even a little child will play with the lions with no fear of being molested. What a glorious day that will be when our Lord reigns on this earth as King of Kings!

Even so, come quickly, Lord Jesus! Amen.

OGNIB

Peter Paulson   **October 26**

The new wine dries up and the vine withers; all the merrymakers groan.

(Isaiah 24:7 NIV)

Imagine a bingo game where the players are given cards already covered with bingo in every direction. The caller steps to the podium and begins to call out numbers. As each number is called, the players must remove the counter over that number. Bingo lineups begin to disappear. Gaps emerge on the cards. Here and there a groan is heard as the last hope for a winning sequence disappears. The hypnotic cadence of the caller continues unabated. People begin to collapse and weep over their empty cards.

Such is Isaiah's vision of the Day of God's Judgement. In the beginning, joy, hope, peace, and blessings filled humankind's card. Then gradually, creation's counters began to disappear. Where there had been joy, sorrow appeared. Hope removed left despair exposed. Peace yielded to before war and spite. Even blessings rolled off the ognib card as sin swept all before it.

Judgement is not a popular topic in today's society. We receive warnings, but seldom personal rebukes for our greed, gluttony, pride, pollution, and our addiction to lethal and lustful entertainment. Life continues, and as the cards empty bit by bit, we shrug it off and pretend that there is plenty left.

God plays ognib, not bingo. You might want to check what game you're sitting in on.

God, when, not if, Your Judgement Day comes, may my heart be ready for You. Amen.

ADVICE

Jennifer Kanode   **October 27**

Pride only breeds quarrels, but wisdom is found in those who take advice.

(Proverbs 13:10 NIV)

I have known one of my friends since we were babies. He and I practically grew up together. So I knew that he loves to tinker around with machines and such. For that, he needed a huge space where he could work. So he rented a house with a large garage.

He recently married, and his wife didn't like the house. They moved into an apartment. Within the first year of their marriage, they were looking for a house with a garage.

How many times, when we are so closely involved in a situation, do we miss the big picture? Our perception gets blurred, and we need an outsider or third party to "tell it like it is." We might not like what they have to say, but we know they are right, and later come to appreciate their honesty.

Lord, help us to be open to what others have to tell us. We might not like what they have to share, but if it's from You, we need to heed and listen. Amen.

SET FREE

Dave Evans   **October 28**

Rustled and roped by enticing lies;
driven, then unwittingly locked
in barren pastures with polluted springs;
languishing and awaiting their demise.

But the locks are broken and the gates
flung open; the Master's voice calls,
and those who choose follow Him to
the branding pen; then are set free
in lush green meadows with
cold, clear running streams
and constant comfort.

For He delivered us from the domain of darkness and transferred us to the kingdom of His beloved Son.
(Colossians 1:13 NAS)

WOUNDED HEALER

Shirley S. Stevens   **October 29**

To another faith by the same Spirit; to another the gifts of healing by the same Spirit.
(1 Corinthians 12:9 KJV)

Madeleine L'Engle speaks of wounded healers. She says that when she is hurt, she is more likely to turn to someone who has been hurt, someone who can understand a little of what she is going through.

I remember my friend Connie writing to me, "Because you have suffered, you are more compassionate with others who suffer."

This is why those who experience the pain of living with a family member who is an alcoholic seek help and understanding by attending Al Anon meetings. There they find people who, in the midst of their suffering, have learned to hold on. Some have kept their sense of humor and can put their experience into perspective.

Madeleine L'Engle adds that just as she looks for a wounded healer in another human being, she looks for the same qualities in God.

Lord, we know that You suffered on the cross for us. You know what it means to be a wounded healer. Help us to reach out to You in our need, and, in turn, to reach out to others in theirs.

JESUS: THE UNSEEN STRENGTH
Carole Lang   **October 30**

At times it takes lots of courage just to live life as it is presented to you. My greatest challenge, and therefore my most courageous act, was to look into the face of the one I loved and tell him that he was okay and that his family would be okay when he left to go to his heavenly home.

My husband of forty-four years had been diagnosed with Caracinoid cancer five years before he passed away. He and I had talked and agreed that when he was tired of fighting, he would quit and rest in the Lord's arms until he went home. A few days before he died, Willard said, "You know what we talked about?" Immediately, I knew and, at my nod, he continued, "I don't want to die, but if Jesus is ready for me, I'm ready for Him!"

A wonderful man, Willard loved and was loved by everyone who knew him. Trusting completely in the Lord, he didn't complain or ask, "Why me?" Never did he seem to blame anyone or anything for his disease. His strength in Christ made it so much easier for me to be courageous when he was ready to leave this earth.

Lord, I trust You to continue to give me strength and courage to live without my life partner. Teach me to trust You as my eternal partner.

OPEN BOOK
Cindy Hawkins   **October 31**

We met with the realtor to sell our house. He hung a lock box on our front door. If a musical soundtrack had been playing at that moment, it would have switched to something ominous. Total strangers would be passing through the front door to view our home. Our lives had now become an open book. I wondered what impression a potential buyer would form of our home...of my housekeeping skills(gulp)...and of our lives (even bigger gulp).

Being a Christian is not unlike putting our house up for sale. Whether we like it or not, once we profess Christ, our lives become an open book. People watch us to see if Jesus makes a difference in our lives. They are watching us in the workplace, in the neighborhood, at school—even at church. People hunger for answers to tough questions and perplexing problems. They are looking to see if we hold the answers. Or if we know Someone who does.

Jesus' life was an open book for all to see. Everywhere He went, devoted believers, curious onlookers, and hardened skeptics followed Him. He used daily opportunities to teach, to challenge, to convict... and to show His love for mankind.

Like it or not, our lives are open books. Let's not put up a charade or false front. Christ calls us to authenticity, where we reveal our struggles and flaws against the backdrop of His all-sufficiency and grace. The background music in our lives, playing over and over again, is the sweeping melody of His redeeming love.

THE NEED OF MUTUAL SUPPORT
Charles A. Waugaman   **November 1**

> *Let us not give up meeting together, as some are in the habit of doing, but let us encourage one another—and all the more as you see the Day approaching.*
> *(Hebrews 10:25 NIV)*

ASH
I stare into the dying campfire
and think of hermits.

And I wonder.

None of the glowing embers
retains its crimson glory
in isolation.

How meaningless is ash.
[Published in *Review of Books and Religions*, Mid-March, 1972]

THE TONGUE
Tiffany Schlichter   November 2

> *Death and life are in the power of the tongue: and they that love it shall eat the fruit thereof.*
>
> *(Proverbs 18:21 KJV)*

The tongue is a weapon or medicine that you carry with you twenty-four hours a day, seven days a week. It can speak kind words of wisdom and love, or it can disperse offensive words of hatred and folly. It can either encourage and strengthen someone or hurt and dishearten a person. We must be aware of this power.

As you go through life day by day, never forget the opportunity you have to brighten someone's day by a simple word of encouragement. And do not disregard the caution that your speech could also dishonor the Lord. Keep it tamed, and God will reward you for this important practice.

> *But I say unto you, That every idle word that men shall speak, they shall give account thereof in the day of judgment. For by thy words thou shalt be justified, and by thy words thou shalt be condemned.*
>
> *(Matthew 12:36-37 KJV)*

TONGUE CONTROL
Martha Rogers   November 3

> *If anyone considers himself religious and yet does not keep a tight rein on his tongue, he deceives himself and his religion is worthless.*
>
> *(James 1:26 NIV)*

My tongue has been a problem since the days of my childhood when I said whatever popped into my head, sometimes to the great embarrassment of my mother. As I contemplate this verse, I remember the many apologies I had to give because my mouth and brain were not in sync. This verse has helped me to think about what I say to or about others.

When we hurt others with words spoken in anger or defense, we are letting our human nature be in control. When we submit our lives to the Holy Spirit, letting Him be in control, our words are kinder and more understanding.

As Christians, we know the power of words to heal, soothe,

and convey love. But they can also hurt, agitate, and convey hate or prejudice. We can build up relationships or tear them down with words. Like wildfire, words spoken in anger or haste can spread quickly, destroying everything in their path. On the other hand, words spoken in love can spread a mantle of kindness over a relationship.

Our words can spread the peace and love of God's Word. We have that opportunity every day with countless lost souls everywhere—on the street corner, at the office, at school, on vacation, and in our churches. With the Holy Spirit in control, our words have the potential to make a tremendous difference in others' lives.

Heavenly Father, may all of our words, written or spoken, be acceptable in Christ's sight. Amen.

SEEKING FAITH

Linda Mae Richardson   **November 4**

I'm sure if I could see You, Lord,
Just look upon Your face,
These many doubts that fill my thoughts
Would leave without a trace.

I'd like to hear You speak to me,
To simply touch Your hand,
To have You tell me what is true,
And then I'd understand.

But would I be so different
From multitudes before,
Who saw Your face and heard You speak
But chose just to ignore?

You've said that greater still is faith
Not based on touch or sight,
But faith that comes by trusting You
With all our soul and might.

So I'll not seek to prove through eyes,
Nor feel with hands of clay
The truth Your Spirit teaches me
Within my heart today.

GOD'S CARE IN A BIRD FEEDER
Annettee Budzban   November 5

Consider the ravens: They do not sow or reap, they have no storeroom or barn; yet God feeds them. And how much more valuable are you than the birds!

(*Luke 12:24 NIV*)

It was a cold, wintry day. My friend called to say that she was coming by for a visit and bringing a gift with her. I had been housebound with an illness for about a year. I could really use some company. Her words were refreshment to my ears.

When my friend arrived, I expected that she would come to the front door bearing her gift. However, I was caught by surprise when she walked around to my backyard, holding a shepherd's hook and a bird feeder to hang from it.

She came to the backdoor and said, "I'll leave these here for your husband to find a place for them." I was impressed by the unique gift my friend offered me.

My husband placed it in an open spot off to the left in our backyard. It was a place that was in full view from both our kitchen windows, and easily accessible for my fine feathered friends. He was attentive to keep it fully supplied for God's little creatures.

Each day, I looked forward to watching the flutter of wings as a variety of birds graced me with a visit. I saw the red-headed woodpecker eloquently dressed in his black and white tuxedo. The bright red cardinal stopped by and brought along his mate. The plain, ordinary, brown and white sparrow came flapping his tiny wings, as well.

I found that watching the birds served as a reminder of God's care for me. The next time you see a fine feathered friend fly by, why not use it as a gentle nudge to trust God for His provision in your life?

THE GREAT AND THE SMALL
Cindy Hawkins   November 6

We make big decisions in life: choosing a career, marrying the love of our life, starting a family, moving to another town, and deciding when to retire. We consider our choices carefully because we realize the impact of our decision in shaping the course of our lives.

In between these major decisions, we face little decisions. We can share a heartache with a friend or suffer alone. We settle an argument with our spouse or stalk away with hurt imbedded in our hearts. We can participate in today's gossip or stay out of it. We blow bubbles with our child or pop in a video for him to watch. We choose whether we witness to a lost neighbor or keep our faith to ourselves. These small decisions alter our lives, one increment at a time.

Some decisions will center us in God's will while others will miss the mark. If we pay attention, the Holy Spirit will nudge us in a certain direction. He is the Wise Counselor, no matter the size of the issue we face. He wants to guide us in every decision we make—from the major to the minute.

> *But the Counselor, the Holy Spirit, whom the Father will send in my name, will teach you all things and will remind you of everything I have said to you.*
> (John 14:26 NIV)

NOW AND FOREVER

Lanette Kissel   **November 7**

How can we consider removing "under God" from
Our Pledge? Such disrespect we are showing.
How can our country afford to alienate
A God who is all seeing and all knowing?

How can we change the words of our wise forefathers?
Yet some are doing all that they can
To forget that this country was founded on religious freedom.
It was a major part of the plan.

There are those of us who realize
That God's blessing is what we need.
As I picture our children reciting the Pledge,
I will pray that this threat not succeed.

Regardless of the outcome of this debate,
There is only one truth I can see:
I *was* under God, am *now* under God,
And under God I will *forever* be.

SPECTATOR CHRISTIANS

Lorena Estep   **November 8**

I have finished the race, I have kept the faith. Now there is in store for me the crown of righteousness, which the Lord, the righteous Judge, will award to me on that day.
(2 Timothy 4:7-8 NIV)

We enjoy the excitement of sitting in the stands to watch a sporting event. When we look around, there are always more spectators than participants. In a track meet, the runners pound down the track, straining to reach the goal of the winner's line at the end of the race. We might be inspired to get more exercise ourselves, then walk away to our busy lives and forget our good intentions.

What about living for the Lord? Are we spectator Christians? We should look around in the churches we attend. Do the same few people do the many necessary jobs? Are we shouldering our share, or staying in our comfort zone on the sidelines, attending the services and nothing more?

Ezra 10:4 (RSV) says: "Arise, for it is your task, ... be strong and do it."

Let's move from the sidelines of our good intentions, and into the action of keeping the faith and running the race for the reward that awaits us in heaven.

NEVER GIVE UP

Marjorie K. Evans   **November 9**

Let us not become weary in doing good, for at the proper time we will reap a harvest if we do not give up
(Galatians 6:9 NIV)

Most of the children in my second grade Sunday school class tried to be attentive during our lesson time. But Randy constantly bothered everyone. He wiggled, poked his neighbors, and talked out of turn. He appeared impervious to correction, and I was sure he never heard the lessons. Extremely discouraged, I felt the time spent in preparing the lessons and teaching was wasted and I should quit.

Then, one Sunday, I told the story of Jesus and His disciples crossing the Sea of Galilee. When a storm suddenly arose, the frightened disciples awakened Jesus. He spoke to the wind and the waves and said, "Quiet! Be still!" (Mark 4:39 NIV). And they were still.

"Children," I asked, "how could Jesus make the wind and the waves be quiet?"

To my utter amazement, Randy's hand shot up. When I called on him, he said, "One Sunday you told us that Jesus made everything—even the wind and waves. So He ought to know how to make them be still."

Randy had been listening! Suddenly I knew the work of preparing and teaching a lesson each week was worth it!

The Bible tells us not to grow weary in doing good, for there will be a harvest if we don't give up. All we have to do is be faithful, do a good job at whatever God has called us to do, and leave the results to Him.

How grateful I am that the Lord used Randy to teach me never to give up.

BORN TO LIVE AND NOT TO DIE
Joe LoBello   November 10

> Conceived by the hand of the Father,
> Our lives are each fearfully made.
> And as time reveals God's wonder,
> It tells of His infinite Love.
>
> Born to live and not to die is His promise,
> A promise that rings so true.
> Born to live and abundantly prosper,
> That is His desire for me and for you.
>
> Though the flesh may age and alter,
> The spirit grows steadily strong,
> And as our flame slowly falters,
> The gift of His grace goes on.
>
> Born to live and not to die,
> It is the foundation of our faith.
> Born to live by His side,
> The Lord reigning with His bride.

HONOR TO WHOM HONOR IS DUE

Dan Nicksich   November 11

Give everyone what you owe him: If you owe taxes, pay taxes; if revenue, then revenue; if respect, then respect; if honor, then honor.

(Romans 13:7 NIV)

A teenager was surprised to hear we had once been at war with Japan. "Who won?" he asked.

Each November 11 is set aside as a day in which we honor our veterans, those who served our country to preserve our freedom. We dare not allow the knowledge of their sacrifice to fade. Scripture says that we are to honor those to whom honor is due. Few would seem more deserving than those who stormed the beaches in such famous places as Normandy, Iwo Jima, or Guadalcanal, and those who risked—and gave—their lives in so many nameless places worldwide.

Make today a little brighter for one who deserves our appreciation—friend, relative, coworker, or neighbor. Express your gratitude to a veteran who is close to you. Make a date for lunch, write a note, pick up the phone; make a connection. It's the least you can do in recognition of what he once did for you.

Lord, although we don't glorify war, we thank You for those who served our country to ensure our freedom. Bless those who risked their lives on our behalf. Amen.

WHOSE PROBLEM?

Marcie Banks   November 12

A Christian friend and I took a communications course together at a community college. During the first session, our instructor said we would learn to acquire the courage to express our views when they disagreed with the view of others. During the semester, the atmosphere seemed to change and so did the goal. In the final session we were told to tell our husband firmly, or whoever disagreed with us, "That's your problem, not mine."

Is it right to snap, "That's your problem, not mine!" then turn again to the computer or television?

Writer Thomas Merton said, "No man is an island."

The Bible tells us, "None of us lives to himself" (Romans 14:7). "We being many are one bread, for we are all partakers of that one bread" (1 Corinthians 10:17). "Bear one another's burdens" (Galatians 6:2). "Comfort yourselves together, and edify one another" (2 Thessalonians 5:11). "Be all of one mind, having compassion one for another, love as brethren, be pitiful, be courteous" (1 Peter 3:8). In the words of Jesus, "This is my commandment, that ye love one another" (John 15:12).

The community college should have returned our money; my friend and I learned more from our time-worn Bibles.

FEELING DOWN
Pat Collins November 13

I will not leave you comfortless: I will come to you.
(John 14:18 KJV)

My heart felt so heavy today; I wondered if anything even matters anymore. *God, where are You? You seem so far away. Please don't leave me; I really need You.*

I felt a tugging at my heart as His words came to me: My child look around you. See that small tender flower that found its way among the weeds? Look at the delicate butterfly land quietly upon the bush. See how the clouds form so many different shapes, and how the sunbeams seem to touch the earth? SEE ME. Listen, do you hear the birds singing? I taught them to sing, to entertain you. The bees and crickets make music of some kind. HEAR ME. Do you feel a slight stirring, when there is no breeze? FEEL MY TOUCH. See, child, I am not far away, I'm closer to you then you think. I am forever near. I live within your heart.

Thank You, dear Lord, for when I become quiet and listen, I do feel Your presence. Help me to be still so You can speak to me. For I am never alone, with You in my heart. Amen.

OH LORD ABOVE
Tune of *O Christmas Tree*

Glenda Joy Race November 14

Oh Lord above, we praise Your Name
For you endure forever.
Oh Lord above, we praise your Name,
For you endure forever.
You made the Heavens and the Earth,
And yet you came through virgin birth.

Oh Lord above, we praise your name,
For you endure forever.

Oh Jesus Christ, Oh Jesus Christ,
Your Priesthood never changes.
Oh Jesus Christ, Oh Jesus Christ,
Your priesthood never changes.
Not only faithful yesterday
But for today and every day.
Oh Jesus Christ, oh Jesus Christ,
Your priesthood never changes.

Oh Lord, Your mercies never cease
Your compassion never fails.
Oh Lord, Your mercies never cease.
Your compassions never fail.
Your faithfulness is good to those
Who trust and wait for You, Oh Lord.
Oh Lord, Your mercies never cease.
Your compassion never fails.

THE AUTHOR AND FINISHER

Judy Barron   **November 15**

Looking unto Jesus the author and finisher of our faith.
(Hebrews 12:2 KJV)

Father God,

You are the instigator and final authority of our faith. Without You in our lives, we could not have faith. We must have faith in You—a belief in You —for anything like grace to come into our lives. And You are the finisher of our faith. You come to take us home at the end of our days here on earth. Without You, and Your promise of salvation, we can never conceive of a "coming home." Without Your Grace, we would die and be dead—period! You finish our faith so gloriously—by overcoming death and providing an eternal home for us where our faith will let us see You face-to-face. What a glorious future we have to look forward to! In the name of our Lord and Savior, Jesus Christ, Amen.

LIGHT IN THE WORD

Marion E. Gorman November 16

Matthew 6:19-34

Driving home from work, my mind relaxed into daydreaming. I thought about people who had won millions in the lottery. What would a person do with all that money? I wondered.

I pondered many things while entertaining this distraction from reality. After tithing at least a tenth, I would buy a lighthouse. They are advertised for sale, very cheap, with the contingency that the buyer have capital to restore and maintain them. I love restoring old things; living on the ocean would be wonderful and surely a lighthouse could bring attention to the Light of the World, Jesus.

Back in real life, the scripture for my devotions that evening read, "You (God) have put gladness in my heart, more than in the season that their grain and wine increased" (Psalm 4:7 NKJ). My daydream burst like the bubble it was, and I knew the "gladness in my heart" could come only from the Lord—not material wealth. Later, as if underlining this truth, I read, "I have rejoiced in the way of Your testimonies, as much as in all riches" (Psalm 119:14 NKJ). I celebrated with praise, knowing the riches I have in Christ transcend anything the world has to offer. Daydreams fade when I listen to God's plan for my life with what He has already given me.

Lord, thank You for shedding Your light on my need to anchor my soul in You.

FOLLOWING OUR GIFTS

Leigh DeLozier November 17

Each man has his own gift from God.
(1 Corinthians 7:7 NIV)

I've always loved to write, but several years ago God began planting the seeds of a new dream in my heart—to write for Him.

I soon found that writing was the easy part—sharing the dream with others was much harder because I felt totally unworthy. With all the accomplished writers out there, why would God want to use me to help share His message?

Then one Sunday our preschool son brought home a large,

cloud-shaped piece of green construction paper with orange strips poking out in every direction. I couldn't imagine what it was, so asked what he'd talked about in class that morning. "Moses," he replied. "This is the bush God used to talk to him."

The simplicity hit me as if I'd seen the burning bush myself. Moses hadn't expected to be called either, and had quite a few "reasons" why he wasn't worthy of the job God gave him. But God had even better reasons for why Moses was the perfect man for the job.

The same holds true today. No matter what God calls us to be, He knows exactly what He's doing. We just need to swallow our excuses and follow His guidance. It's not always easy, but little reminders—like a burning bush—can help.

Lord, thank You for the gifts You've given me. Give me the faith I need to use them as You want.

JEHOVAH-RAAH: THE LORD MY SHEPHERD
Micki Roberts   November 18

The Lord is my Shepherd. . .He restoreth my soul.
(Psalm 23:1, 3 KJV)

As I traveled along the road in my journey with the Lord, I stumbled and I fell. Huffily, I crawled to the edge of the road. I sat, grumbling and crying over my fall. For quite some time, I refused to get up and continue my journey. I was hurt, and I decided that I would not allow myself to be hurt again. So there I sat, complaining to myself and refusing to spend time with my Heavenly Father.

But God had other plans—He was the One who had allowed me to fall. He allowed me to sit on the sidelines for a time. Now, He was reminding me that my journey was not yet done.

So I stopped whining and began praying. I searched God's Word for direction in my life. Suddenly, I felt ashamed that I had allowed hurt to keep me from my daily visits with God. But He gently reminded me that nothing can touch my life without first filtering through His Sovereign, loving hands.

Will I stumble again? Probably. Will I fall again? It's possible. However, my heartfelt prayer is that I will not allow anything to keep me from continuing my journey with Jehovah-raah: The Lord My Shepherd.

The Lord is my Shepherd. . .He restoreth my soul.

A SONG IN MY HEART WAS AN ANSWER TO PRAYER
Delores Hartman   **November 19**

A Scripture for Uncertainty: Psalm 46:1

I had an assignment to write an article on "uncertainty" for a local periodical. While I prayed for the Lord to give me clues as to what to type, a song interrupted my thoughts. At first I struggled to get my thoughts to return to the article. Then I realized God was telling me to look at the words in that song.

I grabbed a 1956 hymn book, looked in the table of contents, and found the song. As always, God supplied my need, because the words were perfect for thoughts on how to handle "uncertainty." Paraphrasing the words, this was the message: Don't fear uncertainty—God's in control; we will be sheltered under His wings of love as He takes care of us every day of our lives. During troubled times, when we think our spirit can't take any more and life seems overwhelming, our heavenly Father is right there with us. Even when agonizing danger is around, He is there to provide all we ever need. Nothing we ask will be denied. No matter what test is present, we can lean on Him, forever...For God will take care of us!

This song, "God Will Take Care of You," was written by W. S. Martin in 1933 and has marvelous meaning. It speaks to us in this world of uncertainty, reminding us of God's wonderful refuge and care.

GOD'S BLESSINGS
Carol Cleal   **November 20**

My heart cries out to the Lord, as life continues with its joys and tribulations. He is the One to give peace, hope, and love. How tolerable is our world when God is with me. He knows when I soar with joy and happiness and plunge with sadness and grief. He is my Rock, my Salvation, my God. He fills me with great peace and gives me hope.

A MAGNET FOR THANKS
Shirley S. Stevens   **November 21**

> *So we thy people and sheep of thy pasture will give thee thanks for ever: we will shew forth thy praise to all generations.*
>
>   (*Psalm 79:13 KJV*)

In the 19th century, the preacher Henry Ward Beecher shared a strong image with his congregation. He told them to imagine a dish of sand mixed with iron filings. Looking at the filings with your eyes, you can't find them. Combing through the sand with your fingers, you still can't find the filings. But if you take a magnet and draw it through the dish, the magnet will be covered with iron filings.

He suggested that the ungrateful person is like our fingers combing through the sand. That person finds nothing to be thankful for. The grateful person, on the other hand, is like the magnet. That person finds hundreds of things to be thankful for.

Thank You, Lord, for reminding us to give thanks each day for the unmerited good that we experience. Help us to begin each day by thanking You for the comfort, well-being, and health which we have. Amen.

OVERLOOKED BLESSINGS

Jana Carman **November 22**

... always giving thanks to God the Father for everything, in the name of our Lord Jesus Christ.
(Ephesians 5:20 NIV)

Dear Lord,

Thank You for the everyday things I usually take for granted, such as hot water, warm clothes, enough to eat, a comfortable bed, and an education. I thank You for people who impact my life: school teachers, parents and grandparents, pastors and Sunday School teachers.

How blessed I am to have my own Bible, freedom of worship, aspirin, hospitals, doctors and nurses, cars, mail service, garbage collection, telephones, radios, music.

Thank You, too, for gifted artists and composers, for people of courage and conviction in all generations, and for those who risked or gave their lives so we could have God's Word and freedom. Thank You for men and women of integrity in government, for policemen and firemen.

Thank You for my country, flawed though it is. Thank You for the love and support I have known from family and friends. And Lord, I am learning to be grateful for discipline, training, and hard times that revealed a strength I didn't know I had.

Help me to make every day Thanksgiving Day, and to spread the contagion of appreciation. Amen.

IN EVERYTHING GIVE THANKS
Joseph Hopkins   **November 23**

In everything give thanks; for this is the will of God in Christ Jesus for you.

(1 Thessalonians 5:18 NKJ)

We had front-row right-field seats in PNC Park for the historic Monday night game between the Pittsburgh Pirates and the Baltimore Orioles. We had arrived early, in time for batting practice. I snapped a picture of home-run king Sammy Sosa as he took practice throws a few yards away. Then, as I was leaning over to read the New Castle News—BAM! A line drive off an Oriole bat bounced off my head. At once I was the center of attention as not only family but fans in nearby seats expressed their concern. For me it was no big deal, nothing to be so excited about. Nevertheless, I reluctantly yielded to their insistence and, accompanied by my granddaughter Alex, followed a staff member to the nearest first-aid station. There a superficial scalp wound was examined and an ice pack provided. Then back to my seat to enjoy the game.

"In—not for—everything give thanks." I wasn't exactly glad I got conked on the noggin by the baseball. But in this incident I found much for which to be thankful.

1. I was wearing a baseball cap, giving my skull a degree of protection.
2. I was looking down, and so was hit on my hard head instead of my soft face.
3. I was the object of friendly concern by dozens of total strangers.
4. I was treated with compassion by the very nice people at the first-aid station.
5. The injury was slight, so I didn't have to be carted off to a hospital and miss the ball game.

Has anything bad happened to you lately? The chances are it could have been worse. Why not make a list of the reasons you have to be grateful to God for sparing you a worse fate—and then thank Him!

AN ATTITUDE OF GRATITUDE

Shirley S. Stevens　　　　　　　　　　　　　　　　November 24

In every thing give thanks: for this is the will of God in Christ Jesus concerning you.
(1 Thessalonians 5:18 KJV)

In her book "The Hiding Place" Corrie ten Boom tells about an incident which taught her the principle of giving thanks in all things. During World War II, Corrie and her sister Betsy were arrested and imprisoned because they had hidden Jewish people in their homes to protect them from the Nazis.

At Ravensbruck Camp, the barracks were infested with fleas. One morning they read in their tattered Bible from 1 Thessalonians the reminder to rejoice in all things. Betsy said, "Corrie, we've got to give thanks for this barracks and even for these fleas."

Corrie replied, "No way am I going to thank God for fleas!"
But Betsy persuaded Corrie to do so.

During the following months they found that the guards left them alone in their barracks where they could study their Bible, talk openly, and even pray. Several months later they learned that the guards didn't enter the barracks because of the "blasted fleas."

Lord, help us to develop an attitude of gratitude, giving thanks each day for the good as well as the bad, the moments of annoyance as well as the blessings. Help us to trust that we will see Your guiding hand in all of our lives. Amen.

A PRAYER IN ALZHEIMER'S

Evelyn Minshull　　　　　　　　　　　　　　　　November 25

Lord,
only You could bring blessings—even from Alzheimer's!

When the husband of my youth
　　became the child of my old age,
my love for him grew more nurturing, more sheltering—
a dim reflection, Lord, of Your love for all Your children.
I thank You that I could release the romantic,
　　and willingly return to the maternal.

As I bathe and shave him—help him to dress,
remind him that our parents are gone, our children grown—
when I assure him once again that this is where we live,
    this house he built—
I thank You, Lord, for patience—
a miniature of Your patience with all Your children.

I praise You for his sweetness, Lord,
his sometimes-expressions of love.

But my greatest praise reverberates for this—
that in his childlikeness, he draws closer to You.
His adult abandonment of all things spiritual
has joined the clutter of other vanished memories.
Did You rejoice, last week—as I did—
    when he asked for the Bible?
I think You must have, as You rejoice
    when any of Your wandering ones return to You.

And when today, though Tuesday,
    he insisted we go to church—
when he walked with me to the lectern,
    and together we read the 23rd Psalm—
did Your heart burst with gladness—as mine did?

Lord, through the years,
You have heard my prayers for his turning to You.
Now, I rejoice in Your answer.
Now, I sense Your yearning to embrace this "child" we love.
Amen.

> *Let the little children come to me ... for it is to such as these that the kingdom of God belongs.*
> *(Mark 10:14 NRS)*

WAY TO THANKSGIVING

Charles A. Waugaman   November 26

Our Father, bless
    the persons that I judge, and those I fear,
    and add the many that I tend to scorn

scattered beneath Your heavens,
>far and near.
I want to come
>with gratitude and praise.
Wishing to sing
>thanksgiving to Your throne
>and gather blessings adequate
>for family and friends,
I am reminded,
>under the bounty of Your sun
>and rain, none are rejected:
>all receive the same,
In Your sweet Name. Amen.

HOMELESS MEN

Elizabeth M. Van Hook November 27

I was a stranger and you invited me in.
(Matthew 25:35 NIV)

The bus was late and the queue waiting had swelled into a crowd. It was the only bus available at this time of night to take us to the north side of Pittsburgh. Wearily, I climbed the steps, and searched for an available seat. There was only one, and it was at the back of the bus between two men with soiled clothes. I cringed about having to sit between them. One of the gentlemen had a dirty blanket draped like a cape around his thin hunched shoulders. They had trash bags resting at their feet. Where were they going? I understood from their conversation that their names were Stanley and Moses. They were homeless, and on their way to a church shelter for a shower, and a clean bed for the night.

I listened with interest as they discussed an incident that had happened earlier in the day in their community of homeless men and women who lived under the Duquesne Bridge. They talked about a turquoise ring that Stanley was wearing. His friend had told him that his ring was worthless. Glancing up from the book I was reading, I tried to get a better look at the ring. I asked Stanley if I could examine it more closely. I knew how distrustful homeless people were of anyone, and how afraid they were that their meager possessions would be stolen, so I was surprised when Stanley handed the ring to me.

During a recent vacation in Arizona, I learned about turquoise jewelry. Searching for the markings on the inside of his scratched worn ring for the Indian artist or tribe that crafted it, I could not see any. The inlaid workmanship, I knew, was authentic. It was similar to one I had purchased on my trip. Handing the ring back to Stanley, I reassured him that the value was more than the $2.98 that his friend had said it was worth!

Father, keep reminding me to look for the "pearl of great price," to search for You as hidden treasure, and I will not be led astray by materialism.

HOMELESS MEN, part 2
Elizabeth M. Van Hook   November 28

Trusting me now, he began to open up about his past. His mother had emigrated to Ohio from war-torn Poland. She worked two jobs to put food on the table, and had sacrificed to send Stanley to college, where he earned an engineering degree. His mother wished for a house of her own with shutters, a fireplace, and a garden of blooming roses. Stanley worked hard to buy his mother her dream house. My heart was going out to this man. What had happened to Stanley, who had had a career, a family, and a beautiful home—to leave him unemployed, estranged from his family, and living under a bridge on the Allegheny River?

As the bus continued to travel through Pittsburgh, we chatted like old friends. Suddenly, Stanley pulled an immaculate white box from his large garbage bag. How could this box stay so pristine when everything about Stanley was so unkempt? He uncovered the box, and took out a shiny harmonica. As he put it to his lips, a soft melancholy melody began to fill the crowded bus. I was so captured by the poignant music and the musician that I nearly passed my stop! I ran down the aisle of the bus, waving good-bye and telling Stanley and Moses what a terrific time I had with them. As I jumped off the bus, I praised God for giving me this unexpected meaningful experience.

Father, I thank You for giving us people in our journey through life who are different from us. Thank You for reminding me that we should not judge a person's character and self-worth by his appearance.

THANKFUL LIVING

Shirley S. Stevens   November 29

Giving thanks always for all things unto God and the Father in the name of our Lord Jesus Christ.
(Ephesians 5:20 KJV)

When I travel, I take time to learn how to say "thank you" in the language of the people whom I visit. Even in The United States, we can make an effort to learn how to say thanks in a Native American language. For example, "Ahéhee'" means "thank you" in Navajo.

When I visited Japan, I learned to say "arigato" and "oishi" to tell my hostess "thank you" and to convey how delicious the food was.

In how many languages can you express your thanks? I have learned the following: "Tack så mycket" in Swedish, "Merci" in French, "Gracias" in Spanish, and "Danke" in German. On the Internet, we can learn how to say thanks in over 465 languages.

Dear Lord, help me to remember to thank others. And please accept my gratitude for all that You do for me.

LOVE IN ANY LANGUAGE

Joan Clayton   November 30

How great is the love the Father has lavished on us, that we should be called children of God!
(1 John 3:1 NIV)

"I called to invite you to my graduation, and I'll be looking for you." I assured Robert that my husband and I would be there. It had been ten years since I had taught Robert when he was a lovable little second grader.

I looked over the program to discover Robert was the valedictorian. I beamed with pride. After he delivered the wonderful speech he had written, imagine my surprise when I heard Robert say, "I want to recognize a teacher I had in second grade who means a lot to me." He reached under the podium and held out a great big cuddly teddy bear. I ran to meet him, and we hugged and cried.

Robert's dad hugged me tight, too, as he handed me a bouquet of carnations. He didn't speak English, and his words in Spanish came so fast I couldn't keep up, but the unconditional love came through loud and clear. The tears in his eyes said it all. I felt love coming from a beautiful sincere heart, and where there is love in the heart, any language is understood.

Love is the language of the heart.

WHAT HAPPENED?

Lorena Estep December 1

> But those who hope in the LORD will renew their strength.
> They will soar on wings like eagles; they will run and not grow weary, they will walk and not be faint.
> (Isaiah 40:31 NIV)

I was sitting in my sunroom, having devotions, when I was startled by a loud thud against a window. I ran over and looked out. A large hawklike bird, resembling a small eagle, lay beak-down in the snow with its wings outspread. As I watched, it slowly raised its head and shook it, then looked around dazedly, as if wondering what had happened. Suddenly with renewed strength, the bird mounted up and flew away.

I was reminded of the verse in Isaiah 40:31, and thought of some of the times in my life I'd soared along thinking all was going well. Then out of nowhere, a traumatic event would pop up and knock me down. There I would be, figuratively reeling, wondering what had happened.

Thankfully, the Lord was always present, as He promises in His word. He strengthened me when I was weak and troubled, and renewed me as the eagle.

LET US REJOICE

Rhonda Hodge December 2

> This is the day the Lord has made; let us rejoice and be glad in it.
> (Psalm 118:24 NIV)

There are 365 days in a year. I can imagine what it would be like to live every single day according to this command. It would be a glorious life! To rejoice and be glad, even when I don't feel like it, requires that I live according to God's promise and not my emotions.

So I have to ask myself why I don't live every day according to this Scripture. My answer is that I have none. I can think of no good reason. The only thing stopping me from living the rest of my days in this manner would be my lack of faith and trust in God.

I should never allow this to happen. So tomorrow when I wake up, I must remind myself that this is the day that the Lord has made; let me rejoice and be glad in it.

Help me, Lord, to live this day to the fullest. Amen.

GOD GAVE US
Betty Redmon December 3

The flowers, mountains, and the trees,
Babbling brooks and the soft spring breeze,
Music, songs, and the birds that fly,
Stars to shine so bright in the sky,

Seashore and oceans to roll evermore—
All these were left at our earthly door.
The riches and wealth of life unfold
Whenever we open our eyes to behold.

These gifts of the Father no one would exceed,
For to see and to know is all that we need.
This Kingdom of happiness God to us lends.
Then to all He adds one more gift to us: Friends!

God, who gives us richly all things to enjoy
(1 Timothy 6:17 NKJ)

ENLIGHTENED BY THE EYES OF A CHILD
Violoa Ruelke Gommer December 4

I pray also that the eyes of your heart may be enlightened.
(Ephesians 1:18 NIV)

It was early in the morning; I was busy setting the breakfast table for my husband and three grandchildren. The oldest one woke up and came to keep me company. I poured my cup of coffee, then filled a glass with juice for her. We went to sit in our favorite spot by the windows that overlook the lake. As I pulled the blinds back, anticipating the beauty of the clouds and sky reflected in the water, all that greeted us was a thick, white fog.

We laughed, realizing that we wouldn't be able to enjoy the anticipated view. Then Madeliene said, "It looks like a piece of white paper from God. What should we draw on it today, Gramma?"

What a delightful insight. The beginning of each day is a white piece of paper from God, who offers me a fresh, new start. I must decide how I will use it. What will I *draw on it* for my life today?

Lord of my days, guide my choices as I seek to serve You this day. Help me to greet each new day with the eyes of a child and the expectation of a child's heart. Amen

A TRUNK OF MEMORIES

Joan Clayton   **December 5**

Then those who feared and loved the Lord spoke often of him to each other. And he had a Book of Remembrance drawn up in which he recorded the names of those who fear him and loved to think about him.
(Malachi 3:16 TLB)

Going through my trunk one day,
I stopped to read and then
Memories of my life appeared,
Blessing me again.

I lingered on some photos
Of those no longer here.
I thanked God for the time I had
With those I hold so dear.

I found Granddaddy's Bible,
Its pages old and torn.
My name was written in this book
On the day that I was born.

I closed the trunk, remembering,
Our lives are short at best.
So fill your trunk with goodness
And God will do the rest.

WHO AM I?

Barbara A. Croce   **December 6**

Do not fear, for I have redeemed you; I have called you by name; you are Mine!
(Isaiah 43:1 NAS)

What matters most in my life? Where do I get my worth? What is my role in society? Am I a wife first, or the owner of a business? A mother, or a member of the body of Christ? An intercessor, a cook, chauffeur, nurse? A woman?

I was mulling over these questions in heart and mind when I came across this verse of Scripture in Isaiah: "You are Mine!" That's what the Lord says about me—I am His! Before I am anything else in life, I am His beloved daughter, and He is jealous for me.

I closed my eyes, took a deep breath, and allowed the thought of being His to permeate every cell in my body, every corner in my mind, every impression in my spirit. All of my worth comes from this simple truth: I belong to the King of the universe.

Yes, by His grace, I will be the best wife I can be. Yes, I am a mother, an employer, an intercessor, and so much more. Foremost, though, He made me His own. He sings over me with joy.

HIS MERCY ENDURES FOREVER

Micki Roberts   **December 7**

(Give thanks) to him which led His people through the wilderness: for His mercy endureth for ever.
(Psalm 136:16 KJV)

This verse refers to the Israelites who wandered through the wilderness (desert) after God delivered them from the bondage of Pharaoh.

When we think about the Exodus account of the Israelites' sojourn in the wilderness, we might wonder why God allowed them to remain there for so long. The answer is simple: because of their disobedience.

Why do we many times find ourselves traveling through a desert place? Could it be due to our disobedience? Perhaps. However, I do not believe this is the only reason God allows us to wander in the wilderness. I believe God allows these times in our lives to: teach us, test us, and mold & shape us into the Christians He wants us to be.

Many times we enter a desert place after making it through one of life's storms. At first we find ourselves feeling confused or disoriented. We long for the comfort of God's peace. Nevertheless, we must be patient and endure this time of instruction.

Do you find yourself in a desert place right now? Cling to the Father and allow Him to guide you through to the other side. Then, reflect on the lessons you have learned. Keep in mind that this desert experience has been allowed by your loving Father.

SNOW

Helen Kammerdiener December 8

    Thank You, Lord, for snow.
    Thank You for
        the light, fluffy snow that
            covers trash and dirt in my world,
        the deep blanket of snow that absorbs
            the raucousness of a noisy city,
        and the soft, packable snow good for
            snowmen and sleds and skis.
    Thank You for
        the unique beauty of each snowflake
        and for the purity of its whiteness
            twinkling in the winter sun.
    Thank You, Lord, for snow.

SONSHINE

Debbie Rempel December 9

I have heard it said
the sun shines on
the other side of the
clouds.

In heaven is where
the Son shines,
and the streets are
made of gold.

Just as in nature,
some days the clouds
hide our view of the Son.
And when a ray of sun
shines through,
Jesus lights the

sky of my life.

Through an open door,
Heaven shines like the
golden sunset.

SNOWFLAKES

Pat Collins December 10

The silently falling snowflakes
cover the ground in a blanket of white.
To watch them twisting and turning,
is really quite a sight.

Drifting down from heaven,
so quietly they fall.
Making a beautiful picture
to be enjoyed by all.

Just another way God reminds us
that He is always there.
No matter what the weather,
we're in His loving care.

THE EASTER PEOPLE

Judy Barron December 11

For the message of the cross is foolishness to those who are perishing, but to us who are being saved it is the power of God.

(1 Corinthians 1:18 NIV)

We are the Easter people. We have been to the cross and to the graveyard. If the action stopped at the cross, then all would be foolishness, death and despair. But we know "the rest of the story!" We have also been to the grave and have seen the stone rolled away, and the grave cloths rolled up, and the empty space. And so, we know the true power of the cross—it is the death of death! It is the power of God. It is resurrection and salvation. It is grace and love. It is the defeat of sin and life for all eternity at the right hand of God.

Abba, Father, we are the Easter people, and so we can look death in the face and praise Your Holy Name. We can say goodbye to our loved ones, and know that we will see them again in a glorious reunion beneath the throne of God. Indeed, we are the Easter people. Praise Thy Holy Name! Alleluia! In Whose Name we are most blessed. Amen.

THE GIFT

Gertrude Wilson　　　　　　　　　　　　　　　　December 12

Years ago a King was born
His fame revealed throughout the land.
Those who surrounded HIM had no
　idea of the mystery God hid in this man.

Decades ago a child was born
Known only as a carpenter's son
Away in a manger he laid unaware
　of the multitude of lives He would spare.

Eons ago, a Son was given
God's gift to all mankind
A blueprint of His life had been scripted
　before the beginning of time.

Centuries ago a Counselor was born
His purpose concealed from common man
For He had a task He'd have to endure,
　standing proxy for sinful man.

Scriptures foretold the life of One
who'd become the redeemer for all.
He did it unselfishly knowing the cost
　the cross He would inevitably haul.

Years ago and years to come
Jesus paid the price in full
He is the reward to all who'll receive
　the greatest gift of God's love.

WHATEVER HAPPENED TO CHRISTMAS?
Florence W. Biros   December 13

Whatever happened to Christmas?
Where did "Christ's mass" go?
How did we let it evaporate
Like the dirty, melting snow?

Remember how we thought of
The wise men carrying gifts from afar,
Treasures meant for the infant child
As they followed the brilliant star?

Remember how we touched our lives
With songs that filled our hearts,
"Silent Night" and words of joy
That could make the tear drops start?

Remember how we made the season
A time to seek out the poor,
And offer praise to our glorious Lord
Because we felt safe and secure?

How did it change to such chaos
And shopping become a mob scene,
When greed causes shoppers
To become violent and mean?

Store owners now forbid workers
To say "Merry Christmas" to us,
For fear some other kind of believers
Will cause a disturbance and fuss.

We seem to forget that Christ
Is the basis, the real reason,
For us to have and enjoy
This special Christmas season.

The Salvation Army's bell ringers
Have been banned from some of the stores,
While shoppers simply pass them by,
Trying their best to ignore.

We need to get back to Christmas
And fill it with worship and praise,
When "holidays" become once more
The season of holy-days.

When once again we all pray for
The need for peace on this earth,
As we celebrate the advent of Christ's coming
And the reason for Jesus' birth.

A MEMORY FILLED EVENING

Pat Rivet   December 14

      The church soloist sang a medley of Christmas songs, ending with one of the most moving renditions I had ever heard of "O Holy Night." Her singing sent my mind back to a time when I was in high school, and a young Korean boy came to our church in the East Liberty section of Pittsburgh, Pennsylvania with his new family, who were members. They had adopted him from a Missionary School since he had no family and was in need of medical attention. He quickly was learning English and teaching us much about his world.

      On Christmas Eve he had been our soloist and singing, "O Holy Night." He told us the melody was the same as the Korean National Anthem. As he sang with feeling and power, it seemed to me no one was breathing. I don't think there were many dry eyes in the congregation that evening.

      After his solo, the congregation stood as one, clapping for this young man's gift to us in his new homeland. I never heard our church members respond like this before nor since.

      The peace of this Sunday evening will stay with me for a long time. It has renewed my attitude of gratitude this Holiday Season.

THE GREATEST GIFT

Carole Lang   December 15

Tis the season—Christ the reason
We have hope and joy today,
Celebrating His arrival
And His birth this Christmas day.

Christ's the answer to life's problems,
Took all sin to Calvary.
Loving us, He died to save us,
Shed His blood to set us free.

Let us worship Christ our Savior.
He is worthy of all praise.
He'll not leave us nor forsake us.
He'll be with us all our days.

He is greater than the greatest.
He is higher than most high.
He will always be there for us
When unto ourselves we die.

Father God, we praise and thank You
For such a love as this,
Though never could we understand
A love as great as His.

ANGELS

Kathy Johnson December 16

Glory to God in the highest.
(Luke 2:14 NIV)

Purchasing a small Mary, Joseph, and baby Jesus to put on my desk, I made my way back into the showroom and picked up a box with an angel. The angel would fill out the scene. As Christmas approaches, we are bombarded with angels. Not only do we visually see portrayals of them, we also sing about the angels' roles in the story of redemption.

Traveling home late in December, from northern Minnesota, we found the two lane road icy. Enjoying the winter scene, I turned my head back from viewing a red barn against the stark white snow, when in front of us an oncoming semi loomed in our lane. My husband fought the steering wheel, but our vehicle kept going because of the ice. I committed us into the hands of the Lord. At what seemed the last moment of our lives, a huge push from the side of the car sent us flying into a ditch filled with snow. We were uninjured.

It is written: "For he will command his angels concerning you to guard you in all your ways" (Psalm 91:11 NIV). Our response to being saved on the icy road was the same as the angels out in the fields on Christmas Day—we glorified God. Our earthly life had been preserved. Even more so, we join the angels and glorify God for sending us His Son to redeem us from our sins so we may live eternally.

CELEBRATING ADVENT
Karen Miller December 17

*And the bow shall be in the cloud; and I will look upon it,
that I may remember the everlasting covenant between God
and every living creature of all flesh that is upon the earth*
(Genesis 9:16 KJV)

When our basement flooded, we lost most of our Christmas decorations. We were sad about our loss of Christmas favorites, but we were blessed when friends and neighbors shared their ornaments and decorations. The figures from our nativity set survived the muddy waters, but we had no stable for them.

One of my children suggested that we use our Noah's Ark. We put hay on the ramp and arranged the animals so that they could watch over the baby Jesus. Angels which had belonged to my mother looked down from a shelf, and a yellow tarnished star from our first Christmas tree glowed atop the roof of the ark.

The baby Jesus smiled in His crib on the deck.

One of my daughters drew a rainbow and colored it with her crayons. We taped it on the wall above the ark.

Thank You, Lord, for reminding us of the connection between two events in the Bible: The Flood and The Birth of the Christ Child in Bethlehem. We remember Your promise in both.

BABY IN THE MANGER
Dave Evans December 18

Winter wind whistles a chilly tune
as it rushes through the canyon;
its melancholy music intrigues our ears—
this Australian Shepherd dog and me,
sitting in my horse's stall,
as he contentedly crops his hay.

On a winter night centuries ago,
perhaps the wind rustled
through cracks in the stable walls
as oxen dined next to a newborn baby,
wrapped and cradled in a manger;
out of the night, after angels sang,
shepherds came and bowed;
the eastern star later led wise men
to bring gifts befitting a king.

This winter night my heart bows
before the baby in the manger,
and my life, unwrapped,
I offer as a gift to the King of Kings.

WORSHIP THE KING

Martha Rogers   **December 19**

While they were there, the time came for the baby to be born, and she gave birth to her firstborn, a son. She wrapped him in cloths and placed him in a manger, because there was no room for them in the inn.

(Luke 2:6-7 NIV)

Toys, Christmas trees and candy canes,
A hint of frost kissing window panes,
Santa Claus with his sleigh bells ringing,
People scurrying from store to store
In a frenzied haste to get it all done.
Children laughing, having great fun,
knowing that Santa is on his way
To bring gifts and toys on that day.

One star outshines them all,
Coming to rest over a simple stall.
A mother's prayer, whispered low,
As shepherds come and bow.
Angels sing in the sky above,
Proclaiming the arrival of peace and love.
Three kings see the star one night
And come to see the source of light.

Bowing down with gifts they brought,
They worship the babe as they ought.

As Christmas comes this year,
which scene will you hold dear?
Will you see a baby small,
Born in a lowly manger stall?
He came to heal our sorrow
And give us hope for tomorrow.
Bow down and worship the King
Who gave His life so we may sing
Of a Savior willing His life to give,
So all who believe may eternally live.

O worship the King, born this day!

THE CHRISTMAS SCRAMBLER

Judy Ferrell   **December 20**

Now his parents went to Jerusalem every year at the feast of the passover.

(Luke 2:41 KJV)

The Christmas Scrambler looked like a foreign language: TAYIINTV, GREAMN, YBTHARID, GLENSA, NMWIEES, OIRVSA. At first glance, none of it made sense. However, knowing the words pertained to Christmas helped unravel the mystery. Soon, I rearranged the letters into meaningful order: NATIVITY, MANGER, BIRTHDAY, ANGELS, WISE MEN, SAVIOR. They all made sense now.

Mary and Joseph were puzzled by Jesus' questions to them in Luke 2:49. They were in the habit of going to Jerusalem every year at Passover, and nothing like this had ever happened. Mary "kept all these sayings in her heart." (v. 51) It may have been years before understanding came to her.

Many people are in the habit of celebrating Christmas with gifts, parties, cards, and trees. The real meaning of Christmas is a mystery to them. However, seeds are planted in their hearts each year. Perhaps this is the year that those seeds will take root, and they will understand that Christmas is the celebration of the birth of the Savior of the world. Perhaps this is the year that NATIVITY,

MANGER, BIRTHDAY, ANGELS, WISE MEN, and SAVIOR will make sense to them.

Father, help me to be faithful, to keep planting seeds with friends and loved ones who don't yet know Jesus as Savior. In Jesus' Name, Amen.

THE WINTER SOLSTICE
Mary A. Koepke — December 21

I was alone most of the day; my husband was out and about. I spent a lot of time at the kitchen table with last-minute card writing and gift wrapping. Taking a break in the rocking chair by the double glass doors, I sensed something different. A dull cloudy day, a heaviness in the air—all eerily empty. Not a living thing in sight except the small blue spruce, planted as a winter bird refuge. Everything looked dead. Leftover wild flowers made dried arrangements through a skim of snow. Even the juncos, the harbingers of winter, hid somewhere in the woods. A draft from a chill wind crept under the door sill, making me grateful for a heated home and cozy sweater.

Our son-in-law's mother died that evening—Tuesday, December 21—The Winter Solstice. Although Mary suffered many years with debilitating Huntington's disease, her death in faraway Nebraska was a shock. So I pondered on Mary's passing on the Winter Solstice—the shortest day of the year, beginning of winter, the turning point. And I recalled legends and festivals of our many different celebrations of light. Our human hope and trust that darkness will pass and spring will break forth as always. Mary passed from darkness to light and now lives in the presence of her Lord. It was His special Christmas gift to her.

THE CHRISTMAS BABY
Elizabeth Irby — December 22

The time came for the baby to be born.
(Luke 2:6 NIV)

"It's time! Allison is at the hospital; the baby is on the way! We'll be there in an hour to pick you up," my parents said. After twenty-four hours of labor, my nephew arrived. I remember holding him and seeing my reflection in his eyes. While I wondered what he thought of me, the corners of his mouth turned up in a slight grin. With that first brief encounter, I experienced a love like never before. After twelve years, he's still one of my favorite people.

Two thousand years ago, another baby was born. With no hospitals or modern conveniences available, this child arrived in a stable. Grandparents and aunts were not his first visitors; animals were. I wonder when this infant named Jesus realized His purpose. What a burden on such a tiny being! I met this Christmas baby twenty years ago when I accepted His gift of salvation. Since then, I try to reflect Jesus' love so others will want to meet Him, too. Each Christmas I rejoice because that Child is now my best friend.

Father, thank You for the gift of family and for giving us Jesus. Amen.

MARY'S LULLABY

Jana Carman — December 23

Little one, who stretched and kicked
beneath my heart (and sometimes hic'd),
precious boy, my pain and joy,
welcome to the world.

I, whom you will call Your mother,
he, whom people call Your father,
even shepherds gladly gather
here to bid you welcome.

Did angels sing Your farewell song?
All heaven's riches were Your own;
now Your mother's breast is home,
and I bid You welcome.

My voice Your choir, my lap Your throne—
hush, my wee one; close Your eyes.
Immanuel, God in disguise,
welcome to Your world.

CHRISTMAS

Gloria Hall Troup — December 24

It is the night before Christmas and all I hear are glorious Christmas carols celebrating the birth of baby Jesus. God sent Himself to earth in the body of an infant so He could save and heal us. Thus Jesus became man, God's only begotten Son. God sacrificed His Son for us so that we could "have everlasting life."

Let the celebration begin! The bells, the drums, the chimes, the organ ... all celebrating His birth. He is the same as He was two thousand years ago. He still heals, performs miracles, and saves people who are hurting. Because of Him our lives are better while we are alive and as Christians, we will be in heaven with Him when we die.

Again, let the celebration begin. Our Messiah, "King of kings and the Lord of lords," has come. He will reign forever and ever. He not only saved my soul, but personally came to heal my body. He will always be my King, my Master, the Great Physician. Prince of Peace and Savior of the World.

Yes, miracles are for today, and Christmas is a time for miracles because nothing is impossible with God. Praise God from whom all blessings flow, and may everyone know that Jesus loves him/her. Amen.

CHRISTMAS ME, LORD

Charles A. Waugaman December 25

Gabriel me this day, O Father,
with personal appearance messages
and help me look
the right direction
before the vision fades.

Anthem me on hillsides of duty
with northern lights of wonder
and startle me awake
before the silences
return.

Mary me, Lord,
with willingness to receive
the pregnancy of love
so startling it will seek
and save
the lost.

Stable me, O Infant Promise,
that those in need of hope
and compassion
may come, find, adore You
in the manger of my life
and dare to leave—
praising and telling.

BEHOLD, HIS GLORY!

Jana Carman   **December 26**

Wisely, they trusted their GPS,
those travelers expecting kings
in palaces, not peasant's home.
But when their Global Positioning Star
pinpointed "Here," they placed their gifts
and themselves in homage at his feet.
(Apart from common lamps within
and uncommon astral glow without,
there was no haloed glory-light,
no nimbus crowning Christ. Not yet.)

But three other awestruck men
would one day see—shining through
as if some shutters, long kept closed,
had opened—light streaming out,
Shekinah glow blazing through His flesh.

The Son shines a glory all His own. And we
behold, bemused, His Glory fills us too.

STRAIGHT

Peter Paulson   **December 27**

Combating world hunger is a passion of mine. So is saving the environment for my grandchildren by keeping things out of landfills. These concerns have combined into a hobby—recycled birdhouses. Scraps of wood from our subflooring, my neighbor's new deck, and my father-in-law's hoary aged apple boxes get cut up and then nailed together. Using odds and ends requires some ingenious cutting to straighten or true up the pieces. An un-square piece of wood, pressed against a straight guide and guided through the whirling blade, results only in a smaller un-square piece of wood. Hand guiding of the board is required.

I have struggled with keeping the blade and my marked cut line in the same hemisphere as I push the wood through. Not so long ago, I found a marvelous trick. Once the cut is started and my ten fingers are out of the way, all I have to do is watch the end point. The saw will cut a straight line to where my eye is focused.

Kind of like heaven, I suppose.

I'm looking, Father.

REJOICING IN HEAVEN

Annette M. Irby   **December 28**

Or what woman, having ten silver coins, if she loses one coin… when she has found it, she calls her friends… saying, "Rejoice with me, for I have found the piece which I lost. Likewise, I say to you, there is joy in the presence of the angels of God over one sinner who repents.

(Luke 15:8-10 NKJ)

Have you ever danced for joy? There have been times I've wanted to, as when we found out we were pregnant with our first baby. I probably shout more often than dance. Dancing just doesn't seem very, what? Adult-like? People look at you funny. But I believe Jesus is describing some rather wonderful celebrating in heaven.

First, who is celebrating? I used to think it was the angels. But Jesus said, "There is joy *before* the angels of God" when someone repents. It looks as though God Himself is celebrating! Imagine what that looks like. God has no inhibitions. When someone accepts Jesus' hard-bought gift of salvation, I believe God celebrates, inviting the angels to join in. What a beautiful display this must be. He celebrates you! And He celebrates every new member of His family. Let's bring more people to Him and join in!

Dear Lord, please show us Your heart for those who would be Yours, and let us partake in the celebration of someone turning from sin to You. In Jesus' name. Amen.

WHAT SONG SHALL I SING?
Connie A. Ansong December 29
Ezra 3:10-13

Father, we pray for Your presence in our new beginning. Lord, without You we can do nothing. As we begin to tread on grounds unknown to us we ask for Your guidance and directions with every decision that we make. We want our decision to match Your will and plan for our lives. Let our actions be the expression of Your will for our lives as well as for Your glorification. Above all, we pray for a spirit of listening in our hearts and being obedient to Your Word.

We also know that this new beginning is an occasion to experience loss. Our old ways of thinking, living, and planning must be abandoned, and, indeed, something new take its place. We cannot be certain what the future will or will not bring, and we also know that we are not alone. Sometimes the old things should be abandoned, for the new beginning is a necessary thing.

We offer each new beginning to Thee, Oh Lord! What song shall we sing?

NOT THE END
Barbara Ann Yonnotti December 30

> eleventh hour
> flowing one into another
> year into year
> I fell asleep
> an eternal lullaby
> not separate or alone
> one with God

In a moment, in the twinkling of an eye, in the last trumpet, for it shall sound, and the dead shall be raised incorruptible, and we—we shall be changed.
(1 Corinthians 15:52)

INTO THE CLOUDS
Dave Evans December 31

One word of command, one shout from the archangel, one blast from the trumpet of God and the Lord himself will come down from Heaven! Those who have died in Christ will be the

first to rise, and then we who are still living on the earth will be swept up with them into the clouds to meet the Lord in the air. And after that we shall be with him for ever. So by all means use this message to encourage one another.
(1 Thessalonians 4:16-18 PHILLIPS)

Slowly the curtain of black is drawn back;
revealing an expanse of billowy clouds,
completely filling the morning sky.
My heart yearns as my ears listen
to hear a shout,
a trumpet call to come
into the clouds
to be with You,
forever;
and I wonder—
will today be the day?

Suddenly, and at any time,
with a shout and the trumpet blast;
in the twinkling of an eye,
those who have died in Christ
and those of us alive, having
received Christ as Savior,
will be caught up into the clouds
to be with the Lord—
what a celebration!
What a reunion!
Could today be th

CONTRIBUTORS OF VOLUME XII:

Connie A. Ansong, RN, began with a professional understanding of human behaviors, which encouraged her to seek a closer relationship with God. Now she wants to share all she's learning. Writing is another step in her exciting, spiritual journey. [3/1, 4/9, 12/29]

Ruth Baldwin's Christian parents were 40 and 52 years of age when she was born. Their teachings have been called old-fashioned, but the Lord's Words are everlasting and never-changing. That's what she proclaims! Always! [1/16, 3/9, 4/23]

Marcie Banks, freelance writer, worked as reporter and church page editor for New Kensington PA Daily Dispatch, did heavy editing for Whitaker House, wrote Aglow Bible Study #9, *The Call of Jesus*. She lives in New Wilmington, PA. [11/12]

Judy Barron is retired from Edinboro University of PA. She attends Trinity Lutheran Church in McKean, PA where she is a communion assistant, lector, altar care attendant, and Worship Committee member. Her prayer journal is central to her devotions. [2/20, 4/8, 8/25, 11/15, 12/11]

Florence Biros saw a longtime dream reached this year when her novel, *Dog Jack*, became a movie. [12/13]

Joy C. Bradford received her Bachelors Degree from the University of Texas. She and her husband have retired to McKinney, TX to be closer to their family. Joy writes for several magazines and has contributed to anthologies. [3/21, 4/27, 5/11, 6/18, 8/29, 9/21, 10/6]

Connie Bretz has sold over 3000 articles, meditations, poetry, interviews, columns. In 2005 she produced a documentary movie called *The Original Dancing Band*. She is an avid bicyclist and bookworm. Her great ambition is to publish more and more and more. [3/3, 4/2, 5/13, 6/10, 10/20]

Helene Burgess lives in Passaic, NJ where she, her 92-year-old mom, and her whole family are enjoying her retirement. She desires to unclutter her home, read more, and take early morning walks in the park. [4/16, 9/28]

Annettee Buzdban is an author, freelance writer, and religion columnist. Her column *Inspirations* is featured each week in the *Daily Herald* and *Zion-Benton News* in Lake County, Illinois. She has been published in various e-zines and magazines. ahrtwrites2u@aol.com [1/10, 2/1, 7/2, 8/20, 11/5]

Jana Carman (Salem, NJ) is a pastor's wife, musician, teacher, and writer. She writes in many genres, including a book of performance poetry and monologues, *People of Faith*, Lillenas Drama. [1/19, 2/9, 3/6, 4/15, 5/15, 7/21, 9/16, 11/22, 12/23, 12/26]

Kay Clark, retired English teacher from Ball State University, a high school, and Anderson University currently supervises student teachers. Widowed from a Disciple of Christ pastor, she is the mother of four, grandmother of eight, and soon-to-be great-grandmother of two. [10/22]

Joan Clayton is a retired educator. Joan's passion is writing. She is presently Religion Columnist for her local newspaper and is also working on her next book. She has been published in many anthologies and in five *Chicken Soup* series. [1/29, 2/2, 3/2, 4/12, 5/5, 6/20, 7/3, 8/9, 8/19, 9/27, 10/18, 11/30, 12/5]

Carol Cleal from Cortland, OH is a Manager of a Mental Health Unit. She serves on her church's praise and worship team and attends a small group Bible study. She is married with two sons and three grandchildren. [5/19, 8/11, 11/20]

Gloria Clover, editor of ten volumes of *Penned From the Heart*, also writes Christian romance. She works in Youth and Cell Ministries through her home church of Emmanuel Christian. [2/19]

Pat Collins, mother of three, grandmother of seven, and great-grandmother, writes children's stories and poems. Her poems have been adapted to music, appear in church bulletins, and have been published by International Library of Poetry. [2/3, 4/20, 5/16, 6/15, 7/28, 8/2, 9/7, 10/2, 11/13, 12/10]

Barbara Croce is a personal trainer, physical therapy assistant and a freelance writer whose work appears in *Chicken Soup for the Soul*, *Signs of the Times*, and other publications. Check her web site out at www.glorywriter.4t.com [12/6]

Flavia Crowner, a former Art teacher, is now spinning stories for Jesus. Her first novel *Pie Pantry*, in her Sunny Farnum series with a wheelchair bound character was published. She lives in Fennville, MI with Jenna her black lab service dog. [3/13, 4/30]

Thomas Dallio lives in upstate New York where he is deepening his relationship with Jesus. [2/27]

Penny Deary lives in Irvine California with her husband, Kevin, along with 2 dogs, 2 cats, and a horse. Blessed by the Lord, she enjoys quilting, writing, walking with her dogs and riding her horse. [3/23, 9/26]

Leigh DeLozier, a freelance writer, editor and Christian speaker, lives in McDonough, GA, with her husband and two children. Her first devotional book, *Work-from-Home Moms' Devotions to Go*, will be published in Spring 2006. Visit her online at www.leighdelozier.net. [6/9, 7/22, 9/1, 10/19, 11/17]

Angie Dilmore enjoys writing for children and inspirational devotions. She is currently working on a year-long devotional for kids. She lives in Pittsburgh, PA with her husband and twin sons. [3/25, 8/3, 9/12]

Marie DisBrow's articles, poetry, and devotions have appeared in numerous Christian publications, including *In Touch*, *The Lutheran Journal*, *The Secret Place*, and *Women Alive!* Marie says, "My desire is that my writing would encourage people and please God." www.wildernesswritings.com. [1/17, 3/15]

Lorena Estep lives near Bellwood, PA with her husband, Charles. She enjoys writing, reading, gardening, and travel. She has been published in *Writers' Journal*, *On the Line*, *The Secret Place*, *Mature Living*, and *Purpose*. She also writes a ten-page bimonthly newsletter for her home church. [1/5, 2/15, 3/17, 4/3, 5/23, 6/11, 7/7, 8/8, 9/6, 10/7, 11/8, 12/1]

Anita Estes wears many hats as a wife, mother of three, teacher: Who's Who Among American Teachers, artist, and writer—published in *Upper Room*, online, and elsewhere. She is also a worship dancer and aspiring novelist. [5/27, 9/17]

Dave Evans is the estimator for a commercial electrical contractor. As a freelance writer, he has had poems and articles published. He and Matt, his therapy dog, visit, cheer, and encourage patients in nursing homes and a retirement center. [1/6, 4/14, 5/26, 6/4, 7/27, 8/24, 9/11, 10/28, 12/18, 12/31]

Marjorie K. Evans is a freelance writer with many published articles. She enjoys her family, church, writing, reading, and needlework. She lives in Stanton, CA. [3/26, 6/3, 9/10, 11/9]

Judy Ferrell is a former elementary school teacher and high school guidance counselor. She's active in her church. She and her husband are blessed with two daughters, two sons-in-law named Dave, and two granddaughters. [9/19, 10/14, 12/20]

Dolores Fruth resides in a faith-based retirement community where she has opportunities to further her love of writing poetry about her personal experiences, family, and devotion to God. Her poems are published monthly and have been adapted to music. [2/8, 6/28]

Viola Ruelke Gommer, RN, MSN, is the mother of two, grandmother of six, and wife of a retired United Methodist pastor. Vi has been involved in mission work in the US, Bolivia, Haiti, Guyana, Zimbabwe, Dominican Republic, Russia, and Cuba. [12/4]

Marion E. Gorman and her husband live in Manns Choice, PA. Retired, they have six married children and 18 grandchildren. She enjoys sharing God's love through her writing, gardening, and scrapbooking. Her new project is a church newsletter. [1/13, 4/7, 5/17, 6/12, 8/16, 11/16]

Charles Harrel lives with his family in Portland, OR where he directs HisPlaceOutreach. He served as a senior pastor for thirty years before pursuing a writing ministry. Charles enjoys writing, teaching, and family camping trips. [1/22, 2/13, 3/7, 5/21, 8/10]

Janice May Harris is a teacher, illustrator/writer living in Portland, Oregon. She is a member of Oregon Christian Writers. [5/30]

Tom Harshbarger, born in Youngstown, OH in 1924, has written poetry all of his life while living: marrying, working in railroad, lumber, and car sales, and retiring. [2/22]

Delores Hartman, artist, photographer, lyricist, retired teacher; past worker and director of the Help Center of SW Blair County is published in *A Tribute for Mothers, The Path, The Sentinel, The Standard, Byline, Guideposts,* and fourteen books desk-top published. [11/19]

Cindy Hawkins makes her home in Irmo, South Carolina, with her husband Tim, a minister. They have three children: Nathan (11), Rachel (6), and Benjamin (1). Cindy has been a freelance writer for four years. [5/8, 7/1, 10/31, 11/6]

Audrey Kletscher Helbling is a freelance writer living in Faribault, Minnesota. She has been published in *God Answers Prayers Military Edition, The Lutheran Digest, Minnesota Moments* magazine, regional poetry anthologies, greeting cards and more. Audrey is married with three children. [2/23, 8/30]

Mary Herron is the wife of a United Methodist minister. They have three grown children and five granddaughters. She does Home Health part time, writes, and works among her flower beds as a hobby. [10/21]

Betty Jane Hewitt, journalist and newspaper columnist for over thirty years, has had daily devotionals published in *The Quiet Hour, These Days,* and numerous other Christian publications. [2/5, 6/14]

Lisa Hill resides in Elmira, NY with her husband, Terry, daughter, Victoria, and her sons, Jesse and Beau. Please feel free to contact her at TLHILL@pkFamily.com. [3/4]

CJ Hitz is a speaker with True Lies, a ministry that challenges people of all ages in the area of media and what we take into our minds. Get to know CJ better by going to www.cjspeaks.com. [2/21, 3/22, 7/17, 7/29]

Rhonda Hodge has been married to a wonderful man named Ken for twelve years. They live in the country with their two shih tzu and cat. She enjoys reading and gardening. [6/26, 12/2]

Joseph M. Hopkins is a musician, missionary, teacher, and Presbyterian minister who has spent his life promoting the Gospel. [1/1, 3/27, 4/13, 5/29, 7/13, 8/12, 10/15, 11/23]

Annette M. Irby is a wife and mother who lives in Washington state and enjoys writing songs, articles, and novels. Her articles have appeared in *Northwest Christian Author, The Christian Journal* and the devotional *The Secret Place.* [12/28]

Elizabeth Irby is a freelancer who writes about spiritual issues for a variety of publications. She and her husband, Houston, recently adopted their first child, Johnny Mac, from South Korea. They reside in Hillsboro, Oregon. [12/22]

Ida Jancso, widow, mother of two, grandmother of two, lives in West Middlesex, PA. She enjoys art, gardening, and church activities. [6/25, 8/22]

Kathy Johnson lives in Minnesota with her husband and six children. Publishing credits include *Christmas in the Country*, *Lutheran Woman's Quarterly*, and devotions in *Portals of Prayer* for adults and *My Devotions* for children. A freelance writer, editor, and speaker. [6/5, 7/11, 8/18, 9/2, 12/16]

Helen Kammerdiener of New Bethlehem, PA, a retired teacher, church association co-coordinator, food pantry site manager, community choir narrator, lay speaker, Sunday School and Bible study teacher, and children's Bible club helper, finds life hectic. She says writing is relaxing. [1/31, 2/6, 3/29, 4/21, 6/6, 7/31, 12/8]

Jennifer Kanode is an English-as-a-Second Language teacher and an announcer on a Christian radio station. She has a Bachelor's degree in Communications and has been writing short stories since she was in elementary school. [1/27, 7/14, 10/27]

Jon Kattenhorn wanted to be a missionary, but because of his Cerebral Palsy, he was unable to serve the Lord in this fashion. He writes for magazines and Sunday school papers, works in Youth ministry, and lives in Shafter, CA. [8/31]

Lanette Kissel, wife, mother, and writer lives in Evansville IN. She enjoys writing short stories, novels, and traditional rhyming Christian poetry. This is her first attempt at devotional writing. [1/12, 3/10, 11/7]

Mary A. Koepke is a freelance writer/illustrator. She lives with her husband of 55 years at the Passavant Retirement Center in Zelienople. She is active in the Arts Program which includes painting, sculpting, journaling, poetry, and literary workshops. [1/11, 4/17, 6/27, 7/12, 9/30, 10/11, 12/21]

Carole Lang is a widow who lives in New Wilmington and works for the Lord through various church groups. [10/30, 12/15]

Joe LoBello was born again in 1976. He is married with six daughters and five grandchildren. His life is dedicated to serving the Lord and spreading the Good News of His love through writing. What a blessing and privilege! [4/18, 6/2, 7/10, 8/28, 9/4, 11/10]

Bonnie J. Manion began writing poetry seven years ago after her six children were grown, has attended SDC writing conferences and placed in various poetry contests, and has published over 100 poems in two dozen journals. [1/18, 4/26, 5/14]

Christi McMath lives in Sharpsville, PA and attends Westside Baptist Church. She is the church prayer coordinator. She leads a weekly home Bible study. She's previously published poems in *Pathway*. She's married with two children and one grandson. [2/25, 5/7]

Karen Delp Miller is studying for a degree in nursing while working at a nursing home and raising four children. They are her best subjects. Karen follows in the steps of her mother who won many awards at the SDCWC. [12/17]

Evelyn Minshull, author of 26 published books, has taught creative writing workshops to all ages. She and Fred have been married for 54 happy years. While they were at home, their three daughters were her "first readers"—her "on-target" critics. [2/28, 4/5, 6/22, 7/16, 9/18, 11/25]

Barbara Myler, a homemaker, and her husband, Jim, live in Mars, PA. Besides her writing, she enjoys creative pursuits: gardening, sewing, crafts, and decorating. With 3 grown children in the area and church involvement—life is full. [3/12, 5/1]

Dan Nicksich is the Senior Minister of First Christian Church in Somerset, PA. He has been a free-lance writer for 17 years with over 200 publishing credits. He also writes for his church's drama ministry. [1/21, 11/11]

Caitlin O'Conner, a 14-year-old homeschool student, looks to make writing her career. Second-born of five children, she enjoys writing, reading, playing guitar, and studying. She resides in Yulee/Fernandina Beach, Florida with her parents, younger siblings and dog. [6/21, 10/24]

Sharon Parrett lives in Florida. Beaver Village Adventures is her first published book in a series of beaver village books in which her sister is co-author. She enjoys writing short stories. She is active in church. She loves working with children. [10/3]

Rev. Dr. Donald L. Patterson is senior minister at The United Methodist Church in Laurel, Mississippi. His congregation and community were devastated during the Katrina hurricane. Much of his time since the hurricane has been in working with the victims. [1/2]

Rev. J. Douglas Patterson is the senior minister of the large Smithfield United Church in downtown Pittsburgh, PA. Married to Ramona and father of three children, he is a popular motivational speaker and prominent clergyman. [5/6]

Peter Paulson is a freelance writer living in Bremerton, WA. A retired pastor, he and his wife enjoy visiting their friends, grown children, and two grandchildren. They met when he asked to borrow a dictionary from her. [2/26, 6/17, 8/27, 10/26, 12/27]

Mary Rose Pearson, Mercer, PA, is author of 29 books and 600+ short pieces. She is the wife of Rev. M. N. Pearson. She taught classes in churches he pastored and held children's crusades in their 35 years of evangelism. [2/4, 6/24, 10/5]

Barbara Peer [6/1, 7/26, 10/17]

Glenda Joy Race enjoys teaching, writing, and singing. She teaches writing skills and GED preparation through Luzerne County Community College. She is involved in children's and music ministries. She enjoys sharing her singing and writing talents with others. [1/30, 3/5, 5/22, 7/18, 9/14, 11/14]

Della L. Ray, at the age of seventeen, gave her life to Jesus. Since then He has taken her on quite a journey that has included teaching, acting, traveling, and now writing. She is blessed to be used by Him. [2/18, 5/9, 10/23]

Betty Redmon, a former resident of New York, employed in millinery design, now lives in Stanton, California. She enjoys friends, writing, and finds life to be an exciting adventure. [1/23, 5/28, 9/20, 10/16, 12/3]

Fara Lynn Reed, a graduate of Northwest Christian College, is currently a mother of three, pastor's wife and a church secretary. A freelance writer and speaker, she enjoys writing devotions and inspirational articles. flreed@yahoo.com [5/31, 6/16]

Debbie Rempel is active in her local church in Dallas, Oregon, and volunteers at the school affiliated with it. She is a member of Oregon Christian Writers and was interviewed in her town's weekly newspaper about her poetry. [1/25, 4/6, 6/8, 8/7, 9/25, 12/9]

Linda Richardson is Assistant Director of Victory in the Valley, Inc. Diagnosed in 1980 with metastatic malignant melanoma, she completed treatment in 1981 and remains in remission. From this experience, Linda writes and shares poems about the journey through cancer. [1/28, 3/11, 4/4, 5/12, 6/13, 7/4, 8/4, 9/23, 10/1, 11/4]

Pat Rivet [12/14]

Micki Roberts and her husband live in Wellborn, FL and have two grown children. Micki's writing includes novels, poetry, and Praise & Worship lyrics. She is a member of RWA and ACFW. [2/11, 4/25, 5/3, 6/7, 7/25, 8/26, 9/22, 10/9, 11/18, 12/7]

Martha Rogers, a retired English teacher and free-lance author of Bible studies, articles, and devotionals, also writes the Verse of the Week for ACFW. Martha and her husband live in Houston, Texas and are active in the ministries of Houston's First Baptist Church. [1/20, 3/30, 4/29, 5/20, 7/8, 10/10, 11/3, 12/19]

Jan Sady, Mayport, PA, President, Writers Fellowship; Editor, *The Path*; Author, *God's Lessons from Nature*. Published in *Small Town Life*, *Upper Case*, *Cross & Quill*. Articles accepted in *Ideals* and *The Writer Magazine*. Certified lay speaker for UMC. janfran@alltel.net. [1/8, 2/7, 3/19, 4/9, 5/18, 6/19, 7/6, 8/14, 9/15, 10/25]

Tiffany M. Schlichter is 17 and lives with her parents and 4 siblings in Montgomery, TX. She publishes the monthly magazine, *Virtuous Daughters*, and has authored and published two books, *Encouragement to the Home School Student* and *Noble Girlhood*. [1/9, 3/16, 5/4, 7/9, 9/15, 11/2]

Anne Siegrist is a volunteer for Faith in Action and Compeer, and her writings have been published in a variety of church publications. Her special interest is in children's literature. She lives in rural upstate New York. [3/24, 9/13]

Audrey Stallsmith is the author of the Thyme Will Tell mystery series from WaterBrook Press. She also writes articles on "Historical Plants" and "Christian Thought: Lewis, Chesterton, et al" for her web site, thymewilltell.com. [1/24, 2/17]

Margaret Steinacker, current worship leader for The Writing Academy, is in her 28th year of teaching GED classes. She is the Organist/Keyboardist for the Traditional and Contemporary worship at the United Methodist Church, Delphi, IN where her husband leads worship. [1/15, 3/8, 4/28, 7/23, 9/9]

Shirley S. Stevens leads a Christian Writers Group, The First Word, in Sewickley, PA. She serves as teacher in residence and mentor for The Writing Academy. Currently secretary of The St. Davids Christian Writers Conference, she enjoys receiving e-mail: poetcat@earthlink.net. [1/4, 1/26, 2/24, 2/29, 3/28, 4/24, 5/10, 6/30, 7/5, 7/30, 8/5, 8/21, 9/24, 10/29, 11/21, 11/24, 11/29]

Jennifer M. Stevenson is a published poet, wife, mother, and Christian dedicated to sharing the Lord through the writing talents He gave her. She lives in Pittsburgh, PA, where she is currently working on a children's story. [9/8]

Tiffany Stuart is married with two children. She is a freelance writer with a passion for sharing the hope of God to others. Visit her blogsite at www.oneofgodsgirls.blogspot.com [8/1]

Louise Sutherland a feelance writer, license minister at Kingdom Life Church in Baltimore, MD, Preschool Director, consultant and a loving wife, mother and grandmother, who writes children stories and up lifting words to encourage people to trust in the Lord. [4/22]

Catherine Szymanski works as a rehabilitation aid in a nursing home where she derives some of her material. [4/10]

Gloria Hall Troup is currently publishing a book with Author House titled, *Jesus Does Heal Today* which contains poetry, prose, and original art. [2/16, 3/18, 9/29, 12/24]

Elizabeth M. Van Hook, a Retirement Specialist in Pittsburgh, is a photographer fascinated with butterflies and flowers. She collects and dresses teddy bears for her Teddy Bear Ministry. When she retires, she plans to chase more butterflies and give away more bears! [2/14, 6/29, 7/19, 8/13, 11/27, 11/28]

Mary Donavan Vish, retired RN, mother of six, member of First Word Writer's group, enjoys writing poetry and prose. She writes often of family and God's gracious guidance. [10/12]

Charles A. Waugaman, poet, was an art director, college art teacher, conference and workshop leader, editor, and served churches in ME, CT, and PA. Retired in Vermont, he delights in long morning devotions where many of his writings begin. [1/3, 2/10, 3/20, 4/11, 5/25, 6/23, 7/15, 8/6, 8/17, 9/3, 10/4, 11/1, 11/26, 12/25]

Martha Kauffman Weaver, taught in Christian Schools 36 years, teaches adult women in Sunday school, is a board member and past president of St. Davids Christian Writers' Association. She lives with her husband at Atglen, PA. [3/31]

Gertrude Wilson is a freelance writer living in Baltimore, MD. She is the mother of three and grandmother of five. Gertrude enjoys writing poetry and praise and worship lyrics. She is a member of PSA and ACWA. [12/12]

Theresa V. Wilson is a minister at Kingdom Life Church, Baltimore, MD. Her freelance work has appeared in *Godly Business Woman* and *Proverbs 31 Magazines.* She is president of the Baltimore Area American Christian Writers Association. Visit her at www.writersinthemarketplace.org [3/14, 7/20, 8/15, 10/8]

Kathleen Wolford, wife, mother of 5 daughters, homemaker, currently lives in Colorado Springs, CO. She enjoys writing poetry and devotionals. [1/14, 10/13]

Cheryl Wyatt, RN turned SAHM, joyful chaos rules her home, and she delights in the stealth moments God gives her to write. She stays active in her church and in her laundry room. [[2/12, 4/1, 5/2, 5/24]

Barbara Ann Yonnotti, RN, enjoys reading, writing poetry, and serving as outreach chairman of Wickliffe Christian Church. She graduated from Austintown Fitch and joined the USN. She has one daughter and lives in Youngstown, OH. [1/7, 7/24, 8/23, 12/30]

Ps. I thought some of you might be interested in my Civil War novel, Dog Jack, is being made into a film production this coming summer. Also, if you haven't read *Tangled Truths,* I guarantee you'll enjoy Gloria's cliff-hanging novel.

$9.95
ISBN 0-936369-47-7

$9.95
ISBN 0-936369-77-9

$14.95
ISBN 0-936369-92-2

$9.95
ISBN 0-936369-35-3

$9.95
ISBN 0-936369-73-6

$10.00
ISBN 0-936369-37-X

1-800-358-0777

Tangled Truths
a romantic novel
by
Gloria Clover

Neil Harrington
Tough, angry Marine Captain Neil Harrington finds himself grasping for the things he had believed he no longer wanted in life – the responsibility of his late sister's twins, the love of a soft-hearted woman, and the forgiveness of a God he's vowed never to speak to again.

Adrian D'Avignon
Level-headed, even-tempered college professor Adrian D'Avignon has always feared the day her adopted children's biological uncle would return. She knew he would disrupt the even tenor of their lives; she never suspected he would wreak havoc on her heart, her security, and her solid walk with the Lord.

Held together by the twins and a desperate desire to discover the past that has brought them to this tangled present, Neil and Adrian search for a compromise only to discover complete dependence on God reveals the way He so lovingly prepared – long before they met and loved.

Available from Son-Rise Publications for $9.95
Call 1-800-358-0777

Precious Memories

As I proofed these blue lines my Aunt Velma had just said good-bye to life, but she leaves a legacy of love to all of us.

Never a birthday or a holiday passed without receiving a call or a note from her.

That's changing, but when it's my turn to see Jesus, I'll expect to have her waiting with Him. Can she make my favorite pumpkin bread in heaven?

Blessings,
Florence Biros